AN AMERICAN MARRIAGE

*The Untold Story of
Abraham Lincoln and Mary Todd*

MICHAEL BURLINGAME

PEGASUS BOOKS

NEW YORK LONDON

AN AMERICAN MARRIAGE

Pegasus Books, Ltd.
148 West 37th Street, 13th Floor
New York, NY 10018

First Pegasus Books cloth edition June 2021

Interior design by Maria Fernandez

Library of Congress Cataloging-in-Publication Data is available.

ISBN: 978-1-64313-734-6

10 9 8 7 6 5 4 3 2 1

Printed in the United States of America
Distributed by Simon & Schuster
www.pegasusbooks.com

To Lois McDonald, beloved soulmate

CONTENTS

INTRODUCTION

A braham Lincoln was apparently one of those men who regard "connubial bliss" as an oxymoron. During the Civil War, he pardoned a Union soldier who had deserted to return home and wed his sweetheart, who reportedly had been flirting with another swain in his absence. As the president signed the necessary document sparing the miscreant's life, he said: "I want to punish the young man—probably in less than a year he will wish I had withheld the pardon."

This book describes and analyzes why Lincoln had good reason to regret his marriage as much as he expected the young soldier to rue his. Lincoln is justly known as a man of sorrows, largely because of the soul-crushing responsibilities he shouldered as president during the nation's bloodiest war. But it is impossible to understand the depth of that sorrow without realizing just how woe-filled his marriage truly was. One of the most poignant discoveries I made in more than thirty years of Lincoln research is an unpublished interview with one of the president's longtime friends and political allies, Orville H. Browning. Even though Lincoln was notoriously "shut-mouthed" about his private life, Browning recalled that during the

Civil War the president often told him "about his domestic troubles" and "that he was constantly under great apprehension lest his wife should do something which would bring him into disgrace." And she did just that by her unethical, tactless, unpopular, scandalous behavior as First Lady. Try to imagine contending with the pressures to which Lincoln was subjected as he toiled to unify the fissiparous Republican party (composed of Whig-hating former Democrats and Democrat-hating former Whigs) and the even more fissiparous North, which included slaveholders (in the loyal Border States) and abolitionists; antitariff free traders and high-tariff protectionists; radical European refugees and nativist bigots; teetotaling prohibitionists and beer-loving Germans; racial egalitarians and dyed-in-the-wool Negrophobes. On top of that, he had to inspire popular morale, to raise armies and find capable leaders for them, to mobilize the economic resources of the North, to distribute patronage wisely while besieged by swarms of importunate would-be civil servants, and to deal with hypercritical newspaper editors, backbiting cabinet members, fractious governors, egomaniacal legislators, and recalcitrant generals—among others. And on top of *that*, he had to cohabit the White House with a psychologically unbalanced woman whose indiscrete and abusive behavior taxed his legendary patience and forbearance to the limit. A few months after Lincoln's assassination, Orville H. Browning, while discussing Mrs. Lincoln's "mental weakness," predicted that "people will never know what Lincoln suffered and endured. He had the wisdom of Socrates and the patience—of Christ."

The sad story of the Lincolns' domestic life has long been glossed over. In 1946, Ellery Sedgwick lamented that writers dealing with Lincoln's "tragic marriage" had drawn "a quiet curtain over a supreme exasperation of his life," and as a result "the full magnificence of his conquest over circumstances remains incomplete." Mary Todd Lincoln, Sedgwick wrote, "was a termagant and a horror, and yet how is she remembered? The other day I turned the pages of a biography which made her the sweet heroine of romance, and even Carl Sandburg is so charitable that he thinks of her as a poet should think of every woman."

Sedgwick's appeal to strip away the "quiet curtain" hiding the truth about Lincoln's marriage has gone unheeded. A few years after his memoir appeared, Ruth Painter Randall published *Mary Lincoln: Biography of a Marriage*, depicting her subject as "an appealing love story" and assuring readers that "the nation can well be proud of this American romance." Many subsequent authors have followed Randall's lead. More recently, historians like Jean H. Baker and Catherine Clinton have "lionized" Mrs. Lincoln, as Jason Emerson wrote, implausibly making her out to be a pioneer feminist. The effect of such romanticized and politicized works has been to create what historian John Y. Simon called the "legend of the happy marriage."

The worst offenders are Mrs. Lincoln's biographers, who resemble defense attorneys and cheerleaders rather than impartial scholars. Michael Burkhimer aptly deems them "apologists for Mary Lincoln." Some of her defenders go so far as to justify the physical abuse she administered to her husband. Louis A. Warren, commenting on her reputation for having "a quick temper and a sharp tongue," concluded: "Possibly she threw coffee at Lincoln and drove him out of the house with a broom and probably he deserved it." Considerable evidence shows that in fact Lincoln's marriage was, as his law partner William H. Herndon observed, "a domestic hell on earth," a "burning, scorching hell," "as terrible as death and as gloomy as the grave." After practicing law with Lincoln for well over a decade in a two-man firm, Herndon exclaimed: "Poor Lincoln! He is domestically a desolate man—has been for years to my own knowledge" because of his marriage to "a very curious—excentric—*wicked* woman."

Although Mrs. Lincoln's biographers have criticized Herndon and his informants, Douglas L. Wilson cogently argued that "the stories Herndon collected" and "his own view of Mary and the Lincoln marriage" differed little "from that of many of Lincoln's other close friends" and "from that of Springfield generally." Similarly, Lincoln historian Paul M. Angle noted in 1930: "As to Lincoln's domestic difficulties, no fair-minded student can disregard what Herndon wrote. The supporting testimony of other contemporaries is too overwhelming."

That supporting testimony, far greater now than what was known in Angle's day, is indeed overwhelming, though it has not been systematically collected and presented to the public, a function that the present book aims to serve. Thanks to the development of word-searchable databases, especially of newspapers, it is possible to learn much more about Lincoln's life in general, and his marriage in particular, than previous writers could. A great deal of the evidence adduced in these pages comes from informants other than those whom Herndon consulted.

The unflattering accounts of Mary Lincoln's character and behavior given by people who knew her are vast, but it might have been greater, for some potential informants refused to share what they knew about her. The best-placed informant was Harriet Hanks, who as an adolescent lived in the Lincolns' home for a year and a half soon after their wedding. But two decades later she wrote to Herndon: "Enny information that I Can give you in regard to the loved and lamented Lincoln will be freely given, but [I] would rather *Say nothing* about his Wife[;] as I Could Say but little in her *favor* I Conclude it best to Say nothing." Lincoln's friend and sometime chess opponent, Judge Samuel H. Treat, similarly balked when an interviewer asked his opinion of Mrs. Lincoln: "beyond the simple admission that he was acquainted with her, coupled with the names of three or four other persons who, he claimed, could adequately describe her 'if they dared to,' he declined to commit himself." Mary Nash Stuart, the wife of Lincoln's first law partner, was equally reticent; when asked about Mary Lincoln, whom she did not like, she refused to say more than: "Oh, she was a Todd." Eliza Francis, wife of Lincoln's close friend Simeon Francis, could have shared much information about Mary Todd, but refused to do so. (Her niece Marietta, perhaps relaying what Aunt Eliza told her, stated that "Mary Todd made Lincoln's life miserable.")

Though Herndon originally portrayed Mary Lincoln unfavorably, in his later years he mellowed, insisting that the "world does not know her, Mrs. L.'s, sufferings, her trials, and the causes of things. [I] Sympathize with her." Indeed, as her eldest sister Elizabeth (who was, in effect, her surrogate mother) told Herndon not long after Lincoln's death, "Mary has had much to bear though she don't bear it well; She has acted foolishly—unwisely and made the world hate her."

Mary Lincoln did indeed have much to bear, so much that she is more to be pitied than censured. Her mother died when she was six, and her father quickly remarried a younger woman who disliked Mary and her siblings. Feeling emotionally abandoned by her father and rejected by her stepmother, she developed an intense psychological neediness. She did not ask to have a childhood that she called "desolate," nor to inherit the gene for bipolar disorder, nor to endure migraine headaches for much of her adult life, nor to suffer from premenstrual disorders, nor to lose three of her four children before they reached adulthood, nor to have her husband murdered by her side at the height of his popularity and influence. As Elizabeth Cady Stanton observed in 1869, "Mrs. Lincoln should call out our sympathy, rather than denunciation. Her unhappy organization, a tendency to insanity (for which she is not responsible), increased and aggravated by the great sadness of her husband, which rested like a dark cloud most of the time on his household, furnish a sufficient excuse for many of her idiosyncracies [sic] of character." This book attempts neither to excuse nor to denounce Mary Lincoln but rather to describe accurately and fully her marriage and her "idiosyncracies of character," and to make the latter understandable.

In trying to comprehend why the Lincolns' marriage was so woe-filled, readers should bear in mind that the depressive, emotionally reserved and uncommunicative Lincoln was far from an ideal husband. As his wife said, despite his "deep feeling" and "amiable nature," he was "not, a demonstrative man, when he felt most deeply, he expressed, the least." Others concurred.

Mary's sister, Elizabeth Todd Edwards, deemed Lincoln "a cold man" with "no affection."

That said, it must be acknowledged that Mary Lincoln's behavior helped make her husband truly "a man of sorrows."

Some of the material included in this volume originally appeared in my earlier books. The present work offers a considerably expanded, updated, and revised version of that material. The extensive reference notes can be accessed at the website of the University of Illinois Springfield https://www.uis.edu. In quoting sources, I have reproduced the spelling and punctuation in the original.

To convert mid-nineteenth century dollar amounts into the rough equivalents of 2021 dollars, multiply by 30. Thus Lincoln's salary of $25,000 in the Civil War would be worth ca. $750,000 in 2021.

AN AMERICAN MARRIAGE

PART I

THE COURTSHIP

1839–1842

1

GIRL MEETS BOY

1839–1840

At the age of thirty, a tall, wiry, up-and-coming Illinois lawyer-politician, Abraham Lincoln, met a short, plump, twenty-year-old, well-educated Kentucky belle, Mary Todd, the cousin of his law partner, John Todd Stuart. He initially encountered her shortly after she had left her family home in Kentucky to live in Springfield, Illinois, with her eldest sister (and surrogate mother), Elizabeth, and her husband Ninian Edwards, son of Illinois's first governor. At parties in the Edwards's home on "Aristocracy Hill," Mary Todd flirted with young men searching for a wife. At the time, Springfield had a dearth of eligible young women.

THE COURTSHIP BEGINS

During the social whirl that accompanied sessions of the Illinois General Assembly, Mary Todd was popular, even though "she was not what you could call a beautiful girl," as a schoolmate remembered. A young man from Springfield termed her "the very creature of excitement" who "never enjoys herself more than when in society and surrounded by a company of merry friends." Among those friends was Kentuckian Joshua Speed, a merchant in his mid-twenties. To social events on Aristocracy Hill, Speed brought along a fellow Kentuckian, his lanky friend and roommate Abraham, and so Lincoln began seeing Mary during the winter of 1839–1840.

Elizabeth Edwards at first encouraged a budding romance, for she considered Lincoln "a rising Man," and thus a possible mate for her sister Mary. As time passed, however, Elizabeth had second thoughts, for he lacked basic social graces; she reported that he "Could not hold a lengthy Conversation with a lady—was not sufficiently Educated & intelligent in the female line to do so—He was charmed with Mary's wit and fascinated with her quick sagacity—her will—her nature—and Culture—I have happened in the room where they were sitting often & often and Mary led the Conversation—Lincoln would listen & gaze on her as if drawn by some Superior power, irresistibly So: he listened—never Scarcely Said a word."

Elizabeth Edwards presciently warned her sister that Lincoln and she were not "Suitable to Each other," for they "had no congeniality—no feelings &c. alike." Mary "was quick, lively, gay—frivalous it may be, Social and loved glitter Show & pomp & power." Elizabeth and her husband "told Lincoln & Mary not to marry" because "they were raised differently." Their "natures, mind—Education—raising &c were So different they Could not live happ[il]y as husband & wife."

Sharing their skepticism was Mary Todd's cousin Stephen T. Logan, who warned her that Abraham was "much too rugged for your little white hands to attempt to polish." But Mary thought that if another of her cousins, John Todd Stuart, found Lincoln to be a suitable law partner, perhaps this Lincoln might also be a suitable life partner.

In Springfield, Lincoln was variously described as "a mighty rough man," "uncouth," "moody," "dull in society," "badly dressed," "ungainly," "careless of his personal appearance," as well as "awkward and shy." Soon after moving to the Illinois capital in 1837, he said that he avoided church because "I am conscious I should not know how to behave myself." His manners were indeed somewhat oafish. Shod in heavy Conestoga boots, he would enter a ballroom and exclaim: "How clean these women look!" In the opinion of Mary Owens, whom he had courted before he met Mary Todd, Lincoln "was deficient in those little links which make up the great chain of woman[']s happiness."

Unsurprisingly, young ladies in Springfield shied away from Lincoln. "We girls," Catherine Bergen Jones remembered, "maneuvered so as to shift on each other the two awkward, diffident young lawyers, Abraham Lincoln and Samuel H. Treat." Lincoln briefly dated Mary's older sister Frances, who recalled that "*he took me out once or twice*, but he was not much for society. He would go where they [we?] took him, but he was never very much for company." At that time, he was considered "the plainest man in Springfield," she said. Another Springfield woman marveled at the "almost prophetic insight" that led Mary Todd to choose "the most awkward & ungainly man in her train," one "almost totally lacking in polish."

LINCOLN'S SOCIAL INEPTITUDE AND LACK OF SEX APPEAL

Lincoln had been uncomfortable around young women from his days in Indiana, where he lived from the age seven to twenty-one. Hoosier maidens liked him but not as a beau, for they thought him "too green." One remembered that "he was so tall and awkward" that "the young girls my age made fun of Abe." Although he "tried to go with some of them," they would "give him the mitten every time," because he was "so tall and gawky." Another young lady complained that he "just cared too much for books."

Similarly, in Macon County, Illinois, and later in New Salem (locales where Lincoln dwelt from the age of twenty-one to twenty-eight), young women thought he "was not much of a beau." One described him as "a very queer fellow," "homely," "awkward," and "very bashful." At social events, he "never danced or cut up."

Although in Indiana Lincoln had refused to dance, explaining that "my feet weren't made that way," later in Illinois he managed to overcome his shyness enough to approach Mary Todd at a party, allegedly saying: "I want to dance with you in the worst way." She accepted his invitation, but his terpsichorean ineptitude was so pronounced that she told him afterwards: "Mr. Lincoln I think you have literally fulfilled your request—you have danced the worst way possible."

MARY TODD'S DETERMINED
PURSUIT OF LINCOLN

Despite that inauspicious beginning, Mary Todd pursued Lincoln, though just how she did so is unclear. In 1875, Lincoln's good friend Orville H. Browning said: "I always thought then and ever since that in her affair with Mr. Lincoln, Mary Todd did most of the courting." Browning added that "Miss Todd was thoroughly in earnest [in] her endeavors to get Mr. Lincoln," and that there was "no doubt of her exceeding anxiety to marry him." Browning knew whereof he spoke, for—as he told an interviewer—in "those times I was at Mr. Edwards' a great deal, and Miss Todd used to sit down with me, and talk to me sometimes till midnight, about this affair of hers with Mr. Lincoln."

Sarah Rickard, sister-in-law of Lincoln's friend and host William Butler (at whose Springfield home/boarding house Lincoln took his meals for several years), recalled that Mary Todd "certainly made most of the plans and did the courting" and "would have him [Lincoln], whether or no." Joshua

Speed, Lincoln's closest friend, testified that "Miss Todd wanted L. terribly." To impress Lincoln, she "read much & committed much to memory to make herself agreeable," according to a member of the Springfield elite.

At first, Mary Todd's strategy worked. Lincoln reportedly admired her "naturally fine mind and cultivated tastes," for she seemed like "a great reader and possessed of a remarkably retentive memory," was "quick at repartee and when the occasion seemed to require it was sarcastic and severe." Her "brilliant conversation, often embellished with apt quotations," made her "much sought after by the young people of the town." Her friends "looked upon her as a well educated girl of bright and attractive manner, when she was not stirred to sharp rejoinder." William Herndon, Lincoln's law partner and biographer, recollected that before she wed, Mary Todd was "a very shrewd girl," "somewhat attractive," "a fine judge of human nature," as well as "polite," "civil," "rather graceful in her movements," "polished," "intelligent," "well educated," "a good linguist," "a fine conversationalist," "highly cultured," "witty," "dashing," and "rather pleasant." Lincoln's friend and physician William Jayne called her "a woman of quick intellect," a "bright, lively, plump little woman—a good talker, & capable of making herself quite attractive to young gentlemen." Lincoln was doubtless impressed that she knew her townsman Henry Clay, Lincoln's *beau ideal* of a statesman. (Clay and Mary's father were good friends in Lexington, Kentucky.)

Moreover, Lincoln may have been drawn to Mary's youthful qualities. A woman speculated that Lincoln saw in his wife, "despite her foibles and sometimes her puerileness, just what he needed." In all likelihood, it was *because* of that "puerileness" rather than *despite* it that he was attracted to her. As Helen Nicolay (daughter of Lincoln's principal White House secretary) noted, Lincoln's "attitude toward his wife had something of the paternal in it, almost as though she were a child, under his protection." Indeed, Lincoln had a deep-seated paternal quality that made him enjoy children and child surrogates, and Mary Todd fit the latter role well. According to one of her most sympathetic biographers, Ruth Painter

Randall, Mary Todd "aroused the paternal instinct that was always so strong an element in his make-up." Randall noted that "in some ways" Mary Todd "never grew up" and "had a timidity and childlike dependence upon the strength and calmness of others." As First Lady, she was, in Randall's view, "a child" in the hands of unscrupulous men and was "as defenseless as a trusting child" among the scheming women of Washington society. After she was married, "nothing pleased her more than having her husband pet and humor her, and call her his 'child-wife.'" In 1848, when Lincoln was a congressman in Washington and she, then staying in Kentucky with her parents, expressed a desire to join him in the nation's capital, he asked her: "Will you be a *good girl* in all things, if I consent?" Two decades later, Mary Lincoln described her husband as "always a father" to her. Her best friend during Lincoln's presidency, Elizabeth Keckly, wrote that when he "saw faults in his wife he excused them as he would excuse the impulsive acts of a child."

Mary's keen desire to wed Lincoln caused her to overlook much, for she had "a bitter struggle with herself" whenever he "would carelessly ignore some social custom or forget an engagement." He occasionally failed to "observe the conventionalities of society," much to her annoyance. When she criticized him "for committing some faux pas," he would "look at her quizzically" as though to say, "How can you attach such great importance to matters so trivial?"

Nonetheless, Mary Todd kept pursuing him. The two could have seen each other in Springfield throughout the first quarter of 1840, but they were apart from April to November; he was then practicing law on the Eighth Judicial Circuit and campaigning for the Whig party throughout southern Illinois, while she spent much of that summer in Missouri visiting relatives. So they courted through the mail. According to Joshua Speed, Lincoln "wrote his *Mary*—She darted after him—wrote him."

Sometime in the late fall of 1840, Abraham and Mary evidently became engaged, though there was no ring, no public announcement, no shower, and no party. Lincoln seems to have proposed because he desired a "child-wife," and because he evidently believed she wanted him to do so.

MARY'S PARENTS SHORTCHANGE
HER EMOTIONALLY

Just as Lincoln may have been attracted to Mary as a surrogate child, she may well have been drawn to him because she desired a surrogate pater-familias to take care of her and provide the love that her father, Robert Smith Todd, had evidently failed to give her after he had remarried soon after becoming a widower. To please his new, much younger wife (Elizabeth Humphreys), he had apparently withdrawn emotionally from Mary, who was only six years old when her mother, Eliza, died. The newlyweds promptly had a child, then eight more in rapid succession. With so many offspring, Robert Todd could pay little attention to Mary, who remembered her childhood as "desolate." She evidently felt betrayed, abandoned, and rejected. Thus a deep-seated, unconscious anger may well have taken root in her psyche as she came to think of herself as unloved and unlovable. Out of those feelings, it would appear, grew a hunger for ersatz forms of love—power, money, fame—and a subconscious desire to punish her father.

Lincoln was well suited to fill the emotional void thus created for Mary Todd; not only was he more than a foot taller and almost a decade older than she, but he also somehow radiated the quality of a wise, benevolent father. A friend said that Lincoln during his early years in Springfield reminded him of "the pictures I formerly saw of old Father Jupiter, bending down from the clouds, to see what was going on below." Mary Todd was predisposed to find a man resembling Father Jupiter highly desirable, someone who might take good care of her.

Once she wed her surrogate father (Lincoln), Mary Todd evidently displaced onto him her unconscious rage at her biological father. As psychologist Linda Schierse Leonard has observed, a "woman's rage" is "often rooted in feelings of abandonment, betrayal, and rejection which may go back to the relation with the father, and which often come up over and over again in current relationships" with men. Such rage "is often mixed with feelings of jealousy and revenge that are strong enough to kill any relationship and the woman's capacity for loving herself as well." Thus "many women destroy their relationships . . . through continued hysterical outbursts." Mary's rage attacks and hysterical outbursts would not destroy her marriage, but they were to undermine it badly.

If Mary Todd felt emotionally shortchanged by her father, she felt even more so by her stepmother. Mary, according to her sister Elizabeth, "left her home in Kentucky to avoid living under the same roof with a stepmother" with whom "she did not agree." Mary recalled that her "early home was truly at a *boarding* school," Madame Charlotte Victoire LeClerc Mentelle's Academy.

Mary's discontent was shared by her younger brother, George, who "complained bitterly" about Betsey Humphreys's "settled hostility" and said that he felt compelled to leave "his father's house in consequence of the malignant & continued attempts on the part of his stepmother to poison the mind of his father toward him." George insisted that Robert Smith Todd was "mortified that his last child by his first wife [i.e., George himself] should be obliged, like all his other first children, to abandon his house by the relentless persecution of a stepmother." George evidently articulated the deep-seated resentment that he and his siblings felt for their stepparent.

Each of Eliza Todd's daughters left Lexington as soon as they could, partly because life in that city was so uninteresting. Mary's cousin Elizabeth Norris recalled that she and her friends "had few privileges & led very dull lives." The first-born daughter, Elizabeth, wed Ninian W. Edwards and settled in Springfield. Her younger sisters followed her there, were introduced into society, and were courted by beaux whom they married. Mrs. Edwards explained that her sisters "had visited her in Springfield because of their differences with their stepmother." Robert and Betsey Todd rarely sojourned in the Illinois capital, and the daughters of Eliza Todd seldom returned to Kentucky.

Mary Todd's niece reported that her aunt "was a bundle of nervous activity, willful and original in planning mischief," who often clashed "with her very conventional young stepmother." When ten-year-old Mary and her cousin Elizabeth used willow branches to convert their narrow dresses into fashionable hooped skirts, Betsey Todd ordered the two girls to "take those things off, & then go to Sunday school." Elizabeth recalled that she and Mary "went to our room chagrined and angry. Mary burst into tears and gave the first exhibition of temper I had ever seen or known her to make. She thought we were badly treated—and expressed herself freely on the subject."

Mary Todd probably resented her stepmother for bearing so many rivals for her father's attention. Her dislike for her half-siblings manifested itself during the Civil War, when all but one of them supported the Confederacy. In 1862, she expressed the hope that her half-brothers serving in the Confederate Army would be captured or slain. "They would kill my husband if they could, and destroy our Government—the dearest of all things to us," she declared, soon after her half-brother Samuel fell at the battle of Shiloh. The following year, when another half-brother (Alexander) was killed, Mary shocked a confidante by stating: "it is but natural that I should feel for one so nearly related to me," but Alexander had "made his choice long ago. He decided against my husband, and through him against me. He has been fighting against us; and since he chose to be our deadly enemy, I see no special reason why I should bitterly mourn his death."

MARY'S PSYCHOLOGICAL DISORDERS

Mary required a lot of care, for in addition to her intense emotional neediness, she suffered from what psychiatrist James S. Brust described as "a significant psychiatric illness, most likely bipolar disorder." Symptoms of that disease appeared early. An intimate childhood friend, Margaret Stuart, observed that Mary Todd in her Kentucky years was "very highly strung, nervous, impulsive, excitable, having an emotional temperament much like an April day, sunning all over with laughter one moment, the next crying as though her heart would break." Orville H. Browning recalled that she "was a girl of much vivacity in conversation, but was subject to . . . spells of mental depression. . . . As we used familiarly to state it she was always 'either in the garret or cellar.'" Later, she displayed classic signs of bipolar behavior: prolonged bouts of depression, excessive mourning for losses, wild spending sprees, ego inflation, and delusions of grandeur.

Like many people with bipolar disorder, Mary had spells of mania and depression that were not a constant feature of her life, but rather came and went. She reportedly suffered from what a Springfield neighbor called "monthly derangements" (i.e., premenstrual stress syndrome, which can cause depression, irritability, and mood swings). Frederick I. Dean, who lived across the street from the Lincolns' home, remembered that in his youth he "noticed strange vagaries on the part of Mrs. Lincoln." He told a Lincoln biographer that "as I grew older, I heard conversations between my mother and neighboring ladies touching upon that subject, and I formed the idea from that source that the vagaries arose from a functional derangement common alone to women, and that they occurred only semi occasionally, but regularly at stated times, & were of but brief duration, and as I grew older these facts were very plainly to be seen by myself." Shortly after Lincoln's death, when Dean asked William Herndon about that pattern, he replied that it "corresponded exactly with his own ideas, and exactly in line with what Mr Lincoln had frequently himself told him, with broken tearful voice." In 1862, Mary Lincoln wrote her husband describing one such episode: "A day or two since, I had one of my severe attacks, [and] if it had not been for Lizzie Keckly, I do not know what I should have *done*—Some of *these periods*, will launch me away."

In addition to bipolar disorder, Mary also exhibited symptoms of narcissism and borderline personality disorder. Her contemporaries did not use such language, which was unknown in the nineteenth century; instead they employed terms like "unsound mind," "madness," "deranged," "brain trouble," and "insane." Orville H. Browning considered Mary Lincoln "demented." Mrs. Norman B. Judd thought her "slightly insane." Margaret Ritchie Stone, wife of the White House physician Robert K. Stone, believed that Mrs. Lincoln "was insane on the subject of money." Mary Lincoln's nephew Albert Edwards, like many others, was convinced that she "was insane from the time of her husband['s] death until her own death." In 1875, an Illinois court, after hearing from numerous witness, adjudged her "a fit person to be sent to a state hospital for the insane." Her son Robert testified at her trial: "She has been of unsound mind since the death of her husband, and has been irresponsible for the past ten years. I regard her as eccentric and unmanageable."

Even before Lincoln's assassination, his wife was thought to be mentally unbalanced. In 1858, Eliza Caldwell Browning, wife of Lincoln's close friend Orville H. Browning, exclaimed: "that woman is not in her right mind!" In 1875, Gideon Welles, secretary of the navy during the Civil War, told Robert Todd Lincoln that he thought his mother should have been committed to a mental hospital long since. That same year, a Springfield paper reported that "[s]ome of the more intimate friends of Mrs. Lincoln date the indications of mental aberration previous to the death of her distinguished husband, beginning with the death of her son Willie" in 1862. A New York newspaper remarked in 1875 that there was "no doubt" that Mrs. Lincoln "has been thus afflicted at least from the time of her husband's elevation to office [in 1860]." From "the day her husband was nominated to the Presidency she was eccentric, if nothing more." She "must have been as insane then as now. Numerous are the incidents of her life hardly fit to publish but are well known."

When Mary Lincoln died in 1882, Chicagoans "who had known her since 1854, and who saw her frequently in 1865, expressed themselves at that time of the opinion that Mrs. Lincoln was insane." Upon hearing of her death, David Davis, Lincoln's close friend, colleague at the bar, political ally, and executor of his estate, wrote: "Poor Mrs. Lincoln! She is at last at rest. She has been a deranged woman, ever since her husband's death. In fact she was so, during his life." Sharing Davis's view was Commissioner of Public Buildings Benjamin Brown French, who worked with Mary Lincoln almost daily in her White House years. Just after Lincoln's assassination, he wrote that "the tragical death of her husband has made her *crazyer* [sic] than she used to be."

In 1867, Springfield's Republican paper remarked that "an impression pervades our general community that she has not been entirely in her right mind for several years." Among other things that apparently led Springfielders to doubt her sanity was her "mania for shopping," which was so strong that "she pitifully carried [it] to the extreme of shop-lifting." Evidently her "family devised schemes to shield her and to protect or reimburse the merchants" (see Chapter 10). David Davis called her "a natural born thief" for whom "stealing was a sort of insanity." In 1875, her sister Elizabeth wrote that the "peculiarities" of Mary's "whole life have been so marked and well understood by me that I have not indulged the faintest hope, of a permanent cure. The painful excitement of the *past years* only added to the malady, [a portion of her letter is missing here] . . . had been apparent to her family for years before the saddest events occurred." Even the defensive editors of her collected letters acknowledged that it "cannot be denied that Mary Lincoln was in some ways mentally disturbed even before her husband's death."

A notable manifestation of Mrs. Lincoln's mental imbalance was what Mary Logan called her "ungovernable temper," so ungovernable that it was "really a species of madness." Others concurred in that judgment, including the journalist Mary Clemmer Ames, who wrote that Mrs. Lincoln's "outbursts of passionate" and "ungoverned temper" actually "verged on insanity" (see Chapter 6).

Mary Todd may well have inherited at least some of her emotional disorders, for several members of her family had psychological problems. Lincoln's friend Isaac Diller said of Mary: "of course she had a temper—the Todds all had a crazy streak." A historian of the family called its members "pampered," "prideful," "quick-tempered," "vain," and "often preoccupied with the surfaces of things and insensitive to the substance." They "made grudges easily" and clung to them. Lincoln poked fun at the family's pretentions by observing that one "d" was good enough for God but not for the Todds.

Dr. George R. C. Todd, the youngest and most disturbed of Mary's full siblings, called himself the "black sheep" of the family. His attorney reported he was "inclined to be abrupt almost to brusqueness in his manner to those whom he did not like." He "took no pains to conceal his dislike for those who had incurred his displeasure" and "refused to consort with his own contemporaries to any great extent." He was "given to moods of deep melancholy." Like his sister Mary, George had an explosive temper. A Union prisoner-of-war called him "the most vicious wretch I ever knew" because of his mistreatment of Yankee patients. During the Civil War, he had "raving fits of madness" in which he assaulted sick and wounded prisoners under his care. A supremely selfish, spiteful drunkard, he evidently killed himself. His daughter, Mattie Dee Todd, "became so disordered" in midlife that she was committed to a sanitarium.

Some of Mary's other siblings were also mentally unstable. Like George, her half-brother David, who as an adolescent had run away from home, mistreated Union prisoners-of-war. At the notorious Libby Prison in Richmond, the eccentric, heavily tattooed David was known as a cruel, sadistic officer. He slashed captives with a saber, kicked Yankee corpses while calling them damned abolitionists, and often said: "I would like to cut 'Old Abe's' heart out." A tactless, unforgiving drunkard, he died in 1871 from wounds reportedly sustained "in a whore house brawl before he went to War."

Mary's older brother Levi, according to his wife, had a cruel and "inhuman manner." In 1864, he drank himself to death, passing away friendless "from utter want and destitution." His granddaughter, Ella Canfield, committed suicide at the age of eighteen. Elizabeth Todd Edwards reported that Ella had "a hereditary liability to insanity," and that her "grandfather died in an insane assylum, [sic] and there are now [date unknown] fourteen members of the Canfield family, in the various assylums."

Ann Todd was "the most quick-tempered and vituperative" of Mary's sisters. A "pugnacious, loud voiced" woman with a face "exactly like a pug bulldog," she was "usually in a temper." In 1861, Mary wrote that Ann "possesses such a miserable disposition & so false a tongue" that "no one respects" her. Ann's "tongue for so many years, has been considered 'no slander'—and as a child & young girl, [she] could not be outdone in false-hood. . . . I grieve for those, who have to come in contact with her malice, yet even that, is so well understood, [that] the object of her wrath, generally rises, with good people, in proportion to her vindictiveness." Ann had a son who was a drunkard, "very peculiar—almost if not quite crazy."

Mary Lincoln's niece Julia, daughter of Ninian and Elizabeth Edwards, also suffered from mental illness. "Insanity," Elizabeth wrote in 1875, appeared "in the case of my own daughter, at the early age of thirteen,—for six months, she was so decidedly flighty, as to be closely guarded." At "no time has she ever been natural in her demeanor. God pity those who are the victims—and who are the anxious sufferers in such terrible afflictions!" Mary Lincoln called Julia a "poor, silly" girl and expressed sympathy for Elizabeth: "How unfortunate a Mother, must consider herself, to so rear, a child—Naturally weak." In 1864, while Julia was visiting Washington, her risqué behavior created a scandal.

Julia's sister, Elizabeth Edwards Clover, inherited much of Mary Lincoln's wardrobe, which she often wore even though the clothes had long since gone out of style. Few people "thought anything of it" because "the Todds had always been eccentric." Julia's niece Georgia died in the Norbury

Sanitarium, a "Private Residential Home for the Treatment of Nervous and Mental Disorders."

Some Todds frankly acknowledged their own eccentricity. Mary's half-sister Elodie warned her fiancé: "I am a *Todd*, and some of these days you may be unfortunate enough to find out what they are." She further confessed: "I cannot govern my temper or tongue, and when I am angry say much that I am very sorry for afterwards and altho' [I] speak my feelings at the time, [and] change them when I get a little cooler, but it is just the same next time. Mother has always predicted that my temper and tongue would get me into trouble, but I say no and if it does, I will stand up to what it utters." Moreover, she added, "I am one of the most unforgiving creatures you ever knew in my disposition, and if a wrong is done me and I am angered, I can never again be reconciled to the offender, altho' that person may have been my dearest friend. My confidence could never be placed again there, and I could not be persuaded to do anything more than speak to them." (If Mary Lincoln had been as self-aware and candid as Elodie, she might well have described herself in similar terms.)

In 1906, the Lincolns' son Robert, then mired "in the depths of gloom," wrote an apology to his aunt: "I was so much out of sorts when your letter came that I could not write you . . . . A good deal of work & bother seem to have brought on again my old nervous breakdown & I am breaking away from business." Two months later, he told a friend about his "nervous breakdown." On other occasions he suffered from what he called "nervous dyspepsia," a condition that resembled depression.

⁂

Just as some of Mary's mental problems stemmed from the early death of her mother, so too did the death of Lincoln's mother wound him psychologically. Nancy Hanks died when Abe was nine years old, leaving a scar on his psyche that predisposed him to depression for the rest of his life. He may well have regarded her death as a deliberate act of abandonment, for as an adult he found it difficult to relate to women and to trust them; he evidently feared that if he got too close to them, they would let him down.

And so Abraham and Mary, both emotionally damaged, brought to their relationship what psychologists call "unfinished mother and father business." It did not bode well for their future together.

2

GIRL LOSES BOY
1840-1841

L incoln's engagement was puzzling, for as Elizabeth Edwards and others noted, he and Mary Todd seemed like polar opposites. A Springfield neighbor recalled that "Mr. and Mrs. Lincoln were not a congenial couple; their tastes were so different that when a boy I often wondered why they were married. She was very fond of show and company and inclined to be extravagant while he was the very opposite." William Herndon said that she was "the exact reverse" of her husband in "figure and physical proportions, in education, bearing, temperament, history—in everything." Mary Lincoln herself referred to "our opposite natures" when discussing their marriage.

Historians as well as contemporaries have been struck by the differences between Lincoln and his wife. Albert J. Beveridge, a close student of Lincoln's prepresidential years, noted that "[f]ew couples have been more unsuited in temperament, manners, taste, and everything else." Ruth Painter Randall acknowledged that the pair "had come into the world endowed with qualities of personality and temperament singularly opposite. In family background and environment up to the time of their meeting there was violent contrast."

Lincoln's background was most unlike Mary Todd's. He called his ancestors "undistinguished," whereas hers included notable figures like her rich paternal grandfather, General Levi Todd. On the hardscrabble Kentucky and Indiana frontier, Lincoln grew up in poverty, while Mary enjoyed a privileged childhood in Lexington, the self-styled "Athens of the West." Robert and Eliza Todd had nine children, eight of whom survived into adulthood. The well-to-do family occupied a comfortable home and exalted social and political positions in Kentucky.

Whereas Lincoln had less than a year's formal education in primitive frontier "blab schools," Mary Todd attended Lexington's most exclusive private schools for over a decade, including Madame Charlotte Victoire LeClerc Mentelle's Academy. In addition to studying traditional academic subjects like reading, foreign languages (French), and math, she also learned such social graces as formal dancing, polite conversation, and proper letter-writing. Lincoln's only sibling, his sister Sarah, wed a backwoodsman; Mary Todd's eldest sister Elizabeth married the son of Illinois's former governor.

In the fall of 1840, when Lincoln returned to Springfield from the political hustings, he began seeing Mary again. He soon realized, in the words of his friend Samuel C. Parks, that they "were not congenial, and were incompatible" and "ought not to marry." Moreover, he was not sure that he really loved her. Joshua Speed explained: "In the winter of [18]40 & 41—he was very unhappy about his engagement to his [future] wife—Not being entirely satisfied that his *heart* was going with his hand—How much he suffered then on that account none Know so well as myself—He disclosed his whole heart to me." In addition, Lincoln may well have doubted that he could meet Mary Todd's emotional demands. Therefore, he broke the engagement.

Even if Lincoln failed to realize that he was too reserved and uncommunicative to satisfy such a woman, he might well have called off the engagement anyway, for in late 1840, he fell head-over-heels in love with Matilda Edwards, the gorgeous eighteen-year-old niece of Ninian Edwards. A resident of Alton, she had come to Springfield like many other young women to attend parties given while the Illinois General Assembly was in session. According to Caroline Owsley Brown, a "legislative winter was as eagerly looked forward to by the ladies of the State as [by] the politicians because it promised a season of constant gaiety and entertainment. An invitation to spend such a time in Springfield was a coveted honor. The pretty girls from all over the State flocked [t]here under the care of fathers, uncles, brothers, cousins, any relation, however remote who could be induced to bring them." Matilda Edwards was under the care of her uncle, Ninian Edwards, at whose home she stayed that winter, along with Mary Todd.

Matilda was "very bright," "something of a coquette," as well as "a most fascinating and handsome girl, tall, graceful, and rather reserved," who "moved at ease among the social and refined classes at Alton." Her "gentle temper, her conciliatory manners, and the sweetness of her heart made her dear to all who knew her." Lincoln was one of the many young men who held her dear; others included Joshua Speed, who described her thus: "Two clear blue eyes, a brow as fair as Palmyra marble touched by the chisel of Praxiteles—Lips so fresh, fair, and lovely that I am jealous even of the minds that kiss them—a form as perfect as that of the Venus de Medicis—a Mind clear as a bell[,] a voice bewitchingly soft and sonorous and a smile so sweet lovely and playful and a countenance and soul shining through it." Speed marveled that all of "these charms" could be "combined in one young lady."

Orville H. Browning, who spoke with Mary Todd about Lincoln's infatuation with Matilda, reported that "Lincoln became very much attached" to Matilda and "finally fell desperately in love with her." Mrs. Nicholas H.

Ridgely, a leader of Springfield society in Lincoln's day, told her grand-daughter "that it was common report that Lincoln had fallen in love with Matilda Edwards." There "was never the least doubt in her mind that this was the case." Matilda Edwards's niece said that it was "an undisputed fact that Lincoln was in love with her." Helen Dodge Edwards, wife of Matilda's uncle Benjamin S. Edwards, recalled that Lincoln "was deeply in love with Matilda Edwards."

That reminiscent testimony is supported by contemporary evidence. In January 1841, Jane D. Bell wrote from Springfield that Lincoln declared "if he had it in his power he would not have one feature in her [Matilda's] face altered, he thinks she is so perfect." Mrs. Bell added that Lincoln and Joshua Speed "spent most of their time at [the] Edwards [home] this winter" and that "Lincoln could never bear to leave Miss Edwards' side in company" because "he fell desperately in love with her."

Though smitten, the notoriously bashful Lincoln was too timid to approach Matilda Edwards, who told her aunt Elizabeth Edwards that he "never mentioned Such a Subject to me: he never even Stooped to pay me a Compliment." Infatuated with Matilda, Lincoln confided to John J. Hardin "that he thought he did not love" Mary Todd "as he should and that he would do her a great wrong if he married her." Hardin shared this information with his sisters Martinette and Lucy Jane, cousins of Mary Todd. Another of Mary's cousins, Elizabeth Todd Grimsley, said that many people in Springfield (herself included) thought Lincoln "doubted whether he was responding [to Mary Todd] as fully as a manly generous nature" should; his feeling for her lacked "the overmastering depth of an early love." When Mrs. William Butler, at whose home Lincoln boarded between 1837 and 1842, "advised him if he had given his promise to marry Miss Todd he must in honor keep his word unless she released him," he told her: "it would just kill me to marry Mary Todd."

Even though it might pain Lincoln's conscience for him to break his word to Mary, he felt honor-bound to call off the engagement because his heart belonged to Matilda Edwards. Just how he did so is not entirely clear. Ninian Edwards, Matilda's host, reported that Lincoln "fell in Love" with her but "did not Ever by act or deed directly or indirectly hint or speak of it to Miss Edwards." Mary Todd "became aware of this—Lincoln's affections—The Lincoln & Todd Engagement was broken off in Consequence of it—Miss Todd released Lincoln from the Contract."

Referring to Matilda Edwards, Joshua Speed remembered that Lincoln "seeing another girl—& finding he did not love his [future] wife[,] wrote a letter saying he did not love her." When shown that document, Speed "tried to persuade Lincoln to burn it up," whereupon Lincoln said: "Speed I always Knew you were an obstinate man. If you won't deliver it I will get Some one to do it."

Speed replied: "I Shall not deliver it nor give it to you to be delivered: Words are forgotten—Misunderstood—passed by—not noticed in a private Conversation—but once put your words in writing" those words "Stand as a living & eternal Monument against you. If you think you have will & Manhood Enough to go and see her and Speak to her what you say in that letter, you may do that."

Taking Speed's advice, Lincoln called on Mary Todd and "told her that he did not love her—She rose—and Said 'The deciever [sic] shall be decieved wo is me.'; alluding to a young man She fooled." Speed reported that "Lincoln drew her down on his Knee—Kissed her—& parted—He going one way & She another—Lincoln did Love Miss [Matilda] Edwards— 'Mary' Saw it—told Lincoln the reason of his Change of mind—heart & soul—released him."

After Lincoln's death, Mary confessed that during their courtship, "I doubtless trespassed, many times & oft, upon his great tenderness & amiability of character." She may have played on his conscience in order to win him back. Elizabeth Edwards recalled that her sister Mary released Lincoln from the engagement with the understanding "that She would hold the question an open one—that is that She had not Changed her mind, but felt as always." So he could renew the engagement if he wanted to; she clearly hoped he would.

It is thus not hard to understand why, as Ninian and Elizabeth Edwards reported, Lincoln "in his Conflicts of duty—honor & his love [—] went as Crazy as a Loon." On January 21, Martinette Hardin McKee told her brother: "We have been very much distressed, on Mr Lincoln[']s account; hearing he had two Cat fits, and a Duck fit." Days later, Jane Bell reported that Lincoln "is in rather a bad way." The "doctors say he came within an inch of being a perfect lunatic for life. He was perfectly crazy for some time, not able to attend to his business at all. They say he does not look like the same person."

Indeed, Lincoln did go "crazy for a week or so" and recuperated at the home/boarding house of William Butler. His friend Orville Browning, who was staying there, recalled that Lincoln "was so much affected as to talk incoherently, and to be delirious to the extent of not knowing what he was doing." This "aberration of mind resulted entirely from the situation he . . . got himself into—he was engaged to Miss Todd, and in love with Miss Edwards, and his conscience troubled him dreadfully for the supposed injustice he had done, and the supposed violation of his word which he had committed." Similarly, Mrs. William Butler told her sister that Lincoln was tormented by "the thought that he had treated Mary badly, knowing that she loved him and that he did not love her." This caused him "an agony of remorse." In 1841, Jane Bell reported that it "seems he [Lincoln] had addressed Mary Todd and she accepted him and they had been engaged some time when a Miss Edwards of Alton came here, and he fell desperately in love with her and found he was not so much attached to Mary as he thought."

Joshua Speed recollected that "a gloom came over" Lincoln "till his friends were alarmed for his life." Some of those friends, fearing that he might kill himself, hastened "to remove razors from his room—take away all Knives and other such dangerous things—&c—it was terrible." Lincoln declared that he "would be more than willing" to die, but said, "I have an irrepressible desire to live till I can be assured that the world is a little better for my having lived in it."

In despair, Lincoln appealed to his good friend, the physician Anson G. Henry, with whom he spent many hours each day from January 13 to 18. If Dr. Henry followed the best practices of that era, he would have subjected Lincoln to a disagreeable regimen of bleeding, leeching, mustard rubs, foul-tasting medicines, and cold water baths. On January 20, Lincoln wrote to John Todd Stuart: "I have, within the last few days, been making a most discreditable exhibition of myself in the way of hypochondriaism [i.e., depression] and thereby got an impression that Dr. Henry is necessary to my existence." Three days later, he added: "I am now the most miserable man living. If what I feel were equally distributed to the whole human family, there would not be one cheerful face on the earth. Whether I shall ever be better I can not tell; I awfully forebode I shall not. To remain as I am is impossible; I must die or be better, it appears to me."

In the legislative session that January, Lincoln was not his usual self. With unwonted testiness, he rebuked a colleague who had criticized him. He poked fun at himself: "if any woman, old or young, ever thought there was any peculiar charm in this distinguished specimen . . . I have, as yet, been so unfortunate as not to have discovered it." Abruptly after making these remarks, he quit attending the General Assembly, failing to answer roll calls on January 13, 14, 15, 16, 18, and 20. On the 19th, he cast a vote on only one of five roll calls; two days later, he resumed voting regularly.

On January 24, James C. Conkling reported that Lincoln seemed so "reduced and emaciated" that he could barely "speak above a whisper." Lincoln's condition reminded Conkling of an ode by Thomas Moore: "Poor L! How are the mighty fallen! . . . I doubt not but he can declare 'That loving is a painful thrill, And not to love more painful still' [evidently referring to Matilda Edwards] but would not like to intimate that he has experienced 'That surely 'tis the worst of pain To love and not be loved again.'" John

Todd Stuart's wife saw Lincoln at the statehouse "with his feet braced against one of the pillars. His face looked like [John] Bunyan's 'Giant Despair' [a character in *The Pilgrim's Progress*]." He "was the saddest man I ever knew."

By late January, Lincoln was on the road to recovery. On the 26th, Sarah Smith Hardin wrote her husband John J. Hardin: "I am glad to hear Lincoln has got over his cat fits[.] we have concluded it was a very unsatisfactory way of terminating his romance[.] he ought to have died or gone crazy[.] we are very much disappointed indeed." After the legislature adjourned, Turner R. King observed Lincoln in Springfield "hanging about—moody—silent." King speculated that the "question in his mind was 'Have I incurred any obligation to marry that woman.' He wanted to dodge if he could."

Lincoln apparently felt unable to dodge, thinking that he ought to wed Mary Todd, even though he did not love her, in order to appease his hypersensitive conscience. James C. Conkling accurately predicted that Lincoln would probably "now endeavor to drown his cares among the intricacies and perplexities of the law."

Throughout 1841 and most of 1842, Lincoln avoided Mary Todd. He perhaps even thought of leaving the country, for in March 1841, John Todd Stuart recommended him for a diplomatic post in South America. The following June, Mary Todd wrote that Lincoln "deems me unworthy of notice, as I have not met him in the gay world for months." She derived some consolation from the knowledge "that others were as seldom gladdened by his presence as my humble self." Yet, she lamented, "I would that the case were different, that he would once more resume his Station in Society, that 'Richard should be himself again,' much, much happiness would it afford me." She told a friend that "after she & Mr L broke off she was very sad." In the spring of 1842, after the party season had ended, a visitor to Springfield found Mary Todd "as lonesome as a gay company loving, girl, could be so situated."

Sometime in 1841, Lincoln paid court to Sarah Rickard, the sixteen-year-old sister of Elizabeth Butler, at whose home she lived, and where

Lincoln boarded between 1837 and 1842. In those years, he often saw Sarah, who was only twelve when they first met. Four years later, he proposed to her, observing that since her name was Sarah, she was bound to marry someone named Abraham. She turned him down because, as she put it, "his peculiar manner and his General deportment would not be likely to fascinate a young girl just entering the society world."

For three weeks in the summer of 1841, Lincoln vacationed at Farmington, the stately home of Joshua Speed in Louisville, Kentucky. That visit helped restore Lincoln's spirits. As he prepared to leave, Speed's mother presented him with an Oxford Bible, which she termed "the best cure for the 'Blues.'" It evidently worked, for in late October, Joshua Speed reported that since Lincoln's return to Springfield, "he has been eminently successful in his [legal] practice" and "is in fine spirits and good health." Three months thereafter, Lincoln declared that recently he had "been quite clear of the hypo."

LINCOLN PLAYS EMOTIONAL
COUNSELOR TO JOSHUA SPEED

That autumn, Lincoln had an opportunity to return Speed's kindness, for Joshua was experiencing the same kind of emotional turmoil that had earlier plagued Lincoln. Speed had proposed to a young neighbor, Fanny Henning, who had accepted him, but he was having second thoughts and undergoing "immense suffering" for fear that he did not really love her. Lincoln acted as an emotional counselor to his friend, playing the same role that Speed had played for him. Lincoln wrote him letters that reveal more about his own emotional state than they do about Speed's. Seeking to convince Speed that his anxiety was unjustified, Lincoln asked him: "How came you to court her? Was it because you thought she desired it; and that you had given her reason to expect it? If it was for that, why did not the same reason make you court Ann Todd [a cousin, not the sister, of Mary Todd], and at least twenty others of whom you can think, & to whom it would apply with greater force than to *her*? Did you court her for her wealth? Why, you knew she had none. But you say you *reasoned* yourself *into* it. What do you mean by that? Was it not, that you found yourself unable to *reason* yourself *out of* it? Did you not think, and partly form the purpose, of courting her the first time you ever saw or heard of her? What had reason to do with it, at that early stage? There was nothing *at that time* for reason to work upon. Whether she was moral, aimiable, [sic] sensible, or even of good character, you did not, nor could not then know; except perhaps you might infer the last from the company you found her in. All you then did or could know of her, was her *personal appearance and deportment*; and these, if they impress at all, impress the *heart* and not the head. Say candidly, were not those heavenly *black eyes*, the whole basis of all your early *reasoning* on the subject?"

This letter suggests that Lincoln may well have entertained some doubts about his feelings for Mary Todd. Perhaps he had persuaded himself that he really loved her because she desired him to do so. Or maybe he worried that he was attracted to her because of her high social status, or that he had permitted his head to rule his heart.

When Speed expressed deep concern about his fiancée's health, Lincoln sought to reassure him: "Why, Speed, if you did not love her, although you might not wish her death, you would most calmly be resigned to it." Evidently referring to his doubts about Mary Todd, he added: "You know the Hell I have suffered on that point, and how tender I am upon it."

Lincoln offered Speed some advice: "remember in the dep[t]h and even the agony of despondency, that verry shortly you are to feel well again. I am now fully convinced, that you love her as ardently as you are capable of loving. Your ever being happy in her presence, and your intense anxiety about her health, if there were nothing else, would place this beyond all dispute in my mind. I incline to think it probable, that your nerves will fail you occasionally for a while; but once you get them fairly graded now, that trouble is over forever. I think if I were you, in case my mind were not exactly right, I would avoid being *idle*; I would immediately engage in some business, or go to making preparations for it." Lincoln was evidently trying to convince himself not to take seriously his misgivings about Mary Todd; but in case he succumbed to them, he ought to busy himself with some project.

Speed overcame his doubts and on February 15, 1842, wed Fanny Henning. Upon receiving Speed's letter announcing his new status, Lincoln opened it "with intense anxiety and trepidation—so much, that although it turned out better than I expected, I have hardly yet, at the distance of ten hours, become calm." He told Speed, "our *forebodings*, for which you and I are rather peculiar, are all the worst sort of nonsense." In response to Speed's expression of fear that the Elysium he had dreamed about "is never to be realized," Lincoln reassured him that "it is the peculiar misfortune of both you and me, to dream dreams of Elysium far exceeding all that any thing earthly can realize. Far short of your dreams as you may be, no woman could do more to realize them, than that same black eyed Fanny. If you could but contemplate her through my immagination [sic], it would appear ridiculous to you, that any one should for a moment think of being unhappy with her. My old Father used to have a saying that 'If you make a bad bargain, *hug* it the tighter'; and it occurs to me, that if the bargain you have just closed can possibly be called a bad one, it is certainly the most *pleasant one* for applying that maxim to, which my fancy can, by any effort, picture."

Apparently Lincoln was trying to convince himself that he should wed Mary Todd even though their engagement might be a "bad bargain" and that he ought not to be disappointed if she failed to live up to his ideal.

The following month, Lincoln rejoiced to learn that Speed was much happier than he had anticipated. But Lincoln said that the good news troubled his conscience, which tormented him about Mary Todd. Alluding cryptically to the "fatal first of Jany. '41," he wrote that since that day, "it seems to me, I should have been entirely happy, but for the never-absent idea, that there is *one* still unhappy whom I have contributed to make so.

That still kills my soul. I can not but reproach myself, for even wishing to be happy while she is otherwise."

In July 1842, Lincoln again told Speed that his guilty conscience was bothering him. He confessed that he could not take Speed's (unidentified) advice: "I must regain my confidence in my own ability to keep my resolves when they are made. In that ability, you know, I once prided myself as the only, or at least the chief, gem of my character; that gem I lost—how, and when, you too well know. I have not yet regained it; and until I do, I can not trust myself in any matter of much importance." Always a fatalist and ever passive in his dealings with women, he announced that he would heed the injunction of Moses: "Stand *still* and see the salvation of the Lord."

And he stood still for the next three months.

3

GIRL GETS BOY
1842

While awaiting the salvation of the Lord, Lincoln was challenged to a duel by a hotheaded Irish Democrat, Illinois state auditor James Shields, who justifiably believed that he had been insulted. In August and September 1842, four satirical letters ridiculing Shields and signed by "Aunt Rebecca of Lost Townships" appeared in Springfield's Whig newspaper, the *Sangamo Journal*. Just after Shields had declared Illinois State Bank notes unacceptable as payment for taxes, there appeared the second "Rebecca" letter, which Lincoln admitted was his handiwork. It described Shields as a "conceity dunce" and "a fool as well as a liar" with whom "truth is out of the question, and as for getting a good bright passable lie out of him, you might as well try to strike fire from a cake of tallow." In addition, Aunt Rebecca quoted Shields saying to some young women: "Dear girls, it is distressing, but I cannot marry you all. Too well I know how much you suffer; but do, do, remember, it is not my fault that I am so handsome and so interesting."

According to the woman who later married Shields, he "became very sensitive about it, for it created a great stir. People twitted him on the streets and when he went into stores he was made the butt of jokes." Indignantly, he demanded to know the identity of "Aunt Rebecca." When Lincoln acknowledged that he was the author of the second letter, the Irishman insisted on a retraction and an apology. That response was understandable, for, as Shields's law partner Gustave Koerner observed: "No man of the least spirit could have taken those insults without seeking satisfaction, even by arms, if necessary." Lincoln accepted the challenge and later acknowledged ruefully that doing so "was the meanest thing that he ever did in his life."

Some biographers, misled by Mary's rather confused account of the affair, have incorrectly asserted that she wrote the "Aunt Rebecca" letters and that Lincoln protected her by gallantly pretending that he had done so and thus paved the way for their reconciliation and marriage. Douglas L. Wilson has shown, however, that her version of the story could not be accurate. Largely thanks to the good offices of Mary's cousin John J. Hardin, the duel was called off, and Shields and Lincoln were reconciled.

A few days later, Hardin helped Lincoln effect another reconciliation, this time with Mary Todd. On September 27, she and Lincoln separately attended the wedding of Hardin's sister, Martinette, in Jacksonville. When the other guests went for a ride, Mary Todd was left behind because she lacked an escort. As she was watching them depart, Lincoln rode up. "She went down & he said he had come for her to join the party." They went off and "a reconciliation followed." Thereafter they rendezvoused at the Springfield home of Simeon Francis, editor of the *Sangamo Journal* and a close friend of Lincoln. Elizabeth Todd Edwards reported that after "the match was broken off between Mary and Lincoln Mrs Francis shrewdly got them together." They resumed courting clandestinely because, as Mary explained somewhat delphically, "the world—woman & man were uncertain & slippery and [we thought] that it was best to keep the secret Courtship from all Eyes & Ears." They may well have done so because Ninian and

Elizabeth Edwards, with whom she was living, had advised the couple not to wed, for they were incompatible and could not live happily as man and wife.

A week after that Jacksonville wedding, Lincoln posed a delicate question to Joshua Speed: "Are you now, in *feeling* as well as *judgement*, glad you are married as you are?" He added: "Please answer it quickly as I feel impatient to know." Lincoln dared not wed Mary Todd unless he received assurance that Speed was happily married. In reply, Speed told him "not to hesitate or longer doubt that happiness would be the result of his marriage to Miss Todd, giving his own experience of depression and melancholy before he and Miss Henning had finally made up and determined to risk their happiness in each other's keeping."

Acting on this advice, Lincoln wed Mary Todd on November 4, 1842. Early that morning, the bride astonished her sister Elizabeth by announcing that "she and Mr. Lincoln would get married that night." At the same time, Lincoln informed Episcopal minister Charles Dresser, "I want to get hitched tonight." Dresser offered to perform the ceremony at his home, but Ninian Edwards would not hear of it. "That will never do," he protested. "Mary Todd is my ward. If the marriage is going to take place, it must be at my house." Ninian's wife Elizabeth told a friend "what a shock the news was to her & how hurt she had been at Mary's want of confidence in her." Elizabeth added that "after she was composed enough to see Mary & talk with her about it," her younger sister "seemed very much disinclined to say anything of it." Elizabeth admonished her: "Do not forget that you are a Todd. But, Mary, if you insist on being married today, we will make merry, and have the wedding here this evening. I will not permit you to be married out of my house."

Only a few people attended the ceremony that evening. Among them were two groomsmen, James H. Matheny and Beverly Powell, and two bridesmaids, Julia Jayne and Ann Rodney. Matheny remembered that "there was more or less stiffness about the affair due, no doubt, to the sudden change of plans and resulting 'town talk,' and I could not help noticing a certain amount of whispering and elevation of eyebrows on the part of a few of the guests, as if preparing each other for something dramatic or unlooked-for to happen." That "something" occurred when the "corpulent, vain, coarse, and effusive" State Supreme Court Justice Thomas C. Browne interrupted the proceedings. A "rough 'old timer'" known as "the Falstaff of the bench" who "always said just what he thought without regard to place or Surroundings," Browne was unfamiliar with the Episcopal service and hence startled when Lincoln turned to Mary and said, "with this ring I thee endow with all my goods and chattels, lands and tenements." Upon hearing those words, the judge blurted out: "Lord Jesus Christ, God Almighty, Lincoln, the Statute fixes all that!" The minister "broke down" and nearly gave way to "an almost irresistible desire to laugh" and "checked his proceeding for a minute or so" but somehow regained his composure and pronounced the couple man and wife.

A LOVELESS MATCH?

A guest at the wedding, Helen Dodge Edwards, told biographer Ida Tarbell that the Lincoln-Todd marriage was a match "made up" by "mutual friends" and not really "a love affair." Tarbell, who interviewed many other friends and relatives of Lincoln and his wife, stated that the bride and groom "were utterly unsuited for sympathetic companionship. I doubt if Mary Todd had the faintest conception of the meaning of the words." Eleanor Gridley, a writer who also spoke with many people who had known the Lincolns, concluded that Mary Todd did not love Lincoln, for "LOVE is the essence of kindness, compassion, tenderness, thoughtfulness, [and] consideration." Gridley rhetorically asked a biographer of Mary Todd: "if she loved him, would she have often annoyed him, confused him and later when her husband became the most distinguished man of the Commonwealth would she have embarrassed and humiliated him, which she often did?" Answering her own questions, Gridley said: "No, rather, if she loved she would have been considerate, thoughtful, careful lest she add another burden to his troubled soul."

The skeptical Gridley may also have asked why Mary Lincoln sometimes spoke of her spouse's death as if it were desirable. Once she told a Springfield friend that if Lincoln were to die, "his spirit will never find me living outside the boundaries of a slave State." In 1857, she wrote her half-sister Emilie Todd Helm: "I often laugh & tell Mr. L[incoln] that I am determined my next Husband *shall be rich*." Four years later, in a similar expression of thinly veiled conjugal discontent, she wrote another half-sister, Elodie, who had just announced her engagement. According to Elodie, Mary sent her "a long letter on the subject of matrimony and adjoins [enjoins] me that I am a great deal better off as I am," namely, unmarried. Elodie remarked: "She ought to know as she committed the fatal step years ago, and I believe another such letter would almost make me abandon the idea."

Lincoln voiced similar thoughts. In 1860, he told an Illinois crowd: "I think very much of the people, as an old friend said he thought of women. He said when he lost his first wife, who had been a great help to him in his business, he thought he was ruined—that he could never find another to fill her place. At length, however, he married another, who he found did quite as well as the first, and that his opinion now was that any woman would do well who was well done by." A journalist wondered what Mrs. Lincoln might "say of her husband's opinion, that her loss can be so easily and satisfactorily replaced."

So did Lincoln love Mary? In addition to Ida Tarbell and Eleanor Gridley, another woman who spoke with the Lincolns' friends and neighbors in Springfield—including one of the bridesmaids at their wedding—believed that the "question whether Lincoln loved her, even when he married her, cannot be answered." A thorough biographer of Lincoln's prepresidential years, Albert J. Beveridge, doubted that he "really 'loved'" Mary Todd.

In response to such skeptics, biographer Ruth Painter Randall cited a "flock of witnesses close to the Lincolns" who "left testimony as to the happiness of their marriage." Those witnesses, among them Henry B. Rankin, are, however, unreliable. Rankin wrote that the Lincolns "were in harmony on the larger affairs in their lives" and that "Abraham Lincoln loved her," statements appearing in his discredited book, *Intimate Character Sketches of Abraham Lincoln*. Randall regarded Rankin as a trustworthy authority because of what she called his "years of pleasant friendship" with the Lincolns, but Rankin flagrantly prevaricated about his relations with them.

Another of Randall's witnesses was attorney Henry C. Whitney, who wrote in his memoirs: "Lincoln thoroughly loved his wife. I had many reasons to know this in my intimacy with him." He added that it "is rare that a man so thoroughly intellectual as Mr. Lincoln, makes a good husband, but there was no flaw in his conduct in this respect, so far as a devotion to matters of intense intellectual application would permit." But Whitney contradicted himself, insisting to Herndon that Lincoln was a poor husband: "so great & peculiar a man as Lincoln could not make any woman happy," for "he was too much allied to his intellect to get down to the plane of the domestic relations." Whitney added: "Lincoln would have greatly enjoyed married life if he had [wed?] either Ann Rutledge or Miss [Matilda] Edwards. I think he would have been very fond of a wife had he had one to suit but I also doubt if he would have been as *great* a man as he was." Moreover, Whitney did not live in Springfield and was unable to observe the Lincolns day in and day out, nor was he an intimate friend of Lincoln's, like Joshua Speed, Orville Browning, or William Herndon.

Randall reasonably asked: "Who knew the truth of the matter better than Mary's sisters?" She quoted Emilie Todd Helm's statement that the Lincolns "understood each other thoroughly, and Mr. Lincoln looked beyond the impulsive words and manner, and knew that his wife was devoted to him and to his interests." Mrs. Helm elaborated: "It has also been said that Mr. and Mrs. Lincoln were not happy. Mrs. [Frances Todd] Wallace denies this emphatically, and the present writer's knowledge bears out Mrs. Wallace's assertion. . . . They lived in a quiet and unostentatious manner. . . . The present writer saw Mr. and Mrs. Lincoln together some part of every day for six months at one time, and saw nothing of the unhappiness which is so often referred to." In December 1854, at the age of nineteen, Emilie Todd had visited the Lincolns and stayed for half a year. Looking back on those days, she wrote: "Any one could see that Mr. Lincoln admired Mary and was very proud of her. She took infinite pains to fascinate him again and again with pretty coquettish clothes and dainty little airs and graces. She was gay and light-hearted, hopeful and happy. She had a high temper and perhaps did not always have it under complete control, but what did it matter? Her little temper was soon over, and her husband loved her none the less, perhaps all the more, for this human frailty which needed his love and patience to pet and coax the sunny smile to replace the sarcasm and tears—and, oh, how she did love this man!" During her stay with the Lincolns, Emilie kept a diary that might have corroborated her account, but she destroyed it. As historian Angela Esco Elder pointed out, Emilie sanitized the account of her sister's marriage: she knew full well that Abraham and Mary experienced "marital discord, but this was not the image of the Todds or the Lincolns that Emilie wanted remembered." Moreover, like Henry C. Whitney, Emilie Todd did not observe the Lincolns regularly over the years the way that Springfield residents did—including neighbors, law partners, servants in the home, political allies, workmen, et al. Moreover, Lincoln was out of town practicing law on the circuit for much of the time that Emilie sojourned as his houseguest.

Like Emilie Todd Helm, Ruth Randall cited the testimony of another sister, Frances Todd Wallace of Springfield, who in 1895 told an interviewer: "I don't see why people should say Mr. Lincoln's home life was not happy, for I certainly never saw a thing there that would make me think either of them was unhappy. He was devoted to his home, and Mrs. Lincoln thought everything of him. She almost worshipped him. . . . And they certainly did live happily together—as much so as any man and woman I have ever known." Mrs. Wallace's credibility is badly undermined by her statement in that same interview: "they say that Mrs. Lincoln was an ambitious woman. But she was not an ambitious woman at all." Based on that wildly inaccurate assessment of Mary's legendary ambition (see Chapter 5), it seems clear either that Frances did not know her sister well or at least was unwilling to tell the truth about her. She, like Emilie Todd Helm, was probably trying to sugarcoat the Todd family history.

Frances and Emilie certainly did not know Mary as well as did their eldest sister, Elizabeth Todd Edwards, a virtual surrogate mother to all three. Mary had lived with Elizabeth during her early years in Springfield as well as her final years. In addition, Elizabeth spent many weeks with the Lincolns at the White House in 1861 and 1862. Did Mary love Lincoln? Elizabeth made no statement one way or the other, but as noted in Chapter 1, she presciently warned Mary that she and Lincoln were not "Suitable to Each other" and, along with her husband Ninian, "told Mary & Lincoln that they had better not Ever marry—that their natures, mind—Education—raising &c were So different they Could not live happy as husband & wife." She said all this in the mid-1860s and did not then or later suggest that her warning had proved unjustified.

Elizabeth Edwards's son, Albert, recalled that in his youth during the 1840s and 1850s, "I used to come to their [the Lincolns'] house Saturdays and Sundays almost every week. I never saw a more loving couple. I never heard a harsh word or anything out of the way." But it was not to be expected that the Lincolns would quarrel before a young relative. Moreover, on most weekends in the fall and spring, Lincoln was away from town on the legal circuit, and when he was back in Springfield, he often spent Sundays at his office.

Following Ruth Randall's lead, Jean H. Baker and others cite a dubious statement to support the conclusion that Lincoln loved Mary: the president allegedly told a woman at a White House reception in 1864 or 1865: "My wife is as handsome as when she was a girl, and I, a poor nobody then, fell in love with her; and what is more, I have never fallen out." In fact, what Lincoln *never* did was to express such sentiments to even his most intimate friends, much less to a comparative stranger. The anonymous source for this quote—a woman who signed herself "C. E. L." and whose claim appeared in 1872—cannot be identified, hence her reliability cannot be checked. The statement she reported is so far out of character that it strains credulity; no one else (aside from Mary herself) reported hearing Lincoln say anything of the sort.

Another questionable source cited by biographer Jean Baker is a statement that Elizabeth Blair Lee *purportedly* made in a letter written to her husband, Samuel Phillips Lee, four days after Lincoln's death: "Mary has her husband's deepest love. This is a matter upon which one woman cannot deceive another." Baker presented these two sentences as a direct quote from a letter by Lee, but they are not; that letter actually says something quite different. It reads: "Some have thought she [Mary] had not his [Lincoln's] affections but tis evident to me she had no doubt about it and that is a point about which women are not often deceived after a long married life like theirs."

Such a garbled version of a key source is especially troubling because Baker relies heavily on the supposed testimony of Lee to show that "[w]artime observers of the Lincoln marriage detected the same mutual understanding that [Mrs.] Lincoln's sister Frances had said about their relationship in Springfield." (See the Appendix)

Ruth Randall, Jean Baker, and their followers to the contrary notwithstanding, a flock of reliable witnesses testified that Lincoln did *not* love Mary. According to William Herndon, "Lincoln knew that he did not love the girl: he had promised to wed her: he knew what would eventually come of it and it was a conflict between sacrificing his honor and sacrificing his domestic peace: he chose the latter—saved his honor and threw away domestic happiness." Joshua Speed believed that "Lincoln Married her for honor—feeling his honor bound to her." Orville Browning said Lincoln "undoubtedly felt that he had made [a mistake] in having engaged himself to Miss Todd. But having done so, he felt himself in honor bound to act in perfect good faith towards her—and that good faith compelled him to fulfill his engagement with her, if she persisted in claiming the fulfillment of his word." Browning "always doubted whether, had circumstances left him entirely free to act upon his own impulses, he would have voluntarily made proposals of marriage to Miss Todd."

John Todd Stuart told Herndon "that the marriage of Lincoln to Mary Todd was a policy match all around," by which he probably meant that it was politically expedient. Herndon guessed it was a "political match" that she desired because Lincoln was "a rising man," while he wished to gain "her family power." Perhaps Lincoln hoped that by wedding Mary Todd he could improve his political chances through an alliance with the Whigs' wealthier faction, but such a calculating approach to marriage seems out of character for Lincoln. He had been engaged to Ann Rutledge and had proposed to Sarah Rickard, neither of whom was politically well connected. His marriage actually hurt his political career in the short run. A few months after the wedding, Lincoln lost his bid for the Whig congressional nomination in part because he was viewed "as the candidate of pride, wealth, and aristocratic family distinction," a reputation he acquired as a Todd family in-law.

THE SEDUCTION HYPOTHESIS

The unusual circumstances surrounding Lincoln's wedding cry out for analysis. It was, according to Elizabeth Edwards, "quick & sudden." The license was issued the day of the ceremony. Lincoln recruited James Matheny as a groomsman that day. Such suddenness was highly unusual for members of the Springfield elite like the Edwardses and Todds, who gave elaborate weddings. Three years earlier, Elizabeth Todd Edwards had put on a wedding for her sister Frances that was "one of the grand affairs of its time." Frances recalled that Elizabeth also "wanted to give her [Mary Todd] a big wedding."

On the day of his nuptials, Lincoln "looked and acted as if he was going to the Slaughter." He told groomsman James Matheny: "I shall have to marry that girl." Matheny remembered that Lincoln "often" confided "directly & indirectly" that "he was driven into the marriage." According to Matheny, Mary Todd "told L. that he was in honor bound to marry her." When dressing for the event, Lincoln was asked where he was headed. "I guess I am going to hell," he replied.

All this evidence, along with the fact that Mary delivered a child (Robert) slightly less than nine months after the wedding, supports the hypothesis of Lincoln scholar Wayne C. Temple, who speculated that she seduced Lincoln. As noted above, the courtship had resumed clandestinely at the home of Simeon Francis. Temple wrote: "Exactly what went on in the Springfield house of the Francises during these secret trysts between Abraham and Mary is unknown. There may have been very little chaperoning done by Simeon or Eliza Francis in the months which followed." Citing Orville Browning's statement that Mary was the aggressor in the courtship and James Matheny's claim that Lincoln said that he had to marry her, Temple concluded that "she may have, in desperation, compromised the shy Lincoln."

Of course, if she did seduce Lincoln, she could not have been certain the next day that she was pregnant, but she might have been, and that would have given her good enough reason to demand that he wed her. In nineteenth-century America, as historian Lawrence M. Friedman explained, "Sex except with her husband 'ruined' a woman, destroyed her life's chances, made her unfit for polite society. 'Virtue' meant chastity for an unmarried woman, total fidelity for a married one. Loss of virtue was an unparalleled catastrophe—the worst thing that could befall a respectable woman."

Wayne Temple's "seduction hypothesis" is plausible though not provable. It helps explain some otherwise inexplicable features of the wedding: why it took place on such short notice; why Lincoln resembled an animal on the way to the slaughter; why he remarked that he was "going to hell;" why he married a woman he said he did not love; why Orville Browning "always doubted whether, had circumstances left him entirely free to act upon his own impulses, he would have voluntarily made proposals of marriage to Miss Todd"; why Lincoln told one of his groomsmen that he "had to marry that girl" and that he "was driven into the marriage"; and why Herndon believed that Lincoln "*self-sacrificed* himself rather than to be charged with dishonor."

Other considerations support Temple's seduction hypothesis. Mary Todd's ethical sense was weak; during her years as First Lady of the land, she took and extorted bribes, padded expense accounts and payrolls, pinched wages from White House staff, attempted to raid the stationery fund, folded personal expenses into government bills, peddled trading permits, expedited pardons, leaked sensitive documents to the press for money, and engaged in other shady activities (see Chapter 9). In addition, at the time of the wedding she was a few weeks shy of her twenty-fourth birthday, rapidly approaching old-maidhood. (In that era, the average age of brides in Sangamon County was nineteen.) The historian Frank H. Hodder plausibly speculated that she "hung on to Lincoln because she knew mighty well that unless she captured some green-horn she would never marry at all." A childhood friend reported that in her youth Mary "did not then appear to be one who would attract the attention of young men, not being as handsome as most of her companions," who "would laugh at her prediction" that she was to marry a president. She may have recalled the laughter of her childhood friends as she sought to get Lincoln to marry her. Martinette Hardin thought that she had "made up her mind that he should marry her at the cost of her pride to show us all that she was not defeated." She would thus assuage not only the present wound (caused by Lincoln's decision to break off the engagement) but also the one sustained during her youth (caused by the skepticism of her friends).

The only other likely marital prospect Mary had at that time was Edwin Bathurst Webb, whom she called her "*principal lion.*" Sixteen years her senior, he was a courtly, "rather aristocratic" Virginia-born state legislator and widower who was desperate to remarry. But Webb did not suit Mary, who described him as "a widower of modest merit" with two "*sweet little objections*" (i.e., children).

Some believed that Stephen A. Douglas was also courting Mary Todd, but as she told a relative years later: "I liked him well enough, but that was all." His most thorough biographer found "no evidence that their relationship went beyond that of friendship." Douglas was obsessed with politics, not romance.

Further support for the "seduction hypothesis" can be inferred from the sexuality of Lincoln and Mary Todd, neither of whom seems to have been undersexed. Herndon called her "the most sensual woman" he ever knew. According to William Jayne, Mary Todd in the early 1840s was a woman of "strong passions." A niece considered her "an incorrigible flirt," and her uncle, Ninian Edwards, said "Mary could make a bishop forget his prayers." A Springfield neighbor recollected that she "dared me once or twice to Kiss her." As that reminiscence suggests, it is possible that Mary Lincoln was unfaithful to her husband. In 1866, Caroline Dall apparently saw evidence in Herndon's memorandum books (no longer extant) that indicated as much. During her White House years, some thought that she committed adultery with William S. Wood, a notorious seducer, as well as with others (see Chapter 8).

Lincoln was "a Man of strong passions for woman," according to David Davis, who thought that Lincoln's "Conscience Kept him from seduction" and "saved many a woman." Herndon witnessed that conscience in action: "I have seen Lincoln tempted and I have seen him reject the approach of women." Lincoln himself described how one day during his presidency his "indignation" came to the rescue: "I believe there is even a system of female brokerage in offices here in Washington, for I am constantly beset by women of all sorts, high and low, pretty and ugly, modest and the other sort." The day before, "a very handsome young lady called" who "would not take a denial" called on him "and began soliciting a certain office" for a man "supposed to be her husband." She was pleading "her cause dexterously, eloquently," and "was almost successful by her importunate entreaties." Gradually "she came closer and closer to me" until "her face was so near my own that I thought she wanted me to kiss her." Then "my indignation came to my relief, and drawing myself back and straightening myself up, I gave her the proper sort of a look and said: 'Mrs. ––, you are very pretty, and it's very tempting, BUT I WON'T.'"

Like David Davis, Herndon also reported that Lincoln had "terribly strong passions for women," and that he "could scarcely keep his hands off them." Lincoln told Herndon that in the mid-1830s he had given in to "a devilish passion" for a girl in Beardstown.

Lincoln allegedly misbehaved once while returning to Springfield after riding the circuit. He was spending the night at the home of a friend; in a nearby bed slept a young woman whose feet accidentally "fell on Lincoln's pillow." Now and then "in her sleep she moved her feet about." That "put the *devil* into Lincoln at once, thinking that the girl did this of a purpose." So he "reached up his hand and put it where it ought not to be." The girl woke up, rose, "and went to her mother's bed and told what had happened." Fortunately for Lincoln, the mother enjoined her to keep quiet about it.

Lincoln regaled his friend James Short with a similar story: while surveying in Sangamon County during his New Salem days, "he was put to bed in the same room with two girls, the head of his bed being next to the foot of the girls' bed." During the night "he commenced tickling the feet of one of the girls with his fingers. As she seemed to enjoy it as much as he did; he then tickled a little higher up; and as he would tickle higher the girl would shove down lower and the higher he tickled the lower she moved." Lincoln "would tell the story with evident enjoyment" but "never told how the thing ended."

Lincoln often said, "about sexual contact, 'It is the harp of a thousand strings.'" A fellow attorney, Oliver L. Davis, reported that Lincoln's "mind run on sexual [matters?]." He liked to tell sexual jokes and stories. In 1859, he asked the newlywed Christopher Columbus Brown, "Why is a woman like a barrel?" When Brown pled ignorance, Lincoln supplied the answer: "You have to raise the hoops before you put the head in."

Lincoln told David Davis a story "about a man and a woman in the old days traveling up and down the country with a fiddle and a banjo making music for their living. And the man was proud of his wife's virtue and was always saying that no man could get to her, and he would trust her with any man who wanted to try it on a bet. And he made a bet with a stranger one day and the stranger took the wife into a room while the husband stood outside the door and played his fiddle. For quite a while he stood there playing his fiddle, and at last sang a song to her asking her how she was coming along with the stranger."

She replied with a song of her own:

"He's got me down,

He's clasped me round the middle;

Kiss my ass and go to hell;

Be off with your damned old fiddle."

During his early adulthood, Lincoln may have patronized brothels. In 1866, Herndon showed a visitor "affidavits from prostitutes" who apparently had serviced Lincoln. In 1832, during the Black Hawk War, he and some colleagues called at a bordello in Galena. Lincoln may not have sampled the wares, for Abner Y. Ellis said that he "had no desire for strange women[.] I never heard him speak of any particular Woman with disrespect though he had Many opportunities for doing so while in Company with J[oshua] F. S[peed] and W[illia]m B[utler] two old rats in that way." But Herndon told Caroline Dall that whereas Lincoln "was a pure perfectly chaste man" before the death of his sweetheart Ann Rutledge in 1835, after that "in his misery—he fell into the habits of his neighborhood." Herndon also recollected that between 1837 and 1842, Lincoln and Joshua Speed, "a lady's man," were "quite familiar—to go no further [—] with the women."

In sum, it is plausible to conclude that if Mary Todd tried to seduce Lincoln in November 1842, he was willing. Many years later, she expressed her belief that he could be seduced. On March 26, 1865, during the Lincolns' visit to the Army of the Potomac, the First Lady asked an officer rhetorically: "Do you know that I never allow the President to see any woman alone?"

"A MATTER OF PROFOUND WONDER"

Lincoln's wedding prompted a little public commentary. Alluding to the duel that he almost fought with James Shields, a newspaper teased the groom: "Linco[l]n, who was to have been flayed alive by the sword of Shields, has given up the notion of dueling, and taken up one no less fatal to bachelors than the sword is to animal existence—in short, he is married! 'Grim visaged war hath smoothed his wrinkled front,' and now he 'capers nimbly in a lady's [chamber].'" Lincoln himself had little to say about the wedding, other than to write to a friend a week later: "Nothing new here, except my marrying, which to me, is a matter of profound wonder."

PART II

THE SPRINGFIELD YEARS

1842–1861

4

A ROCKY START IN TEMPORARY QUARTERS

1842–1844

I n an 1841 legal proceeding, Lincoln represented Mary Shelby, a black woman suing for divorce. While composing a document to submit to the court on her behalf, he indulged in ironic euphemism: though Mr. Shelby had failed to support his wife, the couple had nonetheless "continued to live together (though not in the highest state of connubial felicity.)" Lincoln could not have known then that his own married life, which was to begin the following year, might well be described in similar terms.

Immediately following their nuptials, the newlyweds moved into Springfield's Globe Tavern, where John Todd Stuart and his bride had lived after their wedding, as did Mary's sister Frances and her husband, William Wallace. During the several months that Abraham and Mary spent there, the most corrosive forces that were to undermine their marriage emerged: her ungovernable temper and his emotional reserve. As William Herndon noted, "Mary Todd wanted Lincoln to manifest a tender and a deep love, but poor woman, she did not know that Lincoln was an undemonstrative man in this line." Before Mary Todd wed, she had, in Herndon's opinion, many admirable qualities, but he believed that "after she got married she became Soured—got gross—became material—avaricious—insolent—mean—insulting—imperious; and a she wolf." That wolf "was in her when [she was] young and unmarried, but she unchained it—let it loose when she got married. Discretion when [she was] young kept the wolf back for a while, but when there was no more necessity for chaining it," then "it was unchained to growl—snap & bite at all."

LIFE AT THE GLOBE TAVERN

The Globe was a no-frills hostelry: "a primitive sort of house—a big, ugly frame building" whose proprietor was "extremely prudent and economical, in regard to the burning of tallow candles," and also "in regard to the arrangement of his table." The menu consisted primarily of "buckwheat cakes, corn cakes and short biscuits—the two former often being sour."

Mary Lincoln must have been chagrinned to live in such rude quarters, especially after she had enjoyed relative luxury at the home of her sister and brother-in-law on Aristocracy Hill, not to mention her family's comfortable home in Kentucky. The Globe lacked a parlor where she could receive guests, so when her husband was on the road practicing law or politicking, which took him away for several weeks in the first year of their marriage (and even more in later years), she was stuck in their small room.

The Globe's other women boarders did not like Mrs. Lincoln. Margaret Lanphier reported "that the ladies of that old house used to meet for small parties in their rooms, and not always wishing to include Mrs. Lincoln they would tiptoe up the stairs to the room where they were to meet, in deadly terror of her guessing they were assembling."

Those ladies may have been put off by Mary Lincoln's explosive temper, which they observed in action one morning at breakfast when she arrived late, as usual, thus inconveniencing the other guests. (At the Globe, no one could begin eating until all boarders were seated.) Lincoln "was rather rasped at having the others wait for his wife," so he "somewhat whimsically chided her as she entered and took her place at the table. Whereupon she took a cup of hot coffee from a service tray and threw it at her husband and ran hysterically from the room." Lincoln "sat there in humiliation and silence" while Catherine Early, widow of Lincoln's friend and political ally Jacob Early, helped clean him up. Thus did he get a foretaste of what he would have to endure for the next twenty-three years.

(In December 1860, a similar event took place at dinner one evening when Lincoln "cracked a joke which displeased Mrs. Lincoln because she erroneously imagined it to be at her expense. Quicker than a flash she picked up a cup of hot tea and flung it clear across the table at Mr. Lincoln's head, then jumped up in great fury and rushed out of the room.")

Mary Lincoln was also displeased with her spouse for his failure to come to bed when she did. Just as she was retiring, he would excuse himself to fill a water pitcher. While doing so, he regaled fellow boarders with stories at length. Signaling her impatience as she awaited his return, she coughed, a hint that he sometimes ignored for hours. Thus did she get a foretaste of Lincoln's tendency to avoid her, something she would have to endure for the next twenty-three years. She retaliated by entertaining "gentlemen in her bedroom—with locked doors. [Orville H.] Browning for one. No one imagines anything criminal was done. Her object was to irritate her husband."

The Lincolns' relations with fellow boarders deteriorated after August 1, 1843, when their first child, Robert, was born. (They were to have three more children: Edward "Eddy," in 1846; William "Willie," in 1850; and Thomas "Tad," in 1853. Only Robert lived into adulthood; Eddy died at age three, Willie at eleven, and Tad at eighteen.) Harriet Bledsoe, who was then staying at the Globe, "never cared personally for Mrs. Lincoln" but nevertheless "went every day to her room" and "washed and dressed the baby, and made the mother comfortable and the room tidy, for several weeks till Mrs. Lincoln was able to do these things for herself." Bledsoe's six-year-old daughter Sophia also helped care for little Robert. Sophia liked to carry the rather heavy infant about, "often dragging him through a hole in the fence between the tavern grounds and an adjacent empty lot, and laying him down in the high grass, where he contentedly lay awake or asleep, as the case might be." Sophia "often since that time wondered how Mrs. Lincoln could have trusted a particularly small six-year-old with this charge." She was amazed that "at that early age I missed doing him any damage."

Sarah Beck, a widow who served as proprietress of the Globe Tavern, also helped care for baby Robert; Mrs. Beck's son recalled that Mary Lincoln was "young and inexperienced in caring for babies and needed assistance," so his mother "always went in to assist in preparing him for the night before she went to bed herself."

When Beck and Bledsoe and young Sophia were unavailable to tend the infant, Lincoln helped out. One day as Robert was shrieking, his father picked him up and carried him around the room while his wife sat by, quietly weeping. Beck assured the anxious parents that their child merely had colic and was in no danger. "Does it do any good to pack him round this way?" Lincoln asked. When told it did not, he glanced at his wife "in a manner as though he expected her to protest" and said: "Well, Mary, if it don't do him any good, I'm damned if I don't put him down."

Robert's cries so dismayed the other Globe Tavern boarders that they threatened to leave if the Lincolns remained. So in the fall of 1843, Abraham, Mary, and their baby moved into a rented three-room cottage on nearby South Fourth Street.

LIFE ON SOUTH FOURTH STREET

In their new abode, the Lincolns' immediate neighbors were a tailor, Robert Biddle, and his wife, Maria. The Biddles had gotten to know Lincoln before he wed; Robert made clothes for him in return for his legal services. Lincoln became one of Robert's best friends and took supper at his home several times a month. There Lincoln "stayed far into the night" discussing politics with his host, who was a fellow Whig party activist. The two men regularly visited across the backyard fence. There they "would talk over the news of the day," and Lincoln would "find an attentive listener to his latest story."

Mary Lincoln and Maria Biddle, however, did not become close, even though they were nearly the same age and were both well-educated. Maria's granddaughter wrote that "it would have been quite natural" for the two ladies to have been friends, "but Maria was busy with her babies and her home," and since the two women "did not attend the same church, they seldom met except at some evening party, or an occasional afternoon tea." At those events, Mary Lincoln's "willfulness and cutting sarcasm kept other young women from being as cordial as they might otherwise have been."

Maria Biddle disapproved of the treatment Lincoln received at the hands of his wife, who "seemed to take a special delight in contradicting her husband, and humiliating him on every occasion." Among other things, she criticized her husband's appearance. She felt embarrassed because he "was so plain and dressed so plain" and would often ask him: "Why don't you dress up and try to look like somebody?" Mrs. Lincoln "was always complaining, always criticizing her husband; nothing about him was ever right: He was stoop-shouldered, he walked awkwardly." She also "complained that there was no spring to his step, no grace to his movements; and she mimicked his gate and nagged at him to walk with his toes pointed down, as she had been taught at Madame Mentelle's. She didn't like the way his huge ears stood out at right angles from his head. She even told him that his nose wasn't straight, that his lower lip stuck out, that he looked consumptive, that his feet and hands were too large, his head too small."

Mary Lincoln also criticized her spouse's manners. According to Harriet Hanks, who lived with the Lincolns for over a year in the mid-1840s, Lincoln "seldom ever wore his coat when in the house at home and often went to the table in his shirt sleeves, which practice greatly annoyed his wife." Mary's half-sister Emilie Todd Helm reported that she "complained because L. would open [the] front door instead of having [a] servant do so," and whenever he "would eat butter with his knife," she "raised 'merry war.'" A friend remarked, "Mary if I had a husband with a mind like yours [has,] I wouldn[']t care what he did." She acknowledged: "It is very foolish. It is a small thing to complain of."

In trying to understand Mary Lincoln's belittling of her husband, Maria Biddle made allowances, for the "Lincolns were very poor, at this time, and Mrs. Lincoln was not well: so, considering that she had her pride, her poverty and sickness to contend with, Maria tried to excuse her rudeness for the sake of her husband."

Mary Lincoln was probably suffering from debilitating migraine headaches, which afflicted her for many years. In April 1848, Lincoln asked her: "Are you entirely free from headache? That is good—considering it is the first spring you have been free from it since we were acquainted." She also endured headaches at other seasons of the year. In the winter of 1863, she telegraphed her husband from New York: "Reached here last evening. Very tired and severe headache." The following spring, she wrote a friend: "I was quite unable during several hours yesterday to leave my bed, owing to an intensely severe headache . . . . I believe, you are likewise, a sufferer, from these bilious attacks & know how much inclined to *nausea* they leave you." That summer, she complained of an "intense headache, caused by driving out, in the heat of the day." In May 1864, Lincoln asked the White House doctor to "please send Mrs. L. [a] prescription for one of her cases of bilious headaches." Servants in the Executive Mansion recalled that Mrs. Lincoln was agreeable "when she was not sick with the dreadful headaches she used to have and was not worried about the war and things in general."

In addition to her physical problems, Mary Lincoln in 1843–1844 suffered because of the Millerite craze sweeping Springfield, much to her annoyance. (The followers of the Rev. William Miller of Vermont believed his prediction that the second coming of Christ would occur in that time frame.) She reportedly "had no patience with the people who were responsible for all of this religious turmoil; and it added greatly to her natural nervousness and irritability." (Migraines can cause nervousness and irritability.)

While living on South Fourth Street, Mary Lincoln "always expected her husband to look after Robert (Bob) when he was not at the office or busy with his law practice or politics." He was not a good babysitter, as his friend William G. Greene attested: "when his own son Bob was in the cradle Lincoln used to lie on the floor reading" and let the child "split his lungs yelling to be carried about the house." If his wife "happened to arrive home about this time there was trouble in the family for a few minutes, but no remonstrances or appeals could ever make him a good nurse." Sometimes Lincoln returned from downtown accompanied by Robert Biddle. While the two men halted at the cottage gate to finish their conversation, Mrs. Lincoln would exclaim: "Oh Abe! Abe! Come right home here and take Bob." With a smile, Lincoln would tell his friend: "I reckon the little woman gets pretty lonesome, here at home all day."

Over the next seventeen years, Mary Lincoln would have many occasions to feel lonely, for her husband stayed away from her for longer and longer periods (see Chapter 6). She would tell a businessman's spouse: "You are fortunate in having a husband who is not in politics. A politician is owned by everybody, and his wife has many lonely hours."

5

SETTLING IN AT EIGHTH AND JACKSON STREETS

1844–1849

A new phase of the Lincolns' marriage began in the spring of 1844, when they purchased a six-room, one-and-a-half story frame cottage at the corner of Eighth and Jackson Streets. (It was far smaller than the Lincoln house now to be seen in Springfield; in 1856, Mrs. Lincoln had it enlarged with a second story, doubling the number of rooms.) Located only a few blocks from Lincoln's law office, it was to be his home for the next seventeen years.

LINCOLN'S DOMESTIC DUTIES

Because Mary Lincoln had been raised in a prosperous Kentucky household with slaves to mind children, cook, and clean, she found housewifely chores beneath her dignity and outsourced them as best she could. While washing dishes one day in the mid-1840s, she sighed: "What would my poor father say if he found me doing this kind of work." At their new house, she had the assistance of Harriet Hanks, the adolescent daughter of Lincoln's second cousin (and, in effect, surrogate brother), Dennis Hanks. Lincoln had invited her to Springfield so that she could get a better education than she could in Charleston, Illinois. She stayed with the Lincolns for a year-and-a-half in 1844 and 1845, during which time she helped tend young Robert. But, according to Herndon, when Mary Lincoln "tried to make a servant—a slave" of her, the "high-spirited" Harriet "refused to become Mrs. Lincoln's tool," thereby creating "a fight between Lincoln and his wife." Jesse W. Weik reported that "in time her relations with Mrs. Lincoln became so strained, if not intolerable, she found it a relief at last to withdraw and return to her home."

Just as Mrs. Lincoln tried to make young Harriet Hanks "a servant—a slave," so too was she "quite disposed to make a servant girl" of Lincoln, according to a neighbor. She would demand that he "get up and get the breakfast and then dress the children, after which she would join the family at the table, or lie abed an hour or two longer as she might choose." Similarly, a Sangamon County resident recalled that "Lincoln would start for his office in the morning and she'd go to the door and holler: 'Come back here now and dress those children or they won't be tended to today. I'm not going to break my back dressing up those children while you loaf at the office talking politics all the day.'" Another neighbor reported that Mrs. Lincoln made her husband "take care of the baby," whom he "rolled up and down in [a] baby carriage." When that neighbor told him "that is a pretty business for you to be engaged in, when you ought to be down to your law office," he said: "I promised."

Occasionally, while pulling one of his sons along in a wagon, Lincoln "would become so abstracted that the young one would fall out and squall." If the lad's father did not notice what had happened, someone would alert him and "he would turn back—pick up the child—soothe it—pacify it &c; and then proceed up & down the pavement as before." While performing these duties, he would now and again stop to chat. One Sunday, when Mrs. Lincoln emerged from church and observed her husband doing just that, she screamed at him. He then ran home "and gently took what followed," namely "a hell of a scolding." Herndon felt sorry for his partner: "Poor Abe, I can see him now running and crouching." On Sunday mornings, Lincoln would sometimes bring his boys to the office, work a bit, and "haul his children back home and meet the same old scolding or a new and intensified one. He bore all quite philosophically."

Herndon reported that whenever Mrs. Lincoln "wanted to go to church or to some gathering she would go at all events and leave Lincoln to take care of the babies." According to Dennis Hanks's son-in-law, "Mrs. Lincoln loved the dance, and often left her husband to take care of the children while she enjoyed the pleasures of the ballroom."

Once, while his wife was running errands, Lincoln stayed home to mind their son Tad and to oversee the work of a carpenter. Just as he stepped from the house in response to the carpenter's summons, Mrs. Lincoln returned and was upset to see Tad crying. The carpenter remembered that she "had rather a hasty temper and at once she sought her husband and berated him soundly for letting the child sit on the floor and cry." Lincoln protested, "Why, Mary, he's just been there a minute," then lifted the boy up, took a seat, and snuggled with him.

Lincoln had other domestic duties. His wife had him wash the breakfast dishes and, on occasion, would "pick up a piece of stove wood and drive him out [of the house] to the butcher shop to fetch breakfast meat." A carpenter recalled that Lincoln "always used to do his own marketing" and "before he went to Washington [in 1861] I used to see him at the baker's and butcher's every morning with his basket on his arm."

MARY LINCOLN AS A MOTHER
AND A NEIGHBOR

Mrs. Lincoln pressed her husband into service in part because she found herself overwhelmed by the demands of motherhood, especially when her children fell ill. Her cousin, Elizabeth Todd Grimsley, wrote that Mary was "always overanxious and worried about the boys and withal was not a skillful nurse" and "was totally unfitted for caring for them" when they became sick. A neighbor recalled that Mrs. Lincoln "was nervous and sometimes excitable" and "seemed to always be worried about her children." She grew hysterical whenever anything appeared wrong with her sons. One day, after young Robert developed symptoms of illness, she ordered Charity, the household maid, to fetch a doctor. Evidently convinced that the situation was not serious, Charity paused to chat with a friend. When Mrs. Lincoln observed her dawdling, she shouted: "Charity! Charity! run for your life and I'll give you fifty dollars when you get back."

Elizabeth Lushbaugh Capps, a near neighbor, described Mary Lincoln as "a very nervous, hysterical woman who was incessantly alarming the neighborhood with her outcries. It was a common thing to see her standing out on their terrace in front of the house, waving her arms and screaming, 'Bobbie's lost! Bobbie's lost!' when perhaps he was just over in our house. This was almost an everyday occurrence." Capps recalled a time "when Robert could just barely walk Mrs. Lincoln came out in front as usual, screaming, 'Bobbie will die! Bobbie will die!' My father ran over to see what had happened. Bobbie was found sitting out near the back door by a lye box and had a little lye in his mouth. Father took him, washed his mouth out and that's all there was to it." Capps further recollected that Mary Lincoln "was a bright woman, well educated, but so nervous and crazy acting that she was the laughingstock of the neighborhood."

A servant who worked in the Springfield home called Mrs. Lincoln "half crazy." Once, she repeatedly "screamed 'Murder!'" prompting a neighbor to hasten to her assistance. She "said a big ferocious man had Entered her house." The neighbor "found an old umbrella fixer sitting on the back porch, waiting for 'Mrs.' to come back, as he had seen her go thru the house to the front and supposed she would be right back." The neighbor "took the man by the arm and led him off the porch and told him how he had frightened the woman." As he returned to the street, the umbrella mender exclaimed: "I wouldn't have such a fool for my wife!" Evidently, the "cause of her fright was the man's heavy beard, which was a rare sig[h]t in those days." Another neighbor remembered that one day a peddler "knocked at Mrs. Lincoln's door, as at any door, and had stepped in when she answered the knock and had started to open his pack." She began "to scream and carry on" and repeatedly yelled at him, demanding that he leave. The peddler tracked down Lincoln and told him: "If you have any influence over your wife in God's world, go home and teach her some sense." Mrs. Lincoln once yelled at her neighbor John B. Weber: "Keep this little dog from biting me!" even though the canine was "too small and good natured to do anything." She was also frightened by severe weather. At the first sign of a thunderstorm, she panicked, causing Lincoln to leave his office "to quiet her fears and comfort her until the storm was over." Her cousin Elizabeth Grimsley recalled that Mary "was a very timid woman, usually in times of trial."

Once Mrs. Lincoln cried out, "Fire, Fire!" causing neighbors to rush to her aid, fearing a serious conflagration. Instead, they found "just a little fat burning in a frying pan on the cook stove." She regularly shouted at her husband when she wanted him to build a fire. Once she asked him to do so while he was hoeing their garden; he said he would take care of it as soon as he finished the row he was working on. According to a neighbor, she grew so impatient that she screamed: "Fire! Fire!" In response, local firefighters hastened to the intersection of Eighth and Jackson Streets. The firemen and neighbors soon realized that there was no emergency. A historian of Springfield reported that from "the kitchen door would issue the loud exclamation of 'Fire! Fire! Fire!' The neighborhood understood that there was need for wood in the kitchen" and that Lincoln's "acknowledgment was contained in the simple, mild reply, 'Yes Mary, yes Mary.'" Her agitation so disturbed neighbors that one of them, Mrs. Frederick S. Dean, took pity on her and gently tried to calm her down.

SERVANTS IN THE
LINCOLN HOME

Just as the Lincolns quarreled about Harriet Hanks, so too did they argue about taking in another relative who wanted to attend school in Springfield: Abraham L. B. Johnston, the adolescent son of Lincoln's stepbrother, John D. Johnston. In 1851, Lincoln wrote to John: "I understand he [Abraham] wants to live with me so that he can go to school, and get a fair start in the world, which I very much wish him to have. When I reach home, if I can make it convenient to take him, I will take him." But his wife made it inconvenient. According to Abraham Johnston's brother, she "refused furiously" and "caused hard feelings." Similarly, in 1856 Lincoln agreed to take in Charles Dickey, the thirteen-year-old son of his friend T. Lyle Dickey, just after the boy's mother had died. Even though it would only be for a few weeks, that plan fell through because, as Charles Dickey later reported: "Mrs. Lincoln was taken with one of her attacks of brain trouble and it would not be pleasant to have a boy around."

After Harriet Hanks left in 1845, Lincoln evidently thought his wife would have to make do without domestic help, so he bought her two books by Eliza Leslie: *Directions for Cookery, in its Various Branches* and *The House Book, or, A Manual of Domestic Economy for Town and Country.* But eventually he employed servants, a few of whom got along with Mrs. Lincoln. An African American woman, Ruth Stanton, worked in the home ca. 1849–1852. As she told a journalist, her principal employer—Mrs. John S. Bradford—apparently took pity on the Lincolns, "who were poor then," and "sent me over to help Mrs. Lincoln every Saturday, for she had no servant and had to do her own housework. Then Mrs. Bradford sent me to live with the Lincolns." Ruth Stanton "scrubbed the floors and waited on the table," helped "to clean the dishes and do the washing," and tended to young Robert and Eddy. She called Mrs. Lincoln "a very nice lady" who "worked hard and was a good church member."

Another African American, Mary Brown, who also worked in the Lincoln home, was "a bright, intelligent woman" who "had been educated in a white school" in Paris, Illinois, "but after some color line remonstrance she was finally ousted from the school, and that ended her opportunities for education." Mrs. Brown recalled that she had "milked the cow for Mrs. Lincoln, assisted in the washing and house cleaning and other household duties."

Mary Johnson, who was similarly employed in the late 1850s, was described by Mrs. Lincoln as "a very faithful servant" and "as submissive as possible." A washerwoman working in the home, Mary Gaughan, called Mrs. Lincoln "a good woman"—a "smarter woman than he [Lincoln] was a man"—who "would often help me wash, iron or bake, so that I could get off and play with little Tad."

But those servants were exceptions, for Mrs. Lincoln usually "couldn't keep a hired girl because she was tyrannical," according to Herndon. Even an admiring near neighbor, Julia Sprigg, described her as "headstrong" and confirmed that "stories of her servant troubles are founded on truth." Another neighbor recalled that in dealing with servants, some of whom she referred to as "wild Irish," Mrs. Lincoln was often haughty and "hot tempered." One servant girl "never was reconciled to the aristocratic tendencies of Mrs. Lincoln," and another described her as a "cranky" woman who "often struck" servants.

Ellen Matthews, who as an adolescent worked at the Lincoln home in 1858, recalled that "Mrs. Lincoln was hysterical, high strung and short tempered. She had considerable trouble with maids, and their terms of service were not long. Housekeeping duties and things about the house worried her considerably and she often lost her temper." Lincoln frequently "acted in the role of peacemaker and smoothed out many a domestic fuss." Ellen abruptly quit one Sunday morning when she was attacked while grinding coffee beans. For some reason, that activity upset Mrs. Lincoln, who "rushed into the kitchen, red of face, and heaping invectives upon the head of her maid [Ellen]. She had grasped a broom with the evident intention of striking the girl with it, when Mr. Lincoln appeared on the scene." He "spoke to his wife and taking the broom away from her, he calmed her as best he could." The "terrified girl ran out of the house, not even stopping to collect her wages." Lincoln "took the money to her later with an apology for the manner in which she was forced to leave his employ."

Mary Lincoln attacked a young Norwegian servant, Hannah Knudson, one of whose descendants reported "that Mrs. Lincoln, in anger, pulled a pierced earring" from Hannah's ear, "tearing her earlobe." Similarly, Hannah's sister Mary, who also worked for the Lincolns, was physically accosted by the lady of the house, whose attack left a scar on the girl's arm. Mrs. Lincoln verbally abused another Mary—an Irish servant, Mary Hogan—who was being courted by a young admirer, Michael Kelly. When he called one day at the Lincoln home, he found his sweetheart in tears. She explained that Mrs. Lincoln had tongue-lashed her severely "for allowing one of the children [Robert or Eddy] to stain their clothing with apricot juice." Kelly, insisting that "no one should be treated like that," took Mary Hogan away, and on January 8, 1850, wed her.

Mrs. Lincoln dismissed an unidentified black woman "in the shrew's voice that resounded across Jackson and up Eighth Streets," according to biographer Jean Baker. Once she hired a servant girl to help the two whom she already employed, "but fired them all the next day." On another occasion, she ordered a servant boy, Phillip Dinkel, "to get out, and threw his suit case out the window after him." When a servant girl named Sarah displeased her, she also "promptly had the girl's trunk carried out into the middle of the street."

That Sarah was the niece of Jacob Tiger, a Springfield miller. Herndon described her as "no Common hired girl" but rather a "fine woman, and rather intelligent, pleasant, and social," as well as "industrious, neat, saving, and rather handsome." One day Sarah did something to anger Mrs. Lincoln, who in "one of her insane mad spells insulted and actually slapt the girl." In tears, Sarah fled to the home of her uncle, who called on Mrs. Lincoln to learn what had created the problem. When he asked in "a kind and gentlemanly" manner for an explanation, she "at once blazed away with her sharp and sarcastic tongue" and "abused Tiger shamefully, calling him a dirty villain—a vile creature & the like." She "boiled over with her insane rage and at last struck Tiger with a broom." She had thrown out Sarah's trunk, which Tiger retrieved. Determined to confront Lincoln, he tracked him down and demanded that he "*punish* Mrs. Lincoln and apologize to him." As he listened to Tiger, Lincoln hung his head and finally "said calmly—kindly—and in a very friendly way, mingled with shame and sadness: '*Friend Tiger,* can't you endure this one wrong done you by a mad woman without much complaint for old friendship's sake while I have had to bear it without complaint and without a murmur for lo these last fifteen years?'"

Some of Mrs. Lincoln's less submissive servants fought back. Elizabeth Mischler reported that once a hired girl named Mary "got mad at her mistress and threw the suds water all over her." The young woman then fled down the street, where she encountered Lincoln. He asked what had happened, and when told the story, said of his wife: "Well, I guess it did her good!" Mrs. Frank Murphy claimed that while she was working in the Lincoln home, Mary Lincoln slapped her face, whereupon Mrs. Murphy retaliated and gave her "a good drubbing." (During the Civil War, a White House laundress snapped back at Mrs. Lincoln, according to a soldier in the unit guarding the mansion. He recalled that the First Lady, who was "a little uppish," would "take a notion to go carriage riding, and her long white gloves had to be laundered in a hurry. Then there was trouble below stairs. The laundress was a big, redheaded Irish woman and when she had a little dram she would give Mrs. Lincoln a piece of her mind. Very free spoken she was too.")

One servant who did not fight back, act defiant, or quit abruptly was Margaret Ryan, an Irish woman whom Jesse Weik interviewed. She told him that when Lincoln returned from the office at the end of a workday, he would enter through the kitchen, ask her about Mrs. Lincoln's mood, then retrace his steps and enter through the front door. Weik described an interview with Margaret, whom he unaccountably referred to as "Maria." Margaret/Maria reported that Lincoln clandestinely supplemented her salary, "conditioned on her determination to brave whatever storms that might arise." Weik's interview notes state that "L hired M. and told her he would pay M. 75¢ More than Mrs L to stay there—not to fuss with Mrs. L." She recalled that after she had worked at the Lincoln home for a while, "the madame and I began to understand each other. More than once, when she happened to be out of the room, Mr. Lincoln with a merry twinkle in his eye patted me on the shoulder, urging me: 'Stay with her, Maria [Margaret]; stay with her.'" She obliged him, remaining in his employ for over two years.

Mary Lincoln's sister Elizabeth described a domestic row that the Lincolns had over an unnamed young servant (probably Margaret Ryan): "one day the girl threatened to leave unless She Could get $1.50 per week. Mrs. L. Could [—] rather would [—] not give the Extra 25¢: the girl Said [s]he would leave. Mrs L. Said Leave. Mr L. heard the Conversation—didn[']t want the girl to leave—told his wife so—asked—begged her to pay the $1.50. Mrs L remained incorrigible[.] Mr L slipt round to the backdoor and Said—'Don't leave—Tell Mrs Lincoln you have Concluded to Stay at $1.25 and I[']ll pay the odd 25¢ to you.['] Mrs Lincoln overheard the Conversation and Said to the girl & Mr L: [']What are you doing—I heard Some Conversation—Couldn't understand it—I'm not going to be deceived—Miss[,] you Can leave[,] and as for you Mr L[,] I'd be ashamed of myself.'"

Lincoln also clandestinely supplemented the wages of the family's laundresses. When he learned that his wife was paying Justina De Crastos and Norsis (Narcisa) Donnegan only 50¢ per day for doing the family washing, he increased their pay.

Mary Lincoln's mistreatment of servants had its roots in her Kentucky upbringing. House slaves in the Old South were subject to what historian Eugene Genovese called "the full force of lordship and bondage; that is, the full force of petty tyranny imposed by one woman on another; of expecting someone to be at your beck and call regardless of her own feelings and wishes; of being able to take out one's frustrations and disappointments on an innocent bystander, who would no doubt be guilty enough of something since servants are always falling short of expectations." Young daughters of slaveholders, observing the harsh way that slaves were taught to be submissive, learned early on that "there was no inherent chasm between violence and ladyhood in everyday life."

Mrs. Lincoln's abuse of servants illustrates a point made by some Southern planters' wives, who feared that exposure to the slave system would corrupt their children. In 1849, Anna Matilda Page King of Georgia asked her spouse to "get rid of *all* [his slaves] at *their value* and leave this wretched country" because to "bring up boys on a plantation makes them tyrannical as well as lazy, and girls too." In 1828, Virginia Randolph Cary of Virginia observed that the "habit of despotism is formed almost in infancy. The child is allowed to tyrannize over the unfortunate menial appointed to gratify its wants. Parents allow this abuse of power, without being aware of its fatal tendency. Self-will is fostered from the very cradle."

GENEROUS ABE, STINGY MARY

A disagreement like the one that the Lincolns had over a servant's wages occurred one day when young John F. Mendosa and his father brought to Mrs. Lincoln some blackberries they had spent hours picking. She "started to run them down because they were so small" and balked at the asking price of 15¢ per pint. Mr. Mendosa, a Portuguese immigrant who spoke no English, instructed his son "to tell Mrs. Lincoln that it was the last picking," and hence the berries "were smaller than the first, and furthermore that there were no more to be found, and that father had been [working] all morning since 4 A.M. to find that many." She refused to pay more than 10¢ per pint. When Lincoln observed this haggling, he gave the lad 25¢ for a pint "and told Mrs. Lincoln to take them and put them away." She "did not like that and scolded Mr. Lincoln for taking them." As Mendosa recalled, Lincoln "spoke up and told me to tell father that it was cheap enough, that he had earned every cent of it, and more too."

A similar episode involved young Josiah P. Kent, a neighborhood boy whom Lincoln hired to run errands and serve as a coachman for his wife. One day young Kent desired to attend a circus but did not have the 50¢ admission fee. Mrs. Lincoln owed him that much, but he was afraid to ask her for it. So he explained the situation to Lincoln, who (as Kent recalled) "eyed me closely and seemed deeply interested especially when I mentioned the approaching circus. 'Fifty cents,' he said, 'is rather small pay for the service you seem to have rendered Mrs. Lincoln and you should have been paid long ago.' He smiled and drew from his pocket the money; but it was not the expected fifty, it was seventy-five cents. 'What's the extra twenty-five cents for?' I asked. 'That's interest on your investment,' he laughed."

Mrs. Lincoln's quarrelsome manner alienated vendors in addition to the Mendosas. When she accused the iceman of "swindling her in weight," that gentleman "got mad—cursed—and vowed she should never get ice again." She irritated the family druggist, Roland Diller, whose son called her "very hard to deal with." She "often bought perfume" and after opening it "would send [it] back claiming it [was] not good—did not suit." Diller "would not take it back and ordered clerks not to do so" because she had broken the seals on the bottles, rendering them unsellable. A man who had worked as an apprentice clerk in a dry goods store recalled that Mrs. Lincoln "was a finicky and overparticular customer."

Harriet Hanks observed that "Mrs. Lincoln was *vary* [sic] *economical* So much So that *by Some She* might have been pronounced Stingy." Others in

Springfield noted that while she "put on plenty [of] style," she was "stingy & short in dealing with people" and "of very saving habits." When interviewed after Mrs. Lincoln's death, Springfielders "all spoke of her economies," including her habit of locking away the sugar bowl.

Occasionally Lincoln used guile rather than direct confrontation to cope with his wife's tightfistedness. When some young men asked him to contribute to the local fire department's fund drive, he replied: "I'll do so, boys, when I go home to supper—Mrs. Lincoln is always in a fine, good humour then—and I'll say to her: 'My dear, there is a subscription paper being handed round to raise money to buy a new horsecart. The committee called on me this afternoon, and I told them to wait until I consulted my home partner. 'Don't you think I had better subscribe fifty dollars?' Then she will look up quickly, and exclaim: 'Oh, Abraham, Abraham! will you never learn, never learn? You are always too liberal, too generous! Fifty dollars! No, indeed—we can't afford it; twenty-five's quite enough.'" He told the supplicants to come around the next day to collect $25.

One Sunday during the Civil War, while the Lincolns were attending church, they each placed money into the offering plate. As the collector moved on to the next pew, Lincoln drew him back and whispered: "I want to contribute more than that; come to the White House in the morning." He obeyed the president and next day "received a check upon which was written a goodly amount."

As these anecdotes indicate, Lincoln himself was quite generous. Herndon believed that "Lincoln wouldn't have a dollar to bless himself with if some one else didn't look out for him. He can never say 'No' to any one who puts up a poor mouth, but will hand out the last dollar he has, sometimes when he needs it himself, and needs it badly." Page Eaton described Lincoln as "a very liberal man, too much so, perhaps, for his own good. I am one of the Trustees of the First Baptist Church, and although Mr. Lincoln was not an attendant with our congregation, he would always give $15, $20 or $25 every year to help support the minister. He was sure to give something to every benevolent and charitable purpose that came along. 'Well, how much do you want I should give,' he would say, drawing his purse, 'you must leave me a little to feed the babies with.'" In 1843, Lincoln forgave a debt owed to him by Isaac Cogdal, who had lost a hand in an accident. When Cogdal protested, Lincoln replied: "if you had the money, I would not take it." Charlotte Rodrigues De Souza recalled that Portuguese residents of Springfield thought Lincoln was "a saint sent from heaven," for he would tell "poor people to go ahead and build their house—he would see that it was paid for." Lincoln guaranteed the home mortgage of at least one servant, William H. Johnson (see Chapter 12). Mrs. De Souza also said that Lincoln gave his cook, Frances Affonso, money to buy her wedding dress when she married Manuel de Freitas in 1860. Another servant, Epsy Arnaby Smith, said that she too received a wedding dress from the Lincolns.

When the circus came to town, Lincoln would take not only his sons, but also other children whose parents could not afford the price of admission. For his hard-pressed neighbor, the widow Julia Ann Sprigg, he would provide some wood in the winter and some ice in the summer, explaining to her: "Had more than we needed, so we sent it over."

Mrs. Lincoln, on the other hand, was "stingy & exclusive," according to Herndon, who said she was "cold & repulsive to visitors that did not suit her cold aristocratic blood." That included some of her relatives, among them one young man from St. Louis whom Dr. Albert A. North of Springfield had hired in the later 1850s. According to Herndon, when that unidentified Missourian arrived at the Illinois capital, he called to pay his respects to Mrs. Lincoln, who "told the young gentleman in coarse—cruel and brutish language, that she did not wish her poor relatives to pile themselves on her and Eat her up." He then "tried to explain to her that out of respect he had called to see her and said he had plenty of money and had a good position and did not need her charity and did not deserve her coarse, savage and brutal language. He quickly left the house, deeply mortified, leaving Mrs. Lincoln in one of her haughty, imperious and angry states." After Lincoln apologized to the young man and offered to help him out, he allegedly called the future president "one of the noblest of men" and his wife "a savage."

Another relative who offended Mrs. Lincoln was her cousin, Dr. Lyman Beecher Todd. According to Harriet Hanks, Mary "became very indignant" when told that the doctor "had intimated that Robert L. who as baby was a sweet child but not good looking." To punish him, Mrs. Lincoln excluded his daughter from a party.

Much later, she broke off relations with her favorite half-sister, Emilie Todd Helm, who during the Civil War sought permission to have some cotton shipped from the Confederacy to her Kentucky home. Lincoln had denied her request because of her refusal to take a loyalty oath, as required by law for such applicants. Mrs. Helm reportedly "spurned the proposition," then "abused him to the extent of her vocabulary" and "left in a huff." Back in Kentucky, she wrote the president a bitter letter: "I have been a quiet citizen and request only the right which humanity and Justice always give to Widows and Orphans. I also would remind you that your Minnie bullets have made us what we are & I feel I have that additional claim upon you." (Her Confederate officer husband had been killed in battle.) Thereafter, Mary Lincoln refused to have anything to do with Emilie, rebuffing efforts by her sisters Frances and Elizabeth to effect a reconciliation. Whenever Emilie wrote to Mary, her letters were returned unopened.

Similarly, Mrs. Lincoln feuded with her eldest sister Elizabeth Todd Edwards, who in 1862 had spent weeks in Washington comforting her as she mourned the death of her favorite son, Willie. After Mrs. Edwards returned to Illinois, a letter to her from her daughter Julia arrived at the White House. The First Lady opened it and waxed indignant as she read Julia's criticism of her. Elizabeth Edwards recalled that Mrs. Lincoln "became Enraged at me. I tried to explain—She would Send back my letters with insulting remarks."

MARY LINCOLN'S ABUSE
OF HER HUSBAND

Like Jacob Tiger and some servants, Lincoln endured physical abuse at his wife's hands. When a peddler selling apples approached him, his wife demanded to know "why he was purchasing apples and set upon him with such violence that he feared Lincoln was in actual physical danger from his wife." One day she "became enraged" when her husband returned home from the butcher shop with the wrong kind of breakfast meat. In front of houseguests, she "abused L[incoln] outrageously and finally was so mad she struck him in the face" so hard that she drew blood. After wiping it off, he retreated into town. Once in 1857, when he neglected to stoke the fire despite her repeated urgings, she assaulted him with a piece of stove wood, declaring: "Mr. Lincoln, I have told you now three times to mend the fire and you have pretended that you did not hear me. I'll make you hear me this time." The next day he appeared in court with a bandage over his nose. When someone asked about it, he "made an evasive reply." Late in the Civil War, a White House servant observed Mrs. Lincoln attack her spouse; she reportedly "Struck him hard—damned him—cursed him."

In addition to stove wood, Mary Lincoln used other ersatz weapons, most often a broom, to attack her husband and others. Clara Leaton told her daughter that the Lincolns "were very unhappy in their domestic life" and that Mrs. Lincoln "was seen frequently to drive him from the house with a broomstick." A servant remembered that one day, as Lincoln prepared to leave for a nearby town, his "wife ran him out [of the house] half dressed—as she followed him with [a] broom." Similarly, she "drove off a crowd of painters and decorators with a broom." As they were about to depart, Lincoln returned home, told them a story "that placated them and they returned to work." Mrs. Lincoln once asked a man who soldered fruit cans for her "if he was supporting Lincoln and he said that he was favoring Douglas and she chased him out of the kitchen with a broom."

On yet another occasion, as young Lizzie De Crastos and her mother Justina (one of the Lincoln family's laundresses) approached the back door of the Lincoln home, it suddenly swung open and the head of the household came "rushing out unceremoniously," pursued by his angry wife "showering her wrath on her husband in the form of 'very poorly pitched potatoes.'"

Mrs. Lincoln threw other things as well: neighbors sometimes saw "the front door of the Lincoln home . . . fly open and papers, books, [and] small articles would literally be hurled out." Among the items she reportedly tossed was a small pigeonhole desk, which Lincoln brought to a neighbor in two pieces, asking: "Will you take my old desk and give it room in your house, as it is the first desk I used when I commenced to do business for myself? Mrs. Lincoln in one of her passions, threw it into the street because I upset the ink."

It may seem implausible that five-foot-two Mary Lincoln abused her six-foot-four husband, yet modern studies indicate that it is not uncommon for women to attack their male partners physically. The 2018 National Intimate Partner and Sexual Violence Survey, conducted by the US Centers for Disease Control, indicates that more men than women were the victims of domestic violence in 2015. Earlier surveys had shown that slightly more women than men were victims.

Lincoln seldom turned on his wife, which is not surprising, for battered husbands often do not retaliate against abusive spouses. As sociologist Suzanne K. Steinmetz found in her extensive research into domestic violence, some battered husbands regard any man who hits a woman as a bully. Others hesitate to strike back lest they inflict serious injury. Still others think that by screaming in pain while being beaten, they can make their wives feel guilty. When teased about submitting to his wife's tirades, Lincoln would reply: "If you knew how little harm it does me and how much good it does her, you wouldn't wonder that I am meek."

But Lincoln was not always meek. According to Herndon, he usually paid his wife no heed when she nagged him, but that "sometimes he would rise and cut up the very devil for a while—make things move lively.'" Once, when she grabbed a knife and chased him into their yard, he thought that neighbors could observe them, and so he wheeled about, grabbed her, and marched her back into their home, declaring: "There d—n it, now Stay in the house and don't disgrace us before the Eyes of the world."

Sometimes Lincoln pushed his wife out of the house rather than into it. One Monday, he remorsefully admitted to Herndon that the previous day, when she "had annoyed him to the point of exasperation," he "lost his habitual self-control." She "was in a tirade so fierce" that he grabbed her, "pushed her through the door," and exclaimed: "If you can't stop this abuse, damn you, get out!" Lincoln told Herndon "that he was deeply sorry for this act. He was not accustomed to lose his temper." He "thought it possible that some people on their way to church had seen the incident, and he was greatly depressed that he had permitted himself to do and say what he had done and said."

Occasionally Lincoln fought back verbally rather than physically. When she angrily interrupted a discussion he was having with business colleagues one day, he snapped: "Mary, if you will attend to your business, I will attend to mine." Other times he would mock her. A backyard neighbor, James Gourley, reported that the Lincolns "got along tolerably well, unless Mrs. L got the devil in her," and that she "was gifted with an unusually high temper" which "invariably got the better of her." If "she became excited or troublesome, as she sometimes did when Mr. Lincoln was home," he "would apparently pay no attention to her. Frequently he would laugh at her, which is a risky thing to do in the face of an infuriated wife; but generally, if her impatience continued, he would pick up one of the children and deliberately leave home as if to take a walk. After he had gone, the storm usually subsided, but sometimes it would break out again when he returned."

How often Lincoln had to endure his wife's tirades is hard to say. One historian speculated that the "frequency and intensity" of the Lincolns' "notorious quarrels" are "most likely exaggerated." But Mary Lincoln's closest friend during her White House days, Elizabeth Keckly, recalled that when "in one of her wayward impulsive moods, she was apt to say and do things that wounded him deeply," and she "*often* wounded him in unguarded moments." Keckly also reported that during Lincoln's presidency, his wife created "*many* scenes" when she pressed him to gratify unscrupulous office seekers. A White House playmate of the Lincolns' sons reported that the First Lady "was *often* short tempered and bitter tongued." Turner R. King, a political ally of Lincoln in Illinois, characterized Mary Lincoln as "a hellion—a she devil" who "vexed—& harrowed the soul out of that good man" and "drove him from home &c—*often & often*." As noted above, James Gourley recollected that Mrs. Lincoln "was gifted with an unusually high temper" that "*invariably* got the better of her." John Bunn recalled that Lincoln "*often* left home without his breakfast." Clara Leaton reported that Mrs. Lincoln "was seen *frequently* to drive him from the house with a broomstick." According to Herndon, after dinner parties where Lincoln would spend much time with men telling stories, his wife "would be mad as a disturbed hornet" and "would curtain Lecture [i.e., reprimand] L[incoln] all night, till he got up out of bed in despair and went whistling through the streets & alleys till day &c. &c. It would take a ream of paper to write it all out just as it did *often* happen." James Matheny reported that "Mrs. Lincoln *often* gave L Hell in general." Another Springfield friend recalled "that domestic tiffs were *frequent*" in the Lincoln family. In 1857, Mary Lincoln told her half-sister Emilie: "I *often* laugh & tell Mr. L[incoln] that I am determined my next Husband *shall be rich*." A carpenter recalled that she "was rather quick-tempered" and "very irritable." She "used to fret and scold about *a great deal*" and "would *often* say things she would afterwards be sorry for." Apropos of Mary's acknowledgement that she had "trespassed, *many times & oft*" upon Lincoln's "great tenderness & amiability of character" during their courtship, one of Mrs. Lincoln's more defensive biographers wrote that those words "could well be applied to the *whole of their married life*."

THE LINCOLNS'
PARENTING STYLES

Lincoln was a kindly, indulgent father, but was also absent much of the time. One of the saddest documents in the Lincoln canon is a letter that his eldest son wrote in June 1865: "My Father's life was of a kind, which gave me but little opportunity to learn the details of his early career. During my childhood and early youth he was almost constantly away from home, attending courts or making political speeches. In 1859 when I was 16 and when he was beginning to devote himself more to practice in his own neighborhood, and when I would have had both the inclination and the means of gratifying my desire to become better acquainted with the history of his struggles, I went to New Hampshire to school and afterwards to Harvard College, and he became President. Henceforth any great intimacy between us became impossible. I scarcely even had ten minutes quiet talk with him during his presidency, on account of his constant devotion to business."

The boys' parents had different approaches to childrearing: Mary Lincoln was more punitive, her husband more permissive. He said: "It [is my] pleasure that my children are free happy & unrestrained by parental tyranny. Love is the chain whereby to Lock a child to its parents." Hence he was easygoing with his sons. When Tad was having difficulty learning to read, Lincoln counseled patience: "Let him run, he has time enough left to learn his letters and get pokey."

Lincoln's indulgence of his children shocked some friends, including Judge Samuel H. Treat. One morning, as Lincoln was at his office playing chess with the judge, he failed to note that the noon hour was fast approaching. As the two men sat absorbed in their game, one of Lincoln's sons appeared and, at his mother's request, summoned Lincoln home for lunch. He replied that he would come soon. When he did not do so, the boy returned, repeated the maternal summons, and kicked over the chessboard, sending pawns, rooks, knights, bishops, and other pieces flying. Judge Treat later recalled: "It was one of the most abrupt, if not brazen, things I ever saw, but the surprising thing was its effect on Lincoln. Instead of the animated scene between an irate father and an impudent youth which I expected, Mr. Lincoln without a word of reproof calmly arose, took the boy by the hand, and started for dinner. Reaching the door he turned, smiled good-naturedly, and exclaimed, 'Well, Judge, I reckon we'll have to finish this game some other time' and passed out."

Unlike the forbearing Lincoln, his wife was a harsh disciplinarian, though she would not acknowledge it. Instead, she denied that "in my life I have ever whipped a child." Her boys, she claimed, "never required it," for "a gentle, loving word, was all sufficient with them—and if I have ever erred, it has been, in being too indulgent." Her defensive biographers have echoed those sentiments, praising "that maternal tenderness, that passionate love of children, which was her characteristic throughout life." But according to Springfield neighbors, her language was not always "gentle and loving"; they recalled that she was "turbulent—loud—always yelling at children—could hear her blocks away" and "was prone to excitability and rather impulsive, saying many things that were sharp and caustic, and which she afterward usually regretted."

She lashed out at her offspring corporally as well as verbally. Describing the conduct of his wayward three-year-old son Robert, Lincoln told Joshua Speed that "by the time I reached the house, his mother had found him, and had him whip[p]ed." She did not always rely on others to punish the lad; in fact, she "would whip Bob a good deal," according to a servant. That seems plausible, for Robert "was always running away from home." When Charles R. Post knocked on the door of the Lincoln house, he heard Mrs. Lincoln exclaim: "Bob! Bob! You little scamp! Why don't you behave yourself? I'm going to lick you. Wait till I go to the door!" One day, Mrs. Lincoln bought a new clock, which she warned her sons not to touch. Helen Dodge Edwards recalled that soon thereafter, Mary Lincoln "went into the room and found that two of them had taken the clock to pieces. She whipped them." She once "held a private strapping party" with her youngest son, Tad, after he had fallen into a mud puddle. Elizabeth Todd Edwards said that her sister Mary had a "high temper and after her outbursts normally was penitent. If she punished [the] children [she] would seek to make amends by presents and affectionate treatment." According to DeWitt Smith, one of Robert's boyhood chums, Mrs. Lincoln "in a temper" burned some of her eldest son's toys.

One day in Springfield, Mrs. Lincoln was observed speaking loudly to Tad, "accusing him of having appropriated to his own use a dime which should have been the change to be returned to her" after he had run an errand. "Tad," she scolded, "you are a bad boy, I am afraid you are a thief, you—"

"No, no, mother," the frightened lad protested, "I didn't take that money, I say I didn't; I've lost it."

In a rage, Mrs. Lincoln hurried from the room and soon returned "with a vicious switch" that she used to whip the boy's legs. Just then Lincoln entered the room. Tad "was cringing with fright, the outraged mother stood with the switch held limply in her hand, and Mr. Lincoln was close by them looking first at one and then the other. 'What does this mean?' he asked, simply, addressing his wife."

She replied "in a torrent of almost incoherent words."

"But," asked Lincoln, "are you sure? Perhaps—"

He then "had Tad turning all of his pockets inside out, until, lo and behold, the vagrant dime dropped out of the last pocket!"

Lincoln "said in a voice gentle and tender with understanding: 'Mary! Mary!' That was all he said and his wife made no reply."

Lincoln protected Tad from his mother's wrath on other occasions. Once during the Civil War, the youngster slashed a new pair of copper-toed shoes because they reminded him of the "Copperheads" (Democratic opponents of his father's administration). A White House staffer recalled that when Mrs. Lincoln "was about to whip him, he rushed to his father's office and complained that, because it was against his principles to patronize 'the copperheads,' even with his toes, he was about to suffer. The President caught him in his arms and said, 'I guess I must exercise my Executive clemency a little, and pardon you, my patriotic boy; you shall not be whipped for this offence. Go and explain your case to your mother as it now stands.'"

Mary Pinkerton, who as a young girl often played with the Lincoln children in Washington, recalled that Tad would sometimes tease her and pull her hair. When she complained to the president, he "would dry my tears and tell Tad he should be ashamed for teasing such a little girl—and then maybe for a whole hour Tad and I would be good friends again." But, she added, things were "different when Mrs. Lincoln was the judge. She had a terrible temper—and when I would go to her with my stories about Tad, she would punish him severely." Mary Pinkerton reported that while the president "was always so kind and gentle," his wife "was often short tempered and bitter tongued." If Mary Pinkerton "ran to tattle on Tad to his mother, he would get a whipping. Mrs. Lincoln was a sharp, severe woman." Jane King, a playmate of Tad's in Springfield, felt "actual hatred" for his mother, whom she considered a "horrid woman."

Occasionally the boys' parents would reverse roles, with Lincoln administering corporal punishment and his wife objecting. One day he happened to notice young Robert and his friends putting on a show using dogs in the cast. The boys had secured a rope around the neck of one canine, tossed the rope over a beam, and tugged it to raise the dog. When Lincoln beheld the choking animal, he seized a barrel stave "and immediately began plying it indiscriminately on the persons of such boys as were within reach." Mrs. Lincoln "was very angry, and reproached her husband in language that was not at all adapted to Sunday School." This episode resembles one that Harriet Hanks observed in the mid-1840s. Lincoln "undertook to correct his Child [Bob]" physically while his wife "determined that he Should not" and tried to grab whatever implement he was using to administer discipline. But "in this She failed," whereupon she "tried tongue lashing but met with the Same fate," for (as Harriet Hanks put it) Lincoln "corrected his Child as a Father ought to do, in the face of his Wife[']s anger and that too without even Changing his Countenance, or making enny reply to his wife."

Though Lincoln "was proud of his children," he disliked the way his wife would boast about them. According to Herndon, it "was the habit—custom of Mrs. Lincoln when any big man or woman visited her house to dress up and trot out Bob—Willie or Tad and get them to monkey around—talk—dance—speak—quote poetry, &c. &c. Then she would become enthusiastic & eloquent over the children much to the annoyance of the visitor and to the mortification of Lincoln." After she "had exhausted the English language and broken herself down in her rhapsodies on her children Lincoln would smooth things over by saying—'These children may be something sometimes, if they are not merely rareripes—rotten ripes—hot house plants. I have always noticed that a rare-ripe child quickly matures, but rots as quickly.'"

The Lincoln children had playmates, but their mother "did not like to have them around," according to DeWitt Smith. Another friend, Maggie Blaine, remembered that "Mrs. Lincoln thought we were terrible nuisances." Elizabeth Lushbaugh Capps recollected that Mary Lincoln's frequent outbursts so frightened the neighborhood children that they feared her and therefore, rather than playing with Bob at his house, they would invite him to theirs. One day, while her sons were shooting marbles near their home with a neighborhood pal, Philip Mischler, she called them to dinner. When they failed to heed her, she "burst through the door with her broom, sweeping the marbles into oblivion." Young Mischler "hastily retreated to his own home." Mischler's daughter reported that some friends of the Lincolns' sons "used to sneak Mrs. Lincoln's steak for bait" when they went fishing. She punished them, and as a result they "didn't like her very well."

One exception was Julia Sprigg, a near neighbor who told an interviewer that she had been at the Lincoln home "a great deal of the time. I played there more often than any other place." She described Mrs. Lincoln as "the

kind of a woman that children liked, and children were attracted to her."
Another exception was Fred Dubois, who spoke just as highly of Mrs. Lincoln: "I never knew her to be impatient with us boys, and we were at their
house a great deal and no doubt deserved many scoldings. Instead of being
harsh with us when we were too boisterous in her house or in her yard, she
would give us 'cookies' and other good things to eat and in other ways was
motherly and kindly, and always had the regard of the boys, although not
to the extent that her husband had."

At Washington in 1861, Willie and Tad played with the two young sons
of a Patent Office examiner, Horatio Nelson Taft. They frequently visited
the White House, accompanied by their older sister Julia, and the First
Sons often played at the nearby Taft home. Julia remembered Lincoln as a
kind, avuncular figure, "sometimes quizzical, but always smiling and kind
to 'little Julie.'" He affectionately termed her "flibbertigibbet." But after
Willie died in February 1862, Mrs. Lincoln refused to let the Taft children
enter the White House, for their presence brought back painful memories
of the dead boy. Mrs. Taft then removed her children from Washington
and placed them in a new school; they never saw Tad again, save for a brief
visit in 1864.

Lincoln was indulgent not only to his boys and other children but also
to pets. He was especially fond of cats, which his wife called his "*hobby.*"
According to Herndon, if Lincoln's "children wanted a dog—cat—rat or the
Devil it was alright and [they were] well treated—housed—petted—fondled
&c." A Treasury Department official recalled that Lincoln "was fond of
dumb animals, especially cats. I have seen him fondle one for an hour."
When visiting the Army of the Potomac in 1865, Lincoln was observed
"tenderly caressing" three stray kittens and telling a colonel: "I hope you
will see that these poor little motherless waifs are given plenty of milk and
treated kindly."

Mrs. Lincoln, however, was "not fond of pets and she could not understand how Mr. Lincoln could take so much delight in his goats," according

to Elizabeth Keckly. (The White House goats—Nanny and Nanko—were favorites of Tad.) She also disapproved of the way her husband used Executive Mansion cutlery to feed a cat during one White House dinner. When the First Lady asked a guest rhetorically, "Don't you think it's shameful for Mr. Lincoln to feed Tabby with a gold fork?" the president observed: "If the gold fork was good enough for [James] Buchanan, I think it is good enough for Tabby."

THE LINCOLNS'
MUTUAL AMBITION

The strongest bond connecting Lincoln and his wife was their shared political ambition. Soon after they wed, she urged her husband to pursue a seat in Congress, for she was "anxious to go to Washington." He required little prodding because he was (as William Herndon put it) "inordinately ambitious," a "man totally swallowed up in his ambitions," and the "most ambitious man in the world." Lincoln "thirsted for public notice and hungered—longed for [—] approbation," and "when he did not get that notice or that approbation—was not thoroughly appreciated [—] he writhed under it." Political allies of Lincoln in Illinois shared that view, among them Senator Lyman Trumbull, who said that "a more ardent seeker after office" than Lincoln "never existed. From the time when, at the age of twenty-three, he announced himself a candidate for the legislature . . . till his death, he was almost constantly either in office, or struggling to obtain one."

During his first campaign for office, Lincoln frankly acknowledged his ambition: "Every man is said to have his peculiar ambition. Whether it be true or not, I can say for one that I have no other so great as that of being truly esteemed of my fellow men, by rendering myself worthy of their esteem." Herndon recalled that Lincoln "was flattered in 1833–4, & 5 by Offit [Denton Offutt] & and others in New Salem . . . & made to believe that he would be a great man & *he dreamed of* it then, as he told me—always delicately & indirectly."

Mrs. Lincoln stoked her husband's ambition, for she was even more desirous of fame than he was. As a girl, she had told a friend: "I am going to be the president's wife some day." Another childhood friend, Margaret Wickliffe, recalled that Mary "had always insisted when quite a young girl that her husband would be President of the United States." Margaret reported that Mary's friends laughed at her prediction because she was not good looking enough to attract men. During her courtship, Mary wrote Margaret about Lincoln, "mentioning his unprepossessing appearance and awkwardness, and with a merry appreciation of the humor of the prediction," adding: "But I mean to make him the President of the United States all the same. You will see that, as I always told you, I will yet be the President's wife." A few years after she wed Lincoln, she predicted that he "is to be President of the United States some day; if I had not thought so I never would have married him, for you can see he is not pretty." She often made similar remarks to her sister Elizabeth Edwards, who called her "the most ambitious woman I ever saw," and said that she "spurred up Mr. Lincoln, pushed him along and upward—made him struggle and seize his opportunities."

Several friends and relatives echoed Elizabeth Edwards's opinion, including John Todd Stuart, who thought his cousin Mary was "very ambitious" and that she "had the fire—will and ambition." He told an interviewer that "Lincoln[']s talent & his wife[']s Ambition did the deed." Stuart heard Lincoln's closest friend, Joshua Speed, say that "Lincoln needed driving—(well he got that.)" John H. Littlefield, who clerked in the Lincoln-Herndon law office, recalled that "Mrs. Lincoln had displayed more zeal in regard to the presidential nomination than her husband had. In fact there is no doubt that she was constantly spurring him on for she was very ambitious." Mary Lincoln's friend James Bradwell believed that she "made Mr. L. by constantly pushing him on in his ambition." Charles E. Arnold, who lived directly across Jackson Street from the Lincolns, declared that Mrs. Lincoln was "very ambitious for her husband" and "kept nagging" him on.

Referring to the days when the Lincolns were first married, William Beck said that "Mrs. Lincoln realized better than anyone else did at the time, the greatness of Lincoln's mind. At least her conversation led us to infer that she accepted it as a fact that her husband must eventually attain greatness. It is open to question whether her belief was based on her knowledge of the wonderful powers of his mind, or simply a desire and determination to attain distinction for herself as his wife." Beck opined that "Mrs. Lincoln made Lincoln what he was. At least she was the instrument in the hands of Providence."

Mary Lincoln's ambition became common knowledge, for (according to a neighbor) she "made no effort to conceal her belief that her gifted husband would some day be President. At social functions she would talk confidently of his future, predicting his nomination and election. Lincoln always objected to this." In 1856, when he was urged to pursue the Illinois gubernatorial nomination, his congressional representative remarked that Lincoln "never will be dunce enough to run for governor—(unless his wife makes him.)"

The biography that Jesse W. Weik wrote with Herndon's assistance contains a famous passage: "The man who thinks Lincoln calmly sat down and gathered his robes about him, waiting for the people to call him, has a very erroneous knowledge of Lincoln. He was always calculating, and always planning ahead. His ambition was a little engine that knew no rest." Mary Lincoln did not instill ambition in Lincoln, but insofar as his ambition was in fact "a little engine that knew no rest," she turbocharged it.

In another important way, she indirectly helped promote her husband's political career. According to Milton Hay, she made "his home tolerably disagreeable and hence he took to politics and public matters for occupation. If his domestic life had been entirely happy, I dare say he would have stayed at home and not busied himself with distant concerns." Like Hay,

David Davis and James Matheny agreed that if Lincoln had wed a more amiable woman, in all probability "he would have been satisfied with the modest emoluments of a country lawyer's practice" and "buried in the delights of an inviting and happy home." Joshua Speed also speculated that "if Mr Lincoln had married another woman—for instance Speed[']s wife [—] he Lincoln would have been a devoted husband and a very—*very* domestic man."

As Captain Shotover observed in George Bernard Shaw's *Heartbreak House*, "Who are the men who do things? The husbands of the shrew and the drunkard, the men with the thorn in the flesh."

LINCOLN PURSUES OFFICE

In 1843, Lincoln strove mightily to win the Whig nomination for Congress. After serving four terms in the Illinois House of Representatives and working hard for his party, he felt that he had earned a promotion from the state to the national legislature. It was not just his idea; William Beck reported that in the 1840s, Lincoln's "efforts to get elected to Congress were largely the result of *her* [Mary's] ambition instead of his own."

Two other prominent Whigs also sought the congressional nomination: John J. Hardin and Lincoln's close friend, Edward D. Baker. In the winter of 1842–1843, Lincoln began his quest for the prize, which was to be awarded at the Whig convention in May. As he rode the Eighth Judicial Circuit, he strove to win allies and gain popular support. But at the convention, he lost to Hardin, much to his wife's chagrin. On the day of the convention, "her anger got the better of her, and Lincoln had an unpleasant time in consequence" as she berated him for not trying more vigorously to win. According to William Beck, when Hardin departed for Washington to take the congressional seat that she wanted her husband to occupy, "it was reported about that Mrs. Lincoln 'shed bucketsfull of tears.'"

Three years later, Lincoln did win that seat, much to his spouse's delight. Unlike the wives of most congressmen, she chose to accompany her husband to Washington, where the Lincolns and their two young sons lived at Ann Sprigg's boarding house, near the Capitol. A fellow boarder recalled that Mrs. Lincoln "was so retiring that she was rarely seen except at meals." She evidently did not ingratiate herself with Sprigg's other guests, some of whom found her disagreeable. She left Washington in the spring of 1848 to stay with her family in Kentucky. In mid-April, Lincoln wrote her saying that all the lodgers at the boarding house "or rather, all with whom you were on decided good terms—send their love to you. The others say nothing."

One of the others was evidently the wife of Mississippi congressman Patrick Tompkins. In 1860, Joshua Giddings urged Lincoln to convey his "kind remembrance to Mrs Lincoln. I recollect her with pleasure. I presume she will rem[em]ber the morning when [Congressmen] Dickey and McIlvaine myself and others attended her to the [train] cars and there took our leave of her as she started for home, leaving you in our care. We have all forgotten Mrs Tompkins long since." Poet and historian Daniel Mark Epstein inferred that early in 1848 "there must have been an outburst on Mary's part, an event that so disturbed the peace at Mrs. Sprigg's that the unhappy wife was urged to leave Washington for a spell. That there was such an event seems a certainty; the details are lost to history." Those details probably included Mrs. Tompkins.

Lincoln had mixed feelings about his wife's absence. "In this troublesome world of ours," he wrote her, "we are never quite satisfied. When you were here, I thought you hindered me some in attending to business; but now, having nothing but business—no variety—it has grown exceedingly tasteless to me. I hate to sit down and direct documents, and I hate to stay in this room by myself." The few other extant letters that Lincoln wrote to his wife from Washington are less warm. As the biographer John T. Morse observed, those missives "seem to indicate a little indifference in their general tone. In only one does he seem really to miss her companionship." In that one he wrote: "Come on just as soon as you can. I want to see you, and our dear dear boys very much. Every body here wants to see our dear Bobby."

In 1848, Lincoln did not seek reelection to the House because he had agreed to make way for other ambitious Whigs, but his wife urged him to keep climbing the political ladder. A seeming exception to that pattern occurred in 1849, when he was offered the governorship of the Oregon Territory, a post that he wanted to accept, for it might serve as a stepping stone to a seat in the US Senate after Oregon achieved statehood. When his wife objected, he tried to persuade Joshua Speed to move to Oregon, where he could occupy some government post. According to John Todd Stuart, "Lincoln evidently thought that if Speed, and Speed's wife were to go along, it would be an inducement for Mary to change her mind and consent to go." But Speed was uninterested. Noah Brooks recalled that after Lincoln had become president, Mary "did not fail to remind him that her advice, when he was wavering[,] had restrained him from 'throwing himself away' on a distant territorial governorship."

In 1849, Lincoln waged a vigorous but unsuccessful campaign to become commissioner of the general land office. Upon his failure to win that post, he took a break from political striving. He had sought office in every election cycle for the past seventeen years; now he would sit on the political sidelines for five years, during which he underwent tremendous psychological growth. When, at the age of forty-five, he emerged from his semiretirement in 1854, he would return to the political fray a changed man: instead of a shallow, partisan ridiculer of Democrats, he had somehow been transformed into a highly principled, eloquent, passionate statesman-like champion of the antislavery cause. He had successfully met the psychological challenges of midlife, thus preparing himself to face the immense political crisis of the Union. In so doing, he would not only facilitate the abolition of slavery, preserve national unity, and vindicate democracy; he would also slake his wife's thirst for fame, recognition, and deference.

6

POLITICAL PAUSE
1849–1854

Some writers have detected a change in the Lincolns' marriage during the early 1850s. Jennifer Fleischner noted that between 1849 and 1850, Mrs. Lincoln suffered profoundly dislocating losses: in July 1849 her father died; her beloved maternal grandmother passed away in January 1850; and the following month, so too did her three-year-old son Eddy. These losses probably caused the psychological wounds sustained at the time of her mother's early death to suppurate once again. As Fleischner put it: "She had always been high-strung, demanding, and impulsive," but in the wake of those deaths "she became increasingly fearful, querulous, and self-indulgent; she seemed to act out every anxiety and act on every impulse, good or bad." It "was not just that she was imperiously cutting off whoever she believed crossed her. Reports of papers and books flying out the front door, of Lincoln's spending nights at the office or with friends, of his bandaged nose, of wild chases in the yard and street attest to increasingly violent tirades against her husband."

After 1849, Mary Lincoln may well have become more "high-strung," demanding, and impulsive" than she had previously been, and she may well have abused her husband more often, although it is hard to date her outbursts precisely. Those began as early as the Globe Tavern days, when she flung hot coffee in his face; the South Fourth Street cottage days, when she regularly contradicted and humiliated him; and the early days at Eighth and Jackson Streets, when her rage attacks began driving Lincoln to flee the house.

Between 1849 and 1854, Mary Lincoln had more reason than usual to be disappointed in her spouse, for during those years he ceased running for public office; she must have been bitterly disappointed—and angered—by his reluctance to continue scrambling up the political ladder. How could she achieve fame if he didn't?

HENPECKED LINCOLN

Some Springfield men justifiably regarded Lincoln as "woman whipt," "woman Cowed," and "hen pecked." His wife often erupted in rage attacks that made his domestic life "a burning scorching hell," as "terrible as death and as gloomy as the grave," in the words of Herndon. Others shared Herndon's view. James Matheny, a groomsman at Lincoln's wedding, stated that "Mrs. Lincoln often gave L Hell in general—. . . *Ferocity*—describes Mrs L's conduct to L." Milton Hay, who observed that Mrs. Lincoln "had a very extreme temper and made things at home more or less disagreeable," pitied her husband: "Poor man! I think *some* woman ought to talk kindly to him, and I suppose he has got to go from home to hear it." Sarah Calhoun Forrest, wife of journalist J. K. C. Forrest, called Mary Lincoln "a perfect termagant." A near neighbor, Sarah Corneau, said that Mrs. Lincoln "had locally established the name of being almost a shrew." Two other women—Clara Leaton and Elizabeth Matheny—did not "regard Mrs. Lincoln very highly" because "her temper and disposition generally was not at all commendable." Peter Van Bergen once heard Mary Lincoln "yelling & screaming at L[incoln] as if in hysterics." Judge James Bradwell, who in 1875 helped win Mrs. Lincoln's release from a mental hospital, said "she had an awful temper."

Josiah Kent remembered how Lincoln would flee to his office in response to spousal tirades. Kent reported that it "was never difficult to locate" the "nervous" Mrs. Lincoln, who had a "furious temper." It "mattered not who was present when she fell into a rage, for nothing would restrain her." Her "voice was shrill and at times so penetrating, especially when summoning the children or railing at some one whose actions had awakened her temper, she could easily be heard over the neighborhood." Whenever she erupted in wrath, it was "little wonder that Mr. Lincoln would suddenly think of an engagement he had downtown, grasp his hat, and start for the office." Another Springfield friend recalled that the Lincolns quarreled often, and that "on such occasions Lincoln put on his stove pipe hat and fled to his office, there to remain the rest of the night, spending his time in reading and sleeping on the couch which he had placed there for use in such moments of marital strife." (To enable him to sleep at the office "on nights of domestic discord," Lincoln bought a couch six and a half feet long.)

A woman who interviewed Mary Lincoln's close friends said they depicted her as a person "of violent temper, ungovernable and willful beyond all reason and when her will was defied, she indulged in a series of outrageous tantrums, which so tormented her patient husband that he was well nigh distracted." A Springfield matron who also spoke with friends of the Lincolns reported that "Mrs. Lincoln was sharp and shrewish with an uncontrolled temper," and "every one I met could give me some example of it."

A good example was provided by a neighbor, Adelia Dubois, who told a visiting friend about Mary Lincoln. That friend recalled that Dubois "had a little girl about three or four years of age" who "became angry and threw herself on the floor tore her hair and shrieked and cried violently.

Mrs. Dubois said, 'When I was carrying this child, I was with Mrs. Lincoln every day and I verily believe that she marked this girl, for I have seen Mrs Lincoln have just such a fit of temper as this, many times.'"

Sometimes Mary Lincoln got so mad at her husband that she "would get in a stew and refuse to get his meals for him," according to Page Eaton. Herndon told a friend that Lincoln once lived in their office "for three days at a time on cracker[s] & cheese." Herndon also recollected that Lincoln, after marital squabbles, would come to the office early, "full of sadness," and sit quietly. Surmising that his partner "was driven from home, by a club—knife or tongue," Herndon would discreetly leave in order to grant Lincoln privacy as he struggled to regain his composure. On some mornings of that sort, Lincoln would be accompanied by his young son Robert. Once, after those two had finished breakfast at a local restaurant, Lincoln asked: "Well, Robby, this ain't so very bad after all, is it? If ma don't conclude to let us come back we will board here all summer." One evening Abner Y. Ellis, Springfield's postmaster, swapped stories with Lincoln at the post office until nearly midnight. Finally, Lincoln sighed: "Well I hate to go home." When Ellis invited him to stay at his house, he accepted.

Lincoln often submitted meekly to uxorial tirades, for he believed that "it is better at times to let a woman have her way." His policy was described by one close observer as "immediate surrender." Frances Affonso, who worked for the Lincolns during the summer of 1860, described Mary Lincoln as "a nervous, high-strung woman" who was "very hard to please" and "sometimes tried the unusually mild and gentle temperament of her husband." After Lincoln came home one day and hung up his coat, his wife said sarcastically:

"You're very smart, Mr. Lincoln."

"What did I do?" he asked.

"Why, you go and hang your heavy coat on top of my starched dress."

"Never mind, don't be cross. I'll take my coat away and hang your dress there."

A fellow passenger on a train bearing the Lincolns to Cincinnati recalled that Mary "was almost hysterical about the baggage and fairly forced Mr. Lincoln to walk back three quarters of a mile to Lafayette Junction [Indiana] to see that it was safe—which he did uncomplainingly."

Harriet Hanks described Mrs. Lincoln as "high-strung and quick tempered." She "had her furious spells, but she soon recovered from them, and no apology then was too abject for her to make." Harriet recalled that "one warm afternoon," Lincoln "in his shirt-sleeves" went "out into the hall and threw himself on the floor, his head resting on a pillow, for a nap," from which he was aroused by a knock on the front door. Opening it, "he found two very stylish ladies of Springfield, who had called to pay their respects." He courteously invited them "into the parlor, remarking as they seated themselves that he would trot the woman folks out." When Mrs. Lincoln overheard that "undignified expression," she became "so exasperated" that "she had great difficulty in concealing her rage." Lincoln "at once repaired to his office downtown. At supper time he wasn't hungry enough to go home, and neither did he return until late that night. When satisfied that that his spouse and all else were buried deep in slumber, he quietly slipped in and fastened the front door softly after him."

Most accounts of Mary Lincoln's henpecking are reminiscent, but Lincoln himself described one instance. In February 1857, he wrote to John E. Rosette, editor of a newly founded paper, the Springfield *Republican*: "You know by the conversation with me that I thought the establishment of the paper unfortunate, but I always expected to throw no obstacle in its way, and to patronize it to the extent of taking and paying for one copy. When the paper was brought to my house, my wife said to me, 'Now are you going to take another worthless little paper?' I said to her *evasively*, 'I have not directed the paper to be left.'"

LINCOLN ESCAPES FROM HOME
BY TRAVELING THE
LEGAL CIRCUIT

Because Lincoln's "home was *Hell*" and "absence from home was his *Heaven*" (in Herndon's words), he stayed on the road practicing law for unusually long stretches. That pattern began to emerge during the first year of the marriage, when his wife was pregnant; then he was away from Springfield for nearly ten weeks. To be sure, in April 1843, while on the legal circuit, James C. Conkling found Lincoln "desperately homesick and turning his head frequently towards the south." But as time went by, he betrayed few signs of homesickness and spent longer and longer periods each spring and fall in county seats throughout central Illinois. He so enjoyed life on the legal circuit with his peripatetic colleagues that he rejected a lucrative job offer from a Chicago firm. Instead of returning home on weekends like his fellow circuit riders, he stayed over in the county seats by himself, even though (as a colleague remembered) "nothing could be duller than remaining on the Sabbath in a country inn of that time after the adjournment of court. Good cheer had expended its force during court week, and blank dullness succeeded; but Lincoln would entertain the few lingering roustabouts of the barroom with as great zest, apparently, as he had previously entertained the court and bar, and then would hitch up his horse" and "solitary and alone, ride off to the next term in course." In 1854, David Davis reported that "Mr. Lincoln is so much engaged here [on the circuit] that he will not find time to go home—so that before he gets home again he will have been absent six (6) weeks."

The other circuit-riding attorneys "soon learned to account for his strange disinclination to go home." Lincoln "never had much to say about home," David Davis recalled, "and we never felt free to comment on it. Most of us had pleasant, inviting homes, and as we struck out for them I'm sure each one of us down in our hearts had a mingled feeling of pity and sympathy for him." To his colleagues, it was obvious that Lincoln "was not domestically happy." Davis believed that "Mr. Lincoln was happy—as happy as *he* could be, when on this Circuit—and happy no other place."

Not only was Lincoln the sole Eighth Circuit lawyer to stay away from home on weekends, he was also among the handful who traveled the circuit throughout its entire term. Most attorneys covered only a portion of it. His friend John M. Scott remembered that after 1854, "there was no such thing in central Illinois as 'traveling the circuit' as was done in earlier days. Mr. Lincoln was probably the last one to give it up in the 'old 8th Circuit.'"

Unlike his friends Orville H. Browning, David Davis, Richard Yates, John Todd Stuart, John M. Palmer, Lyman Trumbull, and other attorneys and politicians who wrote home regularly and affectionately, Lincoln seldom corresponded with his wife, who once complained to him: "you are not *given* to letter writing." During the Civil War, she traveled often and rarely heard from her husband except for an occasional brief telegram. In November 1862, in the middle of a thirty-eight-day absence from Washington, she wrote from New York begging him for "[o]ne line, to say that we [i.e., she and Tad] are occasionally remembered." Herndon said that Lincoln "hated" to write letters. On more than one occasion, Lincoln acknowledged that he was a "poor correspondent." Hence relatively few letters from him to his wife are extant.

Mary Lincoln also seems to have disliked writing letters, at least prior to 1865. In the 1850s, she repeatedly apologized to her favorite sister for letting weeks pass before responding to her missives. She was equally unwilling to write her husband. In 1850, David Davis reported that Lincoln, while riding the circuit, had received no word from his wife for seven weeks. Two years later, Davis similarly observed that while Lincoln was on the circuit, he had heard nothing from his wife for six weeks. In Chicago, Mrs. Judd once asked Lincoln about his wife. When he explained that he had gotten no letter from her since he left Springfield weeks earlier, Adeline Judd asked incredulously: "But Mr. Lincoln, aren't you married?"

"No, no," he protested, "if there was anything the matter Mary would write."

Mrs. Judd, whose husband Norman wrote her every day when they were apart, was astounded.

In 1859, instead of writing to Lincoln, Mary appealed to a friend who was about to visit Chicago, asking him to let her husband know that their son Tad was "quite sick." She felt "troubled" by the lad's illness and said, "it would be a comfort to have him [Lincoln], *at home.*"

Lincoln's few surviving letters to his wife are notably less uxorious than those sent by Judd and Lincoln's other friends to their spouses. In 1859, Judd wrote his wife of fifteen years: "I should have you in my arms now instead of being in this stupid town looking after bridges instead of giving you kisses. I cannot yet determine what my stay here will be and have stolen a moment from the examination of papers to scrawl a how do you do and a lot of love to my own dear wife." Two years earlier, Lyman Trumbull, who wrote to his wife every other day when they were separated, told her: "Some husbands care but little for their wives & of course are not troubled if they do not hear from them frequently, but such is not my case." In 1852, John M. Palmer told his spouse: "Men are charged with indifference to their wives and perhaps it is true of many but I declare to you that all my thoughts and feelings and love is far more ardent towards you than they were on the night when I first called you my own dear wife." That same year, Richard Yates wrote his wife: "Caty I am desperately in love with you."

When apart from his "Dearest Eliza," Orville H. Browning wrote her twice a week. In 1844, he expressed keen longing to her: "oh, how I wish you were with me. . . . No man on earth owes more to the devotion of a wife, and I hope God will give me the means to repay it in kindness and affection." When traveling the circuit, he sent his wife letters containing what she termed "Such beautiful poetry, Such Sighing, and Loveing, dearing, and all that kind of thing." Lincoln's Quaker friend and political ally, Jesse W. Fell, wrote his wife from Washington: "How often, and with what absorbing interest have I thought of thee, since we parted. How frequently have I wandered in imagination to the 'Far,' 'far West,' and then fancied myself one of a little group, with my wife and boy by my side." In 1860, David Davis declared to his wife: "All the honors of the world pale before my undying love for you." In 1855, Mary Nash Stuart (Mrs. John Todd Stuart) said that when she and her husband were "separated he has always written to me frequently and affectionately."

Emilie Todd, unlike her half-sister Mary, received warm, loving letters from her husband, Benjamin Hardin Helm, including one in which he declared: "I cannot be happy without *you*[;] *your* presence is essentially necessary to my happiness." Another ardent Kentuckian, Joshua Speed, told his wife of many years: "I wrote to you yesterday, and today, having some leisure, I will write again upon the principle, I suppose, that where your treasure is there will your heart go. My earthly treasure is in you; not like the treasures only valuable in possession; not like other valuables acquiring increased value from an increased quantity; but, satisfied with each other, we will go down the hill of life together as we have risen."

Lincoln's letters to his wife contain nothing of this sort.

As the years went by, Lincoln remained absent more and more often until finally, as he wrote in 1858: "I am [away] from home perhaps more than half my time."

When back in Springfield, Lincoln seldom passed evenings at home. According to Herndon, he left for work between 7 and 8 A.M. and would be "in a good natured cheerful mood—speak pleasantly—tell a good story and thus he would continue" until noon, when he walked home for lunch. (John Billington, who had worked as an office boy for Lincoln, recalled that Mrs. Lincoln "was a high strung, nervous woman who frequently allowed her housecleaning or other activities to interfere with having her husband's lunch on time.") Upon his return to the office, he would be "in a sad terribly gloomy state—pick up a pen—sit down by the table and write a moment or two and then become abstracted & whol[l]y absorbed on some question."

Herndon said that "Lincoln in his abstractions or in his misery *seemed* to me to be a little off." After taking supper at home, Lincoln would return to the statehouse around 7 or 8 P.M. "in a good humor—in one of his best moods—speak kindly & pleasantly" to the lawyers, who were working on their briefs, and regale them with stories till midnight or one o'clock. Herndon reported that sometimes "after one of these festive and companionable evenings Lincoln and I would leave for our homes at the same time, walking to a certain spot where our paths diverged. I recall one occasion. It was much past midnight and Lincoln was still jolly and bubbling over with the merriment and amusing incidents of the evening. Joyous and lighthearted, free from the look of dejection which so often beclouded his face, I believe I never saw him in happier spirits." Joseph G. McCoy believed that Lincoln's "untoward domestic situation" helped make him a better lawyer and political leader, for instead of spending evenings at home, he became "a constant attendant" at the Illinois State Library, where he read widely.

In Springfield, Lincoln spent hours each Sunday away from his wife and children. Fellow attorney Milton Hay, whose office adjoined Lincoln's, recalled that "year after year," Lincoln on Sabbath mornings "would leave his home and walk along the streets with his hands folded behind him" and upon arriving at his office, "would take off his coat and stretch out on a lounge." After staring at the ceiling for a while, he would get up "and look around in some books or papers, or write a letter or two. Then he'd put on his coat and hat and walk home in time for his dinner."

Even when Lincoln was in town, his wife penned letters describing her loneliness. To her good friend Hannah Shearer, she wrote one Sunday in June 1859: "What would I not give, for a few hours conversation with you this evening. I hope you may never feel as lonely as I sometimes do, surrounded by much that renders life desirable." On a Sunday two weeks later, she told that same friend: "I am generally very lonely. Miss Cochran made a little stay of two months, with us, as she was not particularly pleased with her boarding house and as she contemplated a visit during her vacation to

Wheeling, I thought, it would lessen her expenses, and render my evenings less lonely." On both of those Sundays, Lincoln was in Springfield.

To backyard neighbor James Gourley, Mrs. Lincoln complained "that if her husband had Staid at home as he ought to, that She could love him better." When Lincoln was away, she would turn to her neighbors if she were frightened. Gourley recalled one such occasion: "Mrs Lincoln had a bad girl living with her: the boys & men used to Come to her house in L[incoln']s absence and scare her: She was crying & wailing one night—Called me and said—'Mr Gourly—Come—do Come & Stay with me all night—you can Sleep in the bed with Bob and I.'" She also hired neighborhood children to stay the night with her and her sons. Among them was Fred I. Dean, who recalled that Mrs. Lincoln "had me, young as I was, to sleep in the house, with some of the other neighbors' boys." Another child in the neighborhood, Julia Sprigg (born in 1851), remembered packing "her little white ruffled muslin nightgowns to spend the night with Mrs. Lincoln when her lawyer husband was out of town." After Robert Lincoln went off to a boarding school in 1859, Josiah Kent stayed with Mrs. Lincoln while her spouse was absent. "I spent many a night at the house, sleeping usually in the same room which Robert had occupied," Kent said. While on similar duty in the early 1850s, Howard M. Powel noticed that "Mrs. Lincoln was very nervous and subsequently easily scared." One night "some miscreant came and made a hideous noise against the weatherboarding of the house and Mrs. Lincoln promptly fainted."

LINCOLN FINDS OTHER
WAYS TO AVOID HIS WIFE

When in Springfield and not circumnavigating the legal circuit or stumping the campaign trail, Lincoln would sometimes avoid his wife by retreating to his office or to a friend's house; at other times he would leave town to escape her wrath. According to a neighbor, Anna Eastman Johnson, one evening Lincoln, carrying "a prodigious carpetbag," appealed to her father: "Mary is having one of her spells, and I think I had better leave her for a few days. I didn't want to bother her, and I thought as you and I are about the same size, you might be kind enough to let me take one of your clean shirts! I have found that when Mrs. Lincoln gets one of these nervous spells, it is better for me to go away for a day or two." Other neighbors recalled "that they always knew when Mrs. Lincoln was having a tantrum, for Mr. Lincoln would appear at their home with a small desk and say, 'May I leave these papers with you? Mrs. Lincoln is not well today.'"

MARY LINCOLN'S
SOCIAL AMBITION

Mary Lincoln had social as well as political ambition. Her sister Elizabeth Edwards "was the social leader of Springfield and she gave fine parties," next-door neighbor Charles E. Arnold recalled. "Mrs. Lincoln was poor and she resented the way people passed her by. She was hurt and envious." (She may also have envied Elizabeth Edwards's beauty, for one of Mary Lincoln's friends judged that Mrs. Edwards "is ten times better looking than Mrs. Lincoln.") Joseph G. McCoy recalled that Mrs. Lincoln "was ambitious to shine in a social way, beyond Mr. Lincoln's inclination or financial ability to sustain, and was given to scolding and complaining of Mr. Lincoln in a manner and to an extent exceedingly unpleasant to him." Similarly, William T. Baker described Mrs. Lincoln as "a very ambitious woman" whose "tastes and desires demanded larger finances than Mr. Lincoln could arrange for" and who was therefore "dissatisfied with the progress that Mr. Lincoln was making." Baker added that Mrs. Lincoln's "complaints coupled with demands first for one thing then another would have driven anyone but Lincoln crazy."

Preston H. Bailhache, a Springfield physician in practice with Mrs. Lincoln's brother-in-law William Wallace, said Mrs. Lincoln "was very desirous of having a carriage to take herself and packages home, but was unable to persuade Mr. Lincoln to purchase one." She, therefore, "with a view of shaming him," one day "mounted the steps of his office and announced that she had a conveyance at the door to take him home." Manifesting "no surprise," he "quietly started with her down the stairs." On the street there "stood an old fashioned one-horse dray," to which Mrs. Lincoln pointed and said, "There is your carriage." Her spouse, "smiling in his quaint way, climbed on to the dray and invited his wife to join him." She, however, "failed to see the joke," so he instructed the driver "to take him home."

In 1856, using money from the sale of land that her father had given her, Mrs. Lincoln expanded the modest one-and-a-half-story cottage at Eighth and Jackson. That was soon after a tailor had moved into their neighborhood, and she was displeased that a mere tailor should occupy a more handsome residence than hers. John E. Roll, who had helped remodel the Lincolns' home in 1849, reported that "Mrs. Lincoln decided their means justified a more pretentious house." Charles R. Post similarly remembered that because Lincoln was "becoming famous, his wife aspired to something more pretentious and, knowing that his absence would be prolonged, she called to her assistance Mr. [James] Gourley," and together they decided that "it was an opportune time to raise the half story to a full one." In the 1850s, a two-story house was a status symbol that Mrs. Lincoln "was consumed with a desire" to have. The alteration made the house "superior in appearance to those in the immediate vicinity," for it now rose "considerably above the level of the street" and dwarfed "by its great height and size, the adjoining dwellings." Mrs. Lincoln's nephew termed it "one of the more pretentious residences of Springfield."

The expansion puzzled some neighbors, among them Mrs. John Todd Stuart, who told her daughter: "Lincoln has commenced raising his back building two stories high. I think they will have room enough before they are done, particularly as Mary seldom ever uses what she has." In fact, the expansion added so much space that the Lincolns took in a boarder, Stephen Smith, brother of Mrs. Lincoln's brother-in-law, Clark M. Smith.

LINCOLN'S ECONOMIC STATUS

Much as the 1856 home expansion may have gratified Mrs. Lincoln's social ambition, the Lincolns' economic status had not changed much. A year later, she wrote her half-sister Emilie that, as she beheld ships ready to sail for Europe from New York, "I felt in my heart, inclined to sigh, that poverty was my portion." At that time, Lincoln was hardly impoverished, nor was he especially prosperous.

In 1842, he had told Joshua Speed: "I am so poor, and make so little headway in the world, that I drop back in a month of idleness, as much as I gain in a year's sowing." Lincoln's friend Leonard Swett wrote that in the 1840s, Lincoln "was poor," and "his ideas of money were always far from lavish. I never knew him to refuse to spend for anything he needed. Yet he was always rigidly frugal and in no way indulged, in himself or others, idleness or wastefulness." When another friend, Joseph Gillespie, asked him if he ever invested in land, Lincoln "said he did not think he had much more money making sense than a dumb brute," and therefore never engaged in real estate speculation. In November 1858, he wrote a friend: "I am the poorest hand living to get others to pay. I have been on expences so long without earning any thing that I am absolutely without money now for even household purposes." The following year, he lamented: "It is bad to be poor. I shall go to the wall for bread and meat, if I neglect my business this year as well as last."

Compared with other lawyers in Springfield, Lincoln did only moderately well. In the census of 1860, he ranked twelfth of seventeen Springfield attorneys in terms of assets. The five lawyers who owned less than he did—including Herndon—were much younger, their average age being thirty-two; Lincoln was then fifty-one. A scholarly study of Lincoln's finances concluded that during his first twelve years as an attorney, he earned around $1,500 to $2,000 annually and later about $3000 a year. Of 414 Springfield households listed in the 1860 census, the Lincolns ranked 127th in terms of wealth.

Though Mrs. Lincoln pinched pennies when it came to cooking and other domestic expenses, she enjoyed spending money on her wardrobe. Elizabeth Edwards reported that her sister Mary "loved fine clothes and was so close or economical at the kitchen [so] that she might have money for luxuries." She once purchased an entire bolt of special silk to make sure that no other Springfield woman would have a dress like hers. According to Herndon, "Mrs. Lincoln was a very stingy woman" whose "table at home generally was economized to the smallest amount." Lincoln "never dared as a general thing to invite his friends to his house." (Herndon likened that house to "an ice cave" with "no soul—fun—cheer or fun in it.") David Davis told Herndon "that Lincoln never invited him to his house," and Herndon "heard many others of Lincoln's best friends say the same thing." Lincoln did not mind that she "set a poor table," for, as Herndon noted, he "ate mechanically" and "filled up and that is all: he never complained of bad food nor praised the good." John Hay similarly observed that "the pleasures of the table had few attractions" for Lincoln. During the Civil War, the president indirectly complained about his wife's cooking when he praised the coffee served at an army camp that the First Couple was visiting. A soldier recalled that Lincoln told the First Lady, "'Mother, this [is] better coffee than we get at home,' for which remark she did not seem well pleased."

≈≈≈

In 1854, Stephen A. Douglas detonated a political bombshell that rocked the nation and propelled Lincoln back into the political fray. That year the senator introduced a fateful piece of legislation, the Kansas-Nebraska Act, throwing open to slavery millions of acres in the western territories that had been set aside for freedom under the terms of the 1820 Missouri Compromise. Illinois Whigs, Lincoln said, "were thunderstruck and stunned; and we reeled and fell in utter confusion." To help combat the slavery expansionists, Lincoln once again ran for office; his semiretirement from politics was over.

7

POLITICAL SUCCESS AT LAST
1855–1861

When Lincoln reentered politics in 1854, his wife probably rejoiced, for her dream of becoming First Lady now seemed more attainable, but not if he lowered his sights, which he seemingly did by agreeing to run for the Illinois state legislature that fall. He did so to help boost the reelection chances of his friend, Congressman Richard Yates. While he was on a prolonged tour of the legal circuit that year, Springfield Whigs nominated him for a seat in the General Assembly. Upon reading a press announcement of his candidacy, Mrs. Lincoln ordered the newspaper's editors to strike his name from the electoral list. Later, his friend William Jayne asked Lincoln to allow his name to be reinstated. Jayne found the would-be candidate "the saddest man I ever saw—the gloomiest." Practically in tears, Lincoln said: "No—I can't—you don't know all. I say you don't begin to know one half and that's enough." Henry C. Whitney explained that it "was Mrs. Lincoln's opposition which so much disturbed him. She insisted in her imperious way that he must now go to the United States Senate, and that it was a degradation to run him for the Legislature."

Similarly, in 1860 she discouraged talk of her husband becoming vice president. When Lincoln mentioned that the Iowa delegation to the Republican national convention might support him for that office, she "spoke up in a stern, bitter manner and said, 'If you cannot have the first place you shall not have the second.'" Some of Lincoln's friends believed "he would probably have accepted the nomination for the Vice Presidency at Chicago if Mrs. Lincoln had not opposed it with all the power of her will."

Though Lincoln ultimately did run for the legislature, he also pursued the office his wife desired him to obtain: a US Senate seat. In early 1855, just after antislavery forces had gained a majority of the seats in the Illinois General Assembly, it was clear that incumbent senator James Shields, a Democrat, would not be reelected. To supplant him, Lincoln was the first choice of forty-five legislators; he needed only five more to secure victory, but he was unable to gain them because some anti-Nebraska Democrats declined to support a Whig. Rather than allowing the corrupt Democratic governor, Joel Matteson, to capture the seat, Lincoln threw his support to one of the antislavery Democrats, Lyman Trumbull. As a result, Trumbull won, even though he had initially received only five votes.

At a party immediately after the election, when Lincoln was asked if he was disappointed at the outcome, he replied: "Not too disappointed to congratulate my friend Trumbull," and shook his hand. Similarly, Lincoln held no grudge against Norman B. Judd, one of the antislavery Democrats who refused to vote for him. In 1861, when Judd's name came up for a cabinet post and was strongly opposed by Lincoln's friends (and wife), he said: "I can not understand this opposition to Judd's appointment. It seems to me he has done more for the success of our party than any man in the State, and he is certainly the best organizer we have." Lincoln's stoic reaction to his defeat confirmed Richard J. Oglesby's observation that Lincoln "submitted to adversity and injustice with as much real patience as any Man I Ever knew."

Mrs. Lincoln was not so magnanimous; in fact, she was indignant, denouncing Trumbull as a "sordid, selfish creature without *a soul*, almost," who was guilty of "cold, selfish treachery." She also turned on Mrs. Trumbull (her bridesmaid and longtime friend Julia Jayne), deeming her *"ungainly,"* "cold," "unsympathizing," and "unpopular." Shortly after the senatorial election, Mary Lincoln snubbed Julia Trumbull as the two women emerged from church. Julia reported: "I took pains to meet Mary but she turned her head the other way and though I looked her full in the face, she pretended not to see me." Julia persuaded her mother to invite Mrs. Lincoln to a party, but she declined. When the two politicians' wives met by chance in 1856, Mrs. Lincoln was ungracious: Julia Trumbull reported that "I have shaken hands with Mary, her lips moved but her voice was not audible[.] I think she was embarrassed."

Lincoln was uneasy about his wife's snubbing of Julia Trumbull and tried to make amends. One day in 1856, he noticed her aboard the train car that he and John Todd Stuart occupied. As Julia reported to her husband: "I met Mr. L's eye & he started up & came down the aisle to shake hands. 'Why how do you do?' You know his lungs are strong—but he elevated his voice a little as he called out 'Stuart, here, do you know this lady?'" Lincoln then sat down beside Julia Trumbull and rode with her to Springfield.

During the 1860 campaign, politicians eager to smooth relations between Lincoln and Trumbull enlisted the aid of Norman B. Judd's wife, Adeline. At Springfield, Mrs. Judd found neither Mary Lincoln nor Julia Trumbull willing to take the first step; eventually, after much cajoling, Julia consented. But as she prepared to call on her former friend, she balked when Adeline Judd innocently observed, "You are doing a great service to the cause & the country by this act." Flinging down her bonnet, Julia declared that she would not be reconciled merely for the sake of political expediency. Undaunted, Adeline Judd then turned to Mary Lincoln, who eventually agreed to invite Julia Trumbull for a ride. At the Trumbull home, Mrs. Lincoln refused to accompany Mrs. Judd to the door.

"Why didn't Mrs. Lincoln come in?" asked a miffed Julia Trumbull.

"I told her not to," replied Mrs. Judd disingenuously. "I thought it was better."

Despite this inauspicious start, the two women rode about town together and were speaking as they passed by the courthouse, where Lincoln, Trumbull, Judd, and others observed them. Judd blanched as one of the men whispered, "How did she do it?"

In August 1860, Judd told Mrs. Trumbull that "a systematic effort has been made for political purposes to poison Mary[']s mind" against her, that Congressman John A. McClernand and another unnamed Democrat "instigated their wives to do it," that Mrs. McClernand probably "was unconscious of it," that "Mary had been told a great many things & advised if she had any self respect to keep away" from Julia Trumbull; that "Mary fully understood this attempt now & felt how unjust she had been" to Mrs. Trumbull and was "very happy to be again upon the old terms" with her former bridesmaid.

If the two women did manage to effect a reconciliation, it was short-lived. On February 13, 1861, Mrs. Judd reported that her husband had recently visited Springfield and found Mary Lincoln "much more amiable than before." Lincoln had asked Judd to accompany him on his impending train journey to Washington, and the question arose as to whether Judd's wife should join the entourage. Mary Lincoln regarded her as an ally of Julia Trumbull and objected. Adeline Judd then remarked: "My affection for Mrs Trumbull could never hold itself in abeyance to please the Lady [Mrs. Lincoln]."

In 1861, at a White House levee, Mrs. Trumbull paused in the receiving line to chat with the First Lady, who instructed the usher: "Tell that woman to go on."

"Will you allow me to be insulted in this way in your house?" Julia Trumbull asked the president.

In September 1861, while taking passage on a boat, Mary Lincoln loudly disparaged Senator Trumbull. Julia Trumbull reported to her husband that a clergyman who "travelled on the same boat with Mrs Lincoln between N. Y. & Washington," said that the First Lady "talked so as to be heard above every one else & although he was in the Gents. Cabin he could not avoid hearing her; she discussed people freely, even those in private life[;] talked of you & I[;] referred to your first election when Mr Lincoln was defeated & then to last fall when he was honorably elected, with an emphasis on the word which implied that yours was not honorable."

Shortly after Lincoln's assassination, Mary Lincoln complained that Mrs. Trumbull "has not yet honored me with a call, [and] should she ever deign [to do so], she would not be received—She is indeed 'a whited Sepulchre' [i.e., dead to me.]" The estrangement continued through 1868, when Mrs. Trumbull died. Despite all that, in 1870 Senator Trumbull helped persuade his legislative colleagues to approve a controversial bill granting Mrs. Lincoln a pension.

In 1858, Lincoln once again tried to win a Senate seat, this time campaigning throughout Illinois against the incumbent, Stephen A. Douglas, who was accompanied by his beautiful, cultivated, tactful, well-bred wife, the former Adele Cutts. She was such an asset for the senator that Republicans regarded her as "a dangerous element." Horace White, a leading Republican organizer and journalist, said he had "never seen a more queenly face and figure," and did not doubt "that this attractive presence was very helpful to Judge Douglas."

Mary Lincoln served no such function for her husband. With three children at home, she seldom traveled with him, attending only the final debate in Alton. After it concluded, she invited the Republican shorthand reporter covering the campaign, Robert R. Hitt, to spend a few days in Springfield. He declined, stating "that he would never call at her house until she lived in the White House. She laughed at the suggestion, and said there was not much prospect of such a residence very soon."

On the campaign trail a few days later, journalist Henry Villard chanced to converse with Lincoln as the two men waited for a train. Villard recalled that Lincoln "told me that, when he was clerking in a country store, his highest political ambition was to be a member of the State Legislature. Since then, of course, he said laughingly, 'I have grown some, but my friends got me into this business [the senatorial canvass]. I did not consider myself qualified for the United States Senate, and it took me a long time to persuade myself that I was. Now, to be sure,' he continued, with another of his peculiar laughs, 'I am convinced that I am good enough for it; but, in spite of it all, I am saying to myself every day: "It is too big a thing for you; you will never get it." Mary insists, however, that I am going to be Senator and President of the United States, too.' These last words he followed with a roar of laughter, with his arms around his knees, and shaking all over with mirth at his wife's ambition. 'Just think,' he exclaimed, 'of such a sucker [i.e., Illinoisan] as me as President!'"

Though Lincoln narrowly lost his bid for the Senate, he gained national recognition as an eloquent spokesman for the antislavery cause and thus became, in the eyes of fellow Republicans, a viable presidential nominee, living as he did in a key swing state. When his party held its 1860 national convention at Chicago, he was considered the most electable of the major aspirants with solid antislavery credentials. As Mrs. Lincoln anxiously awaited news about the outcome of the balloting, she "said she thought she had more interest and concern in whom the Chicago convention nominated than her husband." A minister in Springfield predicted that if Lincoln won in November, his wife would be so inflated with pride that she "ought to be sent to the cooper's and well secured against bursting with iron hoops." A few days after Lincoln secured the presidential nomination, her sister Elizabeth expressed the hope that Mary's "ambition may be fully gratified in November."

When the news of her husband's nomination arrived, Mrs. Lincoln busily prepared to receive the convention delegates who would formally announce to Lincoln that he had been chosen as the Republican presidential standard bearer. An advance party of that committee included

Ebenezer Peck, who suggested to some Springfielders that Mrs. Lincoln should be informed that her presence when the delegates called would be inappropriate. Hesitating to confront her, the townspeople said: "Go up and tell her yourself." So Peck, along with Gustave Koerner, went to the Lincolns' house, where they were dismayed to find brandy decanters and a champagne basket among the refreshments laid out with the help of a black servant. When Mrs. Lincoln asked the two visitors their opinion of her arrangements, they "told her at once that this would hardly do. This meeting of the committee would be a somewhat solemn business. Several, perhaps, of the Eastern men were strictly temperance people, and they might think treating the committee would not be the proper thing." Koerner recalled that Mrs. Lincoln "remonstrated in her very lively manner, but we insisted on dispensing with this hospitality, which we appreciated ourselves, but which might be misconstrued. I finally told the black man bluntly to take the things out into the back room, which he did. But Mrs. Lincoln still argued with us. Lincoln, being in the parlor opposite, came in, and, learning of the trouble, said: 'Perhaps, Mary, these gentlemen are right. After all is over, we may see about it, and some may stay and have a good time.'"

Upon the full committee's arrival, Mrs. Lincoln, clad in a lowcut dress, came sweeping into the parlor. One committeeman described her as "very ladylike." Another reported that the Lincolns received the delegation "pleasantly and with unaffected diffidence, that does them credit."

Mrs. Lincoln decided that since her husband was a presidential candidate, he had to act more decorously. Soon after winning the nomination, he as usual swung by the local bakery, but this time accompanied by a black servant. He explained to the baker: "I am not ashamed to carry a loaf of bread home under my arm, but my wife says it is not dignified for a president-elect [presidential nominee] to carry bread under his arm through the streets," so in the future the African American servant would come in his place. She also considered it undignified for her husband to milk their cow, but he insisted on performing that duty because he thought the servant girl should not be exposed to the harsh winter weather.

On election night in November, Lincoln and some friends gathered at the telegraph office to follow the returns. When victory appeared certain, he excused himself, saying he must return home because "there is a little short woman there that is more interested in this Matter than I am."

PRESIDENT-ELECT LINCOLN

Lincoln spent almost all of the next three months in Springfield, answering mail, meeting callers, following the ominous news from Dixie, choosing a cabinet, and drafting an inaugural address. Meanwhile, his wife received positive coverage from Northern journalists. In mid-November, Henry Villard reported that Mrs. Lincoln "by the easy grace and dignity with which she receives those who call upon her daily . . . shows that she possesses the necessary qualifications to assume the higher duties of the President's wife at Washington."

In January 1861, a month during which five Southern states voted to secede from the Union, newspapers announced that Mrs. Lincoln was visiting New York "to make purchases for the White House." (Her Springfield friends reportedly thought her shopping spree, when she bought clothes for herself as well as items for the White House, "quite unnecessary in the present state of political affairs" with "the country in a sad condition.")

Writing from Washington, journalist Herman Kreismann said Mrs. Lincoln's New York sojourn "is considered very much out of place. The idea of the President[']s wife kiting about the country and holding levees at which she indulges in a multitude of silly speeches is looked upon as very shocking. . . . Among other interesting speeches of Mrs L. reported here is that she says her husband had to give Mr Seward [New York senator

William Henry Seward] a [cabinet] place. The pressure was so great; but he did it very reluctantly."

As Lincoln pondered cabinet choices, his wife sought to influence his thinking. (Years later she asserted that such meddling was something that "never once occurred to me to do in my good husband's time.") She disliked Seward even before Lincoln named him secretary of state. In December 1860, when her husband suggested to a visitor that he might appoint the New Yorker to head the state department, she exclaimed: "Never! Never! Seward in the Cabinet! Never. If all things should go on all right—the credit would go to Seward—if they went wrong—the blame would fall upon my husband. Seward in the Cabinet! *Never!*" A fortnight after the election, she told dinner guests: "The country will find how we regard that Abolition sneak Seward." According to one of those guests, that comment resembled several others she made "with more force than logic." Lincoln "put the remarks aside, very much as he did the hand of one of his boys when that hand invaded his capacious mouth."

Mrs. Lincoln failed to block Seward's appointment, but she did help thwart Norman B. Judd's bid for a cabinet post. She deeply resented Judd's refusal to vote for her husband in 1855, when the Illinois General Assembly was electing a US senator. From New York, where she was sojourning in January 1861, she wrote to David Davis, warning that Judd's nomination "would cause trouble & dissatisfaction," and reporting that Wall Streeters thought that "his business transactions, have not always borne inspection." People "were laughing at the idea of *Judd*, being in any way, connected with the Cabinet in *these times*, when honesty in high places is so important." Judd complained that his opponents were using all possible means to defeat him, "including female influence." According to Gideon Welles, who became Lincoln's secretary of the navy, "Mrs. Lincoln has the credit for excluding Judd of Chicago from the Cabinet." Herman Kreismann observed Lincoln tell Judd: "I could sleep better nights if you were not in the cabinet. I wish I could take care of you outside of the cabinet. You know what I mean."

The president "glanced significantly toward Judd. He was referring, as Judd knew, to a dislike that Mrs. Lincoln had for him." When Judd indicated that he desired a European mission, Lincoln agreed to name him minister to Prussia.

The journalist J. K. C. Forrest ascribed Mary Lincoln's opposition to both Judd and Jesse K. Dubois to a different cause: "She desired no Illinois stateman and his family in Washington to detract from her exclusive societary [sic] position." (Forrest's wife Sarah believed that Dubois "was kept out of office by Mrs L[incoln]'s contempt for his manners.")

When Lincoln was told that some men complained about his wife's meddling in the selection of a cabinet, he remarked: "Tell the gentlemen not to be alarmed, for I myself manage all important matters. In little things I have got along through life by letting my wife run her end of the machine pretty much in her own way."

Like Herman Kreismann, Mrs. Lincoln's sister Elizabeth Edwards complained about Mary's conduct between the time of her husband's election and his departure for Washington. Mrs. Edwards wrote her daughter in early February 1861: "I cannot express my surprise, at your Aunt Mary's most singular, and undignified conduct—it is really mortifying, to see that she is making herself so ridiculous, in the eyes of the public." Elizabeth Edwards further objected to some disparaging public remarks that Mary Lincoln evidently made about the financial woes of Ninian Edwards, who had fallen on hard times, and about the likely inability of his wife to afford a "fine and elaborate" dress for the inaugural ball. To her daughter, Elizabeth criticized Mrs. Lincoln for giving "vent to feelings so unamiable, with regard to her family—if the remarks attributed to her are true, she deserves, severe condemnation. It is a mistaken pride, to discover [i.e., reveal] to others, that our immediate family are objects of mortification—and no language, should ever convey the truth, that such is the case." Mrs. Lincoln's "fear that my trousseau, would not come up to her ideas, of the elegant, would make her unwilling to *have me cross* the threshold of the White House."

On the train journey back to Illinois, Mrs. Lincoln got into an argument about tickets. She had used free passes on most legs of the journey, but at Buffalo, where she found herself without a pass for one stretch, she was asked to pay. She indignantly protested, causing her son Robert to appeal to the superintendent of the railroad company: "the old woman is in the cars raising h—l about her passes—I wish you would go and attend to her!" This embarrassing episode was widely mentioned in the press and may have been the "most singular, and undignified conduct" that Elizabeth Edwards referred to.

Mrs. Lincoln and Robert arrived back in Springfield later than originally scheduled; because she did not inform her husband about the change in plans, he "proceeded to the railroad depot for three successive nights in his anxiety to receive them, and that in spite of snow and cold." Henry Villard wondered whether "she got a good scolding from Abraham for unexpectedly prolonging her absence."

As Lincoln prepared to leave for Washington, his wife misbehaved. One Isaac Henderson, part-owner of a leading New York newspaper, sought to win a juicy patronage plum (see Chapter 8). To improve his chances, he sent diamond jewelry to a Springfield merchant with instructions to give it to Mrs. Lincoln if she persuaded her husband to appoint him to a leadership post in the New York Custom House.

(Mary Lincoln had been receiving other gifts. On February 11, a young woman visitor to Springfield told her sister: "Mrs. Lincoln has had a present of a set of furs worth $600. Won't she cut a dash in Washington? She is very fond of dress and loves to show off.")

And so Mrs. Lincoln lobbied her husband on behalf of Henderson. He resisted her appeals until finally, on the morning of February 11—just as he was about to leave for the depot where a Washington-bound special train awaited him—she threw a tantrum that held up his departure. To inquire about the delay, Herman Kreismann called at the room of the hotel where the Lincolns had been spending their final days in Springfield. As he told a reporter years later, Kreismann "found Mrs. Lincoln had thrown herself upon the floor and was crying and saying: 'I will not go. I will not go—I will not go.'" Lincoln explained to his startled visitor: "Kreismann, she will not let me go until I promise her an office for one of her friends." The president-elect managed to calm his spouse "by agreeing to what had apparently been a subject of controversy. Mrs. Lincoln then stopped crying, got up cheerfully, shook out her skirts, gave a push or two to her hair, and went to the station with Mr. Lincoln." Kreismann subsequently heard that she desired to have a certain person (Isaac Henderson) "appointed naval officer at the Port of New York. Lincoln had refused to promise until the crisis at the latest moment before he left for Washington" (see Chapter 8).

(Edgar Welles, the son of Lincoln's Secretary of the Navy Gideon Welles, recalled a similar episode. As a young boy, he stood outside a shop on Washington's Pennsylvania Avenue and overheard Mrs. Lincoln tell her husband that if he did not appoint the man of her choice to an office, she would descend from their carriage and roll about on the sidewalk. According to Welles, Lincoln gave in.)

After capitulating to his spouse, Lincoln joined his son Robert and an entourage of journalists, secretaries, friends, bodyguards, and a servant (the black man William H. Johnson) aboard the presidential train. Mrs. Lincoln and her younger sons did not accompany them; the following day she and the two boys caught up with Lincoln in Indianapolis.

Mrs. Lincoln graciously tolerated the hardships of that memorable journey; toward its end, however, she caused trouble when Lincoln was informed that assassins awaited in Baltimore. To avoid them, he agreed to sneak though that city at night on a regular train, accompanied by a single bodyguard. Utmost secrecy was necessary if the plan was to work, but that secrecy was jeopardized when Mrs. Lincoln learned she would be excluded from that leg of the trip. She "became very unmanageable," according to Alexander K. McClure. She insisted on joining her husband and, McClure recalled, "spoke publicly about it in disregard of the earnest appeals to her for silence. Prompt action was required in such an emergency, and several of us simply hustled her into her room with Col. [Edwin V.] Sumner and Norman Judd" and then "locked the door on the outside. The men with her explained what was to be done and forced her to silence as she could not get out of the door." McClure "thought Mrs. Lincoln was simply a hopeless fool and was so disgusted with her conduct that evening" that he had nothing to do with her thereafter.

On February 23, Lincoln arrived safely in Washington, and soon thereafter his wife and the rest of the party did too, having experienced some unpleasantness in Baltimore. As their train entered the Maryland metropolis, an unruly mob greeted it with three cheers for Confederate president Jefferson Davis and three groans for Lincoln. Most of the crowd did not realize that Mrs. Lincoln and her boys had detrained before reaching the depot and taken a carriage to the home of John S. Gittings, president of the Northern Central Railroad. Some hecklers learned of this and greeted her with "yells and catcalls, mingled with hurrahs for the Confederacy" as she alighted at the Gittings' residence. Despite the heckling, Mrs. Lincoln told her hosts "that she felt at home in Baltimore." She added that "her husband was determined to pursue a conservative course."

As Lincoln prepared to assume the presidency, David Davis predicted that the "cares & responsibilities of office will wear on him." The "cormorants for office will be numerous & greedy." Davis added that Mary Lincoln, who "is very ambitious, and is in high feather," was "not to my liking. I don[']t think she would ever mesmerise any one." Although Davis feared that she "will disgrace her husband," he nonetheless hoped "that she will not give her husband any trouble."

It was to prove a vain hope.

PART III

THE
WHITE HOUSE
YEARS

1861–1865

8

THE "FEMALE PRESIDENT" STICKS HER FINGER IN THE GOVERNMENT PIE

During the Civil War, Elizabeth Comstock, a Quaker leader whom Mrs. Lincoln heard preach, offered advice to the First Lady about ways in which she might help her husband: "Thou hast it in thy power to strengthen his hands in the great work in which he is engaged, to encourage him in seasons of deep discouragement; to soothe & cheer him in times of depression; to divert his attention in seasons of relaxation, from the heavy pressure of care & the weight of Government; to train his sons to honor their father & their father's God, to shield him from all little cares & annoyances in his home." Mrs. Lincoln did not take that well-intentioned advice, causing her husband to lament in 1863: "I am the loneliest man in America. There is no one to whom I can go and unload my troubles, assured of sympathy and help."

Rather than providing "sympathy and help," Mrs. Lincoln was an endless source of anxiety and embarrassment to the president, who often discussed "his domestic troubles" with a close friend, Orville H. Browning. As Browning recalled, Lincoln "several times told me there [in the White House] that he was constantly under great apprehension lest his wife should do something which would bring him into disgrace."

ROGUES FLATTER AND
BRIBE MRS. LINCOLN

Lincoln had good reason to fear that the First Lady would disgrace him. She considered herself "a sort of sub-President" entitled to influence the selection of public officials. (Horace Greeley referred to her as "the female president.") A Springfield resident joked about her ambition, speculating that if her husband died before taking office, she, "like another [Queen] Boadicea [of England], will repair to the 'White House' and assume the reins of government!" Two days after her husband's inauguration, she reportedly seemed "to feel her station is as high as that of any of the Queens of the earth." In 1880, Emily Briggs, a journalist friend of Mrs. Lincoln, wrote that "the wife of our President has more real political power than Queen Victoria." Mrs. Briggs described how a presidential spouse "waits carefully in an ante-room, and when Cabinet sessions are over, seizes upon the head of any of the Departments, and then and there, like a Catharine [the Great of Russia] or Elizabeth [the First of England], makes known her command." Mrs. Lincoln "inaugurated this excellent plan of doing business, because the exigencies of the war wholly occupied the mind and time of the President, and it became necessary for the 'first lady' to look after the minor affairs of the country."

In the initial weeks of the new administration, Washington buzzed with rumors that Mrs. Lincoln's lobbying efforts so annoyed the president that his "hollow cheeks, sunken eyes and woe-begone expression" were due to "her caprices and interference." Henry Villard recollected that early in Lincoln's presidency, he appeared "so careworn as to excite one's compassion," in part because of "the inordinate greed, coupled with an utter lack of propriety, on the part of Mrs. Lincoln," who "allowed herself to be persuaded, at an early date, to accept presents for the use of her influence with her husband in support of the aspirations of office-seekers." Less than a week after the inauguration, Charles Sumner, chairman of the Senate Foreign Relations Committee, regaled a friend with stories about how "Mrs. Lincoln was meddling with every office in the gift of the Executive." Months later, David W. Bartlett of the Springfield, Massachusetts, *Republican* reported that she had "made and unmade the political fortunes of men. She is said to be much in conversation with cabinet members, and has . . . held correspondence with them on political topics. Some go so far as to suggest that the president is indebted to her for some of his ideas and projects." She was "ambitious of having a finger in the government pie." Among Massachusetts visitors to Washington, the First Lady's political influence was a prime topic of conversation. One young Bostonian considered her just "as meddling & injuriously officious as she is conceited & ill-bred."

Mary Lincoln's best friend in the White House, her African American dressmaker Elizabeth Keckly, told a journalist "that politicians used to besiege Mrs. Lincoln, and that presents would be sent to her from people whom she had never seen." The donors attended White House receptions, where the First Lady "would often be surprised to be asked by a perfect stranger: 'Mrs. President Lincoln, I hope you admired that set of furs I sent you lately.'"

She would reply: "Oh, was it you who sent them; really I am at a loss to thank you for your kindness."

"Not at all, madam, it was but a slight and worthless token of the deep esteem I have for the talents of one whose intrinsic merit would, irrespective of your present exalted position, make you an ornament in the highest circles of the most civilized society."

Gratified by such "fulsome flattery from a vile politician, who would insidiously ask for a favor, she, after receiving his present and believing his flattery, would find it difficult to refuse" his request for assistance in obtaining an office or contract.

The First Lady was especially susceptible to insincere praise. In March 1861, Horace Greeley noted that she "enjoys flattery—I mean deference." That same month, William Howard Russell of the London *Times* exclaimed that Mrs. Lincoln "was surrounded by flatterers and intriguers, seeking for influence for such places as she can give!" Later that year, he observed: "She is accessible to the influence of flattery, and has permitted her society to be infested by men who would not be received in any respectable private house in New York." The First Lady's intervention led to what another journalist in 1862 called "some very curious appointments, more curious than suitable."

THE CASE OF ISAAC HENDERSON

Isaac Henderson was a case in point; his selection as naval agent in the New York Custom House was emblematic of Mrs. Lincoln's meddling in patronage distribution on behalf of gift-givers (see Chapter 7).

Patronage battles were to bedevil Lincoln throughout his presidency, especially in the spring of 1861, while he was struggling with momentous issues of war and peace. He understood the necessity of uniting the Republican party (and, by extension, the North) by judiciously dividing the spoils among the various elements of that fissiparous coalition. The greatest challenge was to persuade the feuding Radicals and Conservatives to cooperate with each other.

In no state was the battle more intense than New York, where Conservatives led by William Henry Seward and Thurlow Weed fought Radicals led by Horace Greeley and William Cullen Bryant. The most coveted patronage plums were jobs in the Custom House, where the collector, naval agent, and naval officer stood to earn handsome sums not only from their generous salaries but even more from "indefinite (or rather infinite) fees."

The First Lady wanted to control some of those key appointments, though she denied it. According to Charles A. Dana, during a White House meeting that he, James S. Wadsworth, and other New York Radicals were holding with Lincoln in the early days of his administration, an usher with a message from the First Lady "bolted into the apartment and rudely said to the President, 'You are wanted!'"

"'Yes,' curtly responded Lincoln, impatient at the intrusion." He ignored the summons, and the conversation resumed.

A few minutes later, the usher returned "and with marked emphasis said to the President, '*She* wants you!' and nodded to the company with an air that more than intimated, 'You are *not* wanted.'"

Lincoln "hastily retired, throwing some apology behind him." Wadsworth then "proposed that the committee themselves should pay their respects to the lady of the mansion. Cards were sent in, and the gentlemen soon followed. The manner in which that lady received her distinguished visitors plainly showed that she was ready for an encounter with the heads of the anti-Seward faction. Bridling up, she informed them that she learned it had been reported that she interfered with her husband's affairs, but she wanted them to distinctly understand that this was not true." The icy interview soon terminated when the First Lady sailed out of the apartment. As the Radicals descended the White House steps, Wadsworth sarcastically remarked that "before he took part in electing another President he would inquire into the nature of his conjugal relations." Lincoln, Dana reported, "was so mortified at this affair, that he told the New York Radicals he wished them to make out a list of those persons whom they desired for important positions in their State." He assured them, "I shan't let [William H.] Seward gobble up all these fat things; he and [Treasury Secretary Salmon P.] Chase must ride and tie [i.e., cooperate with each other]."

Among the final New York Custom House slots to be filled was naval agent, a civilian employee of the Navy Department and also a disbursing officer under Treasury Department supervision. (Benjamin Brown French called it a "good place—fat salary and no work!") The Seward-Weed faction proposed Simeon Draper or Silas B. Dutcher, while the Greeley-Bryant forces backed Philip Dorsheimer of Buffalo. As a compromise candidate, Thurlow Weed suggested John Bigelow of the *Evening Post* or the prominent entrepreneur and financier Isaac Sherman. Lincoln favored D. D. T. Marshall, an abolitionist and former Democrat, known for his strict integrity.

But none of them won the job; instead, it went to Mrs. Lincoln's candidate, Isaac Henderson, the wealthy publisher and part-owner of the New York *Evening Post*. In January 1861, Henderson told influential friends that he wanted the position of naval officer (more lucrative than naval agent), though his business partner William Cullen Bryant—a leading poet, editor of the *Evening Post*, and a close friend of Henderson—warned him against applying for a Custom House appointment. Bryant feared that the avaricious Henderson might be tempted by the many opportunities for graft available to Custom House officials. Nonetheless, Bryant and his son-in-law Parke Godwin supported Henderson's bid, as did John Bigelow, who had recently sold his one-third interest in the *Post* to Godwin.

Henderson was known as "the wicked partner" of the *Evening Post* as well as a man who "had the sharpness of a Yankee horse-trader" with "mercenary tastes." As noted in the previous chapter, he sent diamond jewelry to Springfield to help persuade Mrs. Lincoln to lobby her husband on his behalf, which she did. And so, with the help of the First Lady, Henderson became naval agent in the New York Custom House.

In that post, he justified Bryant's suspicions by extorting money from contractors, leading to his arrest and a public scandal. In 1864, Assistant Secretary of the Navy Gustavus Fox and a special commissioner for the Navy Department discovered Henderson's misdeeds while investigating a supplier who had sold adulterated oil to the navy. On June 20, Navy Secretary

Gideon Welles noted in his diary that Henderson "has been guilty of mal-feasance although standing high in the community as a man of piety and probity." Only reluctantly did Welles conclude, "that it was my duty to ask his removal and take measures against him." That Henderson, like all naval agents, "was getting rich at the public expense I have not doubted—that there were wrong proceedings in this matter I fully believed, and yet to break with old friends was and is unpleasant." Democratic congressman Moses Odell, Henderson's congressional representative, friend, and fellow church congregant, examined the case and concluded that Henderson had "committed great frauds."

Others agreed, including New Hampshire legislator William E. Chandler (a future secretary of the navy) and Iowa senator James Grimes. In May 1864, Senator Grimes publicly charged that Henderson and others associated with the naval supply system in New York "have been debauched by bribes."

When Lincoln asked Welles if he felt sure that the charges against Henderson were valid, the secretary replied in the affirmative. Although the 1864 election campaign loomed, during which the president could ill afford to alienate influential newspapers like the New York *Evening Post*, Henderson was nonetheless arrested on June 22.

Bryant stoutly defended his partner, protesting to Lincoln that the "effect of these proceedings upon Mr. Henderson's reputation, hitherto spotless, cannot but be very damaging, since they imply that in the view of the government, he is indisputably and grossly guilty." It was important "that men of integrity and capacity should understand that, when they accept posts of trust, they are not to be capriciously turned out, on charges preferred against them by any rogue, who may fancy that his interest will be promoted by their removal." Moreover, Bryant noted, Henderson was supporting Lincoln's reelection bid.

Vexed by the *Evening Post's* recent criticism of his administration, Lincoln wrote back: "Whether Mr. Henderson was a supporter of my second nomination I neither knew, or enquired, or even thought of. I shall be very glad indeed if he shall, as you anticipate, establish his innocence; or, to state it more strongly and properly, 'if the government shall fail to establish his guilt.' I believe however, the man who made the affidavit [Joseph L. Savage, proprietor of a Brooklyn hardware store] was of as spotless reputation as Mr. Henderson, until he was arrested on what his friends insist was outrageously insufficient evidence. I know the entire city government of Washington, with many other respectable citizens, appealed to me in his behalf, as a greatly injured gentleman." Lincoln went on to express some irritation: "While the subject is up may I ask whether the Evening Post has not assailed me for supposed too lenient dealing with persons charged of fraud & crime? and that in cases of which the Post could know but little of the facts? I shall certainly deal as leniently with Mr. Henderson as I have felt it my duty to deal with others, notwithstanding any newspaper assaults."

In May 1865, when a judge dismissed the case against Henderson, Welles deplored "attempts to cover the tracks of guilt by technicalities of law, which may perhaps arrest the arm of justice, but cannot suppress the righteous judgment of an honest public opinion." William E. Chandler, who had examined the evidence closely, told Welles: "The result of the cause, although Henderson is acquitted, is the universal public belief of his guilt and the entire vindication of the Department."

Bryant exulted in the judicial vindication of his friend Henderson, though Parke Godwin was understandably convinced of his guilt, for the evidence was compelling. Five years later, Godwin's unfavorable opinion of Henderson had not improved. "I regard Mr. Henderson as a far-seeing and adroit rogue," he told Bryant; "his design from the beginning has been and still is to get exclusive possession of the *Evening Post*, at much less than its real value." Bryant, however, continued to have faith in Henderson until 1877, when he learned that Henderson had been defrauding him for decades. To repay Bryant for all that he had stolen over the years, Henderson was forced to sell his shares in the *Evening Post*, which he did quietly "to avoid another criminal prosecution."

Lincoln may well have scolded his wife for her role in the appointment of Henderson. As Elizabeth Keckly reported, "many scenes" occurred "when his wife was goaded on to ask for [a] place [desired] by office-seekers." Eventually, the president "shut down on it (to use his own phrase)."

THE CASE OF GEORGE DENISON

The position that Henderson had originally sought—naval officer—went to another "adroit rogue" whom Mrs. Lincoln championed: George S. Denison, a handsome, unaccomplished attorney in his late thirties who, at the time of his appointment, was working as a lowly bill collector in New York.

Denison's greatest asset was his connection with twenty-nine-year-old William Henry Marston, son-in-law of Lincoln's close friend and banker, Robert Irwin. A native of Greenfield, New Hampshire, Marston had moved to New York in 1851 to work for a bank established by fellow townsman Frederick P. James. In the mid-to-late-1850s, Marston lived near Lincoln in Springfield, which served as his base of operations as he helped establish branches of James's bank throughout Illinois. While in the Prairie State capital, he befriended Lincoln, who collaborated with him on a successful plan to thwart a Chicago banker who was extorting one of Frederick James's branches. In 1860, Marston moved back to New York, where he teamed up with Denison. Together they induced Robert Irwin to lobby the president on behalf of Denison, who aspired to become naval officer in the Custom House.

Robert Irwin inserted himself into Lincoln's patronage battles evidently because he wanted to help his daughter Liza, who had wed Marston in 1859. The following year, the young couple moved to New York, where Liza gave birth to her first child, Robert Irwin Marston.

On February 15, 1861, Marston and Denison formally agreed to divide the handsome income that Denison would derive from his anticipated government position. (Marston's ethical sense was weak. In 1862, he founded a brokerage firm and became a major player on Wall Street, acquiring a shady reputation while making and losing fortunes. A few years later, he served as a close ally of Diamond Jim Fisk and Jay Gould in their struggle against Daniel Drew and Cornelius Vanderbilt for control of the Erie Railroad. In 1898, Marston committed suicide immediately after investors in his gold mining company learned that it was worthless.)

Just how Denison and Marston knew each other is uncertain. They both lived in New York in 1861 and were lobbying for bank note companies. Since no evidence of any relationship between Denison and Irwin is extant, it is fair to surmise that Irwin was lobbying on Denison's behalf as a proxy for his son-in-law Marston in order to aid his daughter Liza and his namesake grandson.

Marston recalled that just after the 1860 election, he went back to Springfield, where Lincoln told him: "Pick out any office in New York except the Collector of the Port and Postmaster, and you shall have it." (Lincoln was thus offering to indirectly help Irwin, whom he described as a friend "who has served me all my life, and who has never before received or asked anything.")

Marston replied that he was so busy that he "could not afford to accept any office."

The president-elect said: "Then look around among your friends when you return to New York and send me word what I can do for the best one of them."

Marston suggested Denison, who was unknown to Lincoln. Soon after the inauguration, Seward proposed a slate of candidates for New York offices, which included Silas B. Dutcher for naval officer in the Custom House. According to Marston, the president listened to Seward's explanation of that list and said "in his gentle and quiet way that it was all right with one exception, and that was the naval officer, which he had already promised to a young Wall Street friend of his, whose name he had forgotten for the moment, but that he knew he was all right and would fill the position with credit, as I had told him so, and that was enough for him."

According to Marston, Seward "became very angry, and intimated that it was a high-handed piece of business on the part of the president, and that unless Mr. Lincoln consented to appoint his friend [Dutcher] to that post he would not be responsible for the Republican Party in the state [of New York]." The president's "only reply was he had never broken his word, and that he was too old to commence then, remarking further that he would not act upon any of the other names until he had assurance that my friend [Denison] would be confirmed by the Senate." Seward "brought every power at his command to bear on Mr. Lincoln, and Mr. T[hurlow] Weed came over here [to New York] to try to persuade me to give up the office and save the grand old party. Finally, finding nothing could change the president, the names were all acted upon at the same time."

Lincoln asked only one thing of Marston in return: "to have his Springfield shoemaker's son, Harry Gourley, appointed to a clerkship." Shortly after the 1860 election, Lincoln had told his friend and neighbor James Gourley: "Jim, you have not asked me for anything, but I cannot forget the many kindnesses my family have had at your family's hands. What would you like?"

He replied, "Nothing for me but if you would give [my son] Harrison a lift, I'd be glad."

Lincoln evidently told Robert Irwin that he wanted young Gourley, a schoolmate of Robert Lincoln's, appointed a clerk in the New York Custom House. Irwin wrote the president-elect in February 1861: "I have arranged for the Clerkship for Gourl[e]y, if Mr Denison is appointed." In the spring of 1861, Harrison Gourley received a clerkship at the New York Custom House, where he toiled for decades.

Robert Irwin forwarded to Lincoln some recommendations for Denison that, he claimed, "will certainly satisfy you of his good moral character and capacity for the situation asked for. And now my friend I ask you for his appointment as the only one I have any interest in. I have been a consistent and warm political friend of yours from your first to your last race, and have at all times been for you against all others. Socially I shall not speak of. I ask this as a Republican, and for a working Republican, nor do I think you can have an applicant who will be more strongly recommended."

But in fact, Denison was not strongly recommended. As Lincoln told Irwin: "I am scared about your friend Dennison. The place is so fiercely sought by, and for, others, while . . . his name is not mentioned at all, that I fear appointing him will appear too arbitrary on my part."

Unmoved by the president's appeal, Irwin importuned him once again: "Now my friend for the last time—as I do not want to bore [i.e., pester] you [—] cannot you consistently give my Friend Denison the appointment he has solicited you for[?] I hope you will for my sake as I shall feel mortified and humbled in your not doing it— from the newspapers I gather that there is considerable squabling for it (as well as all others) and I hope you will end all feuding by appointing my friend."

There were indeed several others were contesting for the naval office, which was, next to the collectorship, the most lucrative post in the Custom House. Among the aspirants, in addition to Silas B. Dutcher (Seward's choice), were New York state treasurer Philip Dorsheimer, a prominent German leader from Buffalo; ex-congressman Abram Wakeman, backed by New York congressman Roscoe Conkling; and another former congressman, Henry Bennett, the favorite of many influential New Yorkers.

Denison, on the other hand, had few backers and many critics. Secretary of the Treasury Salmon P. Chase protested against his appointment strongly, writing to Lincoln: "I fear, if you make this appointment, you will regret it. When it was first proposed I had heard so little expression either way that I did not feel myself called upon,—though I felt that setting aside so many prominent men for a gentleman so little known in political or financial circles was of questionable expediency,—to say any thing against it." But recently "many of the most eminent and influential gentlemen of New York have expressed to me such unfavorable opinions of Mr. D– and such strong convictions that his appointment to so high an office will affect the Administration injuriously in quarters whose good opinion is most valuable that I feel myself constrained to say that were the responsibility of decision mine, I should not put my name to the commission."

In reply, Lincoln explained to Chase that "the urgent solicitation of an old friend" (Robert Irwin) led him to support Denison: "His (Mr. Dennison's) good character was vouched for from the start by many at New York, including Mr. [George] Opdyke."

Chase was right; prominent New Yorkers (other than Opdyke) questioned the integrity of Denison, a Massachusetts native who had for a few years practiced law in DeKalb, Illinois. There his "profits were small—in fact could hardly keep the pot boiling, and he left the town rather suddenly, and by no means pleasantly." He "came to New York a poor young man" in the late 1850s and worked as a bill collector for the New York *Evening Post* and other clients.

In January 1861, Denison met Mrs. Lincoln during her shopping trip to Manhattan. She stayed at the Metropolitan Hotel, where Denison and his wife were boarding and where he was "doing the collecting business of the proprietors." There, according to a press account, "his charming lady, by kind attentions to Mrs. L., (who patronized that hotel) won her kind regards." Denison himself won Mrs. Lincoln's kind regards not only because he was "genial and handsome" but also because he presented her with a $1,500 "full-dress coach" that was "luxuriously fitted-up." In May 1861, he accompanied the First Lady on another shopping expedition to New York, where a journalist reported that the "prospective naval officer [in the Custom House]—whom she has had appointed to that lucrative sinecure in spite of the politicians—has been untiringly attentive to her ladyship." According to another journalist, "some of the wealthy friends of Seward had a splendid carriage built for the president's wife, to which the Greeley gang were not allowed to contribute their mites. Of course, the letter tendering this present to Mrs. Lincoln was signed in full by all who helped to pay for it, and they alone. And won't the 'old woman,' as Bob Lincoln called her [Mary Lincoln], see that they are provided for."

(The chairman of that committee was Rufus Andrews, who soon thereafter received a juicy patronage plum: surveyor in the New York Custom House. Years later, as Mrs. Lincoln was urging Andrews to help settle her debts, she told a Springfield friend: "In the *halcyon* days, amongst the first appointments my noble & good husband made—was that of Mr. Andrews to one of the most lucrative places in New York." She claimed credit for helping him win that post.)

Denison was identified in the press as the "ambitious individual who endeavored to steal into the affections of Mrs. Lincoln by presenting her with a beautiful carriage." He "did not mean that his name, as the donor, should leak out; but somehow it always happens that these things do get ventilated, and without seriously lacerating the feelings of the benevolent party." In addition to giving her what she called a "*very luxurious*" carriage, Denison opened for Mrs. Lincoln a $5,000 line of credit in New York.

Prominent Republicans like New York senator Preston King, a supporter of Philip Dorsheimer's unsuccessful bid to become the naval officer, complained to the president about Denison's unseemly tactics in pursuit of office. After his White House interview, the senator concluded that Lincoln was "weak and unequal not only to the present crisis but to the position he holds at any time."

Parke Godwin of the New York *Evening Post* told Lincoln: "It is exceedingly important that the appointment of Mr G. Denison, as naval officer at New York should be delayed. I think I can show that he is a dishonest man, and therefore unworthy of a public trust." Others questioned Denison's credentials. James A. Briggs said that he "only cares to make money. He knows nobody, & nobody knows him. His appointment was a party outrage." A New York merchant alleged that Denison was an unqualified, "good looking boy about 25 years of age [actually 39], whose only naval experience was obtained as a runner, or collecting clerk" for the New York *Evening Post.*

On May 27, less than a week after his wife's return from her New York shopping trip, Lincoln officially appointed Denison as naval officer of the Custom House. On that sojourn, she had purchased a coach and, according to Horace Greeley, improperly charged the $600 cost to the contingency fund. She also attended a service at the church of a celebrity minister, Henry Ward Beecher, where she created a "great sensation."

In addition to his desire to please Robert Irwin, Lincoln was influenced by Mrs. Lincoln. Though no direct evidence of her lobbying on Denison's behalf survives, Charles A. Dana, the well-informed managing editor of the New York *Tribune* and a leading member of the Empire State's Radical faction, recalled that Lincoln "minutely inquired as to the extent and value of the patronage and perquisites of the Naval Office at the Port of New York, a position which he subsequently worse than threw away in pursuance of a bargain, to which he was not an original party, but to which he felt constrained to yield in order to keep the peace in his household." That bargain was doubtless the one concluded between Marston and Denison to share the income of the latter.

Others reported that Mrs. Lincoln had facilitated Denison's appointment. The Democratic press sneered: "George Dennison [sic], who presented Mrs. Lincoln with a carriage, last spring, has received his reward in the shape of the appointment of naval officer at New York." The New York *Daily News* remarked: "We hear that Mr. George Dennison [sic] has received his appointment at last as naval officer of this port. Mr. Dennison is a close and intimate friend of Pres. Lincoln's family." Many years later it was reported that "William Marston was a friend of Abraham Lincoln, and has always been credited with having persuaded Lincoln to throw over Thurlow Weed's candidate for Surveyor [actually naval officer] of the Port and appoint his own candidate instead."

It is not hard to understand why Mrs. Lincoln favored Denison. Aside from the fact that he had presented her with a luxurious coach and a generous line of credit in New York, he was handsome and ingratiating and may have flirted with her. Sam Ward, a Washington insider known as "King of the Lobby," suggested that there was something unsavory about the relationship between Denison and the First Lady. In addition, she had befriended Denison's wife and was close to Liza Irwin, Robert Irwin's daughter and the spouse of Denison's associate, William Marston.

In office, Denison managed to enrich both himself and Marston. By law, the naval officer was entitled to augment his annual salary of $4,950 with one-sixth of the money collected as fines, penalties, and forfeitures for frauds committed on the public treasury. During his first twenty-five months in office, Denison netted $44,640.67 from those supplementary sources, according to an indignant William Cullen Bryant. When added to his salary, that meant Denison took in even more than Lincoln, whose annual pay of $25,000 was five times greater than Denison's.

Like Isaac Henderson, Denison proved an embarrassment to Lincoln. In office, he abused his power by engaging in extortion, seizing ships promiscuously, and pocketing cash from out-of-court settlements that should have flowed into the government's coffers. After the Civil War, he grew wealthy as a "buccaneer operating on the fringes of a legally organized business."

THE CASE OF WILLIAM S. WOOD

Under pressure from the First Lady, Lincoln nominated yet another "adroit rogue" from New York to a lucrative government post: William S. Wood, who had organized and supervised the First Family's train journey from Springfield to Washington in February 1861. At that time, he was a lobbyist for the American Bank Note Company and an aspirant for the post of commissioner of public buildings.

A native of upstate New York, Wood had been a clerk and jeweler there before moving to Manhattan, where he established a jewelry store and prospered until it burned down. He later moved to Syracuse, where he became involved in the railroad business, dominated by his relative, Erastus Corning, president of the New York Central line. According to journalist and historian David Rankin Barbee, Wood was a "scoundrel" who was "sent to Springfield by the Eastern Railroads to entice Lincoln" to choose an indirect, northerly route from the Illinois capital to Washington via Cleveland, Buffalo, Pittsburgh, Albany, New York, Trenton, Philadelphia, Harrisburg, and Baltimore. "By lies and other propaganda," Wood convinced Lincoln that it was too dangerous to take the more direct southerly route over the Baltimore & Ohio Railroad. In January 1861, Wood appeared at Springfield to take charge of the train trip. He was supplied with credentials from William Henry Seward's alter ego, Thurlow Weed, who in 1853 had been instrumental in winning legislative approval for the merger that created the New York Central. Lincoln said that he knew nothing about Wood, but that Seward had recommended him "as being all right."

While acting as superintendent of arrangements for the inaugural rail journey, Wood devoted most of his attention "to the whims and caprices of Mrs. Lincoln." A journalist aboard that train described Wood as "a man of comely appearance, greatly impressed with the importance of his mission and inclined to assume airs of consequence and condescension." Mrs. Lincoln reportedly "became smitten with his handsome features, luxuriant whiskers and graceful carriage." Wood, seeing "how well he 'took' with my lady," determined "to cultivate her favor as much as possible." So he "danced with her at the Inauguration ball, and then complimented her for her gracefulness." In addition, he "praised her children for their beauty, and reverenced her husband for his prudence and firmness."

To further ingratiate himself with Mrs. Lincoln, Wood on March 6 presented her with a pair of "perhaps the finest coach horses that were ever matched in America" to draw the "magnificent visiting coach" that friends of Seward had recently purchased for her (the one that George Denison had presented). Wood did so "in the most delicate manner" with "the request that if she preferred any other color, she would specify it." Mrs. Lincoln "was highly gratified at the esteem and delicacy of feeling manifested by the donors."

Wood had "played his cards remarkably well," so much so "that Mrs. Lincoln declared him a paragon of manly excellence, and resolved that he should have whatever office he wanted." But when he applied for the post of commissioner of public buildings, he was chagrinned to learn that Lincoln had already promised it to a Springfield friend. The First Lady then "stormed and scolded," demanding that Wood be appointed. Because "there was such a tempest made about his ears," Lincoln capitulated on May 30, shortly after the First Lady and Wood returned from their shopping excursion to New York. William Howard Russell heard that the First Lady "has the devil[']s temper & made Abe surrender & appoint one of the men (Wood) as Comr of Public Bldgs [Commissioner of Public Buildings] by shutting herself in her room." Wood began serving as commissioner-designate in June, replacing the incumbent, James Blake. The Senate, then out of session, would consider his nomination when congress reconvened the following month.

To help ensure Wood's confirmation, the First Lady recruited assistants. In April, she urged Lincoln's close friend and fellow Illinois attorney Ward Hill Lamon to speak to the president in favor of Wood, whom she called "a clever man," well qualified to "make an efficient Commissioner." Lamon, who regarded Wood "as a high toned honorable gentleman," complied immediately. In addition, she reportedly persuaded two leading Republicans from Indiana—Thomas H. Nelson and Congressman Schuyler Colfax—to cooperate in a scheme to win Lincoln's approval. She would invite them to an intimate supper at the White House, where they would dine with only the First Couple. During the meal they were to refrain from lobbying;

after dessert, she would excuse herself, at which point they were to urge the president to appoint Wood. The Hoosiers agreed, and the dinner went according to plan. After they finished making their postprandial appeal, Lincoln said: "Well, gentlemen, you can say to Mrs. Lincoln that to-morrow I will send in to the Senate Mr. Wood's name." When Colfax and Nelson reported this news to the First Lady, "she was greatly pleased."

Wood's name was submitted on July 5, the day after the Thirty-seventh Congress first met. Mrs. Lincoln told Senator Orville Browning that he "would always find a very true friend in her" if he would support the candidacy of Wood, who "was very popular and very worthy[.]"

But Lincoln surreptitiously told a senator that, appearances to the contrary notwithstanding, he did not favor Wood's nomination. Senators then raised objections, ostensibly because of Wood's lobbying efforts on behalf of the American Bank Note Company, and the Committee on the District of Columbia did not report favorably on Wood's nomination, which was laid over till Congress reconvened in December. Meantime, the office of commissioner of public buildings was officially vacated. In effect, Wood's nomination was defeated by the Senate's refusal to act on it before the adjournment of Congress in early August.

Lincoln had sabotaged Wood's appointment apparently because, as he told David Davis in May, "it would be ruinous to appoint him—*ruinous to him.*" (Davis called the nomination of Wood "incomprehensible.") It is unclear what Lincoln meant; perhaps he was influenced by rumors that the First Lady was having an affair with Wood. In June, the president received a letter signed "Union" about a "scandal" involving Mrs. Lincoln and Wood, who together had gone on a shopping trip to New York in May. "Union" warned Lincoln that if rumors about that scandal appeared in the press, it would "stab you in the most vital part." The president spoke sharply to his wife about Wood; Schuyler Colfax recalled "the war she had with Mr. Lincoln" about him. According to Colfax, the First Couple "scarcely spoke together for several days." The "war" may have erupted when Mrs. Lincoln found out (if in fact she did find out) that Lincoln had torpedoed Wood's nomination.

Lincoln might have had a possible adultery scandal in mind when he told Orville Browning that he was afraid that the First Lady would bring him into disgrace. An Iowan, evidently referring to Wood, asserted that Mrs. Lincoln "used to often go from the White House to the Astor House in New York to pass the night with a man who held a high government office in Washington, given to him by her husband." Benjamin Brown French termed Wood a "libertine" and "a disgrace to the Nation, to Lincoln & to the office." French, who had a friend "whose wife he [Wood] undertook to seduce," called Wood a "damned infernal villain." Wisconsin senator James R. Doolittle termed Wood "a great scamp."

Mrs. Lincoln may have been unfaithful with others as well as with Wood. John Watt, the White House gardener, told a journalist in 1867 that "Mrs. Lincoln's relations with certain men were indecently improper" and claimed to be well informed about "the secrets of Mrs. Lincoln's domestic affairs" (see Chapter 9). Rumors circulated that Watt himself had "too great an intimacy" with her. In 1870, Illinois senator Richard Yates, a longtime friend and ally of Lincoln, suggested that Mrs. Lincoln had been unfaithful; he told his legislative colleagues that "there are recollections and memories, sad and silent and deep, that I will not recall publicly . . . Amid all the perils of life, and its devastation, amid good and evil report, a woman should be true to her husband. . . . I shall not . . . go into details."

Edward McManus, a White House doorkeeper, evidently made a similar allegation. In early January 1865, Mrs. Lincoln had him fired and called him a "serpent" for spreading rumors about her. She confided to her friend Abram Wakeman (rumored to be romantically linked with her) that soon after McManus's dismissal, she and her husband had a "*scene*" which caused some "coolness," but that by the end of January "the storm" had "cleared away." It is not certain that McManus's firing caused the domestic discord, but if it did, it may have resembled the First Couple's quarrel about her relations with Wood in 1861 (see Chapter 10).

The press covered the First Lady's role in Wood's case. In June, it reported that he had won appointment "at the special request of Mrs. Lincoln." In early August, after Congress adjourned, she urged her husband to reappoint Wood to the office that had been vacated. He obliged her by doing so on August 12. A Washington correspondent stated that the First Lady "has her way . . . in reference to Wood, the commissioner of public buildings. He was a favorite with Mrs. L., and she desired his appointment. Certain senators did not like the nomination, and he was not confirmed. The women, however, will have their way, and the president has reappointed Wood." But hers was a Pyrrhic victory, for Lincoln reinstated Wood only temporarily, with the understanding that he would resign on September 1, when Benjamin Brown French would succeed him. (Wood allegedly was "deeply dejected by his mortifying repulse" and "implored the President for the sake of his family to reappoint him for a month only" so "that he might have the credit of resigning." Lincoln "good-naturedly consented to this strange request, and at the end of the month Wood was, accordingly, desired to send in his resignation." But he balked. The press reported in early September that his "conduct in Washington has been so strange that the notion began to be entertained that his common sense has been nearly exhausted."

That strange behavior was evidently described in a report that a congressional committee gave the president indicating that Wood was corrupt. In July, while serving as commissioner-designate, Wood told one Samuel A. Hopkins: "I understand that you are here . . . trying to get work from the government in the way of engraving. I want to tell you, as a friend, that there is no use at all of trying; that the work will be given to the American Bank Note Company and the National Bank Note Company." When Hopkins protested that his firm could perform the work better and cheaper than those providers, Wood explained the situation: "I am interested in the American Bank Note Company myself, and have been at work for them here, and have got things all right; and [George] Dennison [sic], the naval officer of New York, and his friends, F. P. James and William H. Marston, are interested in the National Bank Note Company, and they have got the thing figured all right."

Hopkins then said he was trying to sell the government some cannons for $500 apiece. Wood replied: "Well, I can help you in that matter. Say nothing about the price; we can make something out of that. If the government wants them, they can as well afford to pay more as less. I will take you down and introduce you to Mr. Leslie, the chief clerk of the War Department." (Hopkins's testimony links Wood with Marston and Denison, though their connection is murky). After Hopkins told this story on August 30 to the House Select Committee on Government Contracts, chaired by New York congressman Charles H. Van Wyck, Lincoln was informed that Wood had "made himself an instrument for plundering the government."

By September, the First Lady had abruptly turned on Wood, denouncing him as "a very bad man" who "does not know, what *truth* means." Everyone, she claimed, regarded him as "a most unprincipled man." She may have made her *volte-face* because of these new revelations, but William Howard Russell thought that she had earlier soured on Wood "because he would not put down the expense of Plon Plon's [i.e., Prince Jerome Napoleon's August 1861] dinner to public ac[coun]t as manure money for [the White] House" (see Chapter 9). She also resented Wood's criticism of White House gardener John Watt, with whom she was colluding to pad payrolls and engage in other shady practices (see Chapter 9). On August 8, five days after the dinner for Prince Napoleon, it was reported that Lincoln would remove Wood and name Benjamin Brown French in his stead. Finally, on September 6, Wood "declined the tender of a reappointment," and French became his successor.

NEPOTISM: THE FIRST LADY HELPS
RELATIVES WIN GOVERNMENT JOBS

Lincoln was accused of appointing members of his own family to government posts, but in fact he awarded patronage plums to his wife's relatives, not his. Well before she became First Lady, Mrs. Lincoln had intervened to protect her brother-in-law, Benjamin S. Edwards, who sought an office coveted by David Davis. Davis complained: "Lincoln hadn't the manhood to come out for me in preference to Ben Edwards whom he despised . . . because Ben was in the family. I had done Lincoln many, many favors—Electioneered for him—spent money for him—worked for him—toiled for him—still he wouldn't move." According to Herndon, Lincoln feared that if he had "gone for Judge Davis," then "Mrs. Lincoln would have clim[b]ed in his hair and he Knew this and Knew it well."

One of the most controversial beneficiaries of the First Lady's favoritism was Benjamin Edwards's older brother, Ninian, who received a government job and became a major embarrassment for the president. In a letter no longer extant, Edwards asked for a patronage appointment. Belatedly, Lincoln responded: "It pains me to hear you speak of being ruined in your pecuniary affairs. I still hope you are injured only, and not ruined. When you wrote me some time ago in reference to looking up something in the Departments here, I thought I would inquire into the thing and write you, but the extraordinary pressure upon me diverted me from it, and soon it passed out of my mind. The thing you proposed, it seemed to me, I ought to understand myself before it was set on foot by my direction or permission; and I really had no *time* to make myself acquainted with it. Nor have I yet. And yet I am unwilling, of course, that you should be deprived of a chance to make something, if it can be done without injustice to the Government, or to any individual. If you choose to come here and point out to me how this can be done, I shall not only not object, but shall be gratified to be able to oblige you."

Edwards had been an ally of Lincoln in the Illinois General Assembly during the 1830s and 1840s, but in 1851 he joined the Democrats, a shift which "deeply mortified" Lincoln. In 1858 and 1860, Edwards supported Stephen A. Douglas, to whom he wrote letters with the closing "Your friend." Despite that, Lincoln appointed him captain and commissary commissioner for Springfield, a job which entailed the letting of contracts for provisioning troops. Some of Lincoln's friends endorsed Edwards, among them David Davis and Orville Browning.

But other party allies and Springfield friends of the president objected "in the most emphatic manner." Ozias M. Hatch, William Butler, and Jesse K. Dubois wrote Lincoln in the summer of 1861, alleging that Edwards would be the tool of corruptionists, "with Gov [Joel] Matteson at their head." (As governor from 1853 to 1857, Democrat Joel Matteson had fraudulently enriched himself at public expense.)

In 1854, when Ninian Edwards found himself in political limbo, Matteson had come to his rescue, appointing him to government posts. Returning the favor, Edwards as commissary commissioner awarded contracts to Matteson and his friends, thereby eliciting further indignant howls from Dubois, Hatch, and Butler, who wrote the president on October 21, 1861: "We again insist that this outrage against common decency be corrected. We protest that Mr Edwards is not, or ought not to be permitted to make such contracts, and we respectfully ask that he be assigned to duty, elsewhere, and be required to contract directly with honest men, and not indirectly with thieves and scoundrels."

That same day, John G. Nicolay wrote the president from Springfield "Mr. Edwards starts for Washington to-night to obtain further authority to make *all contracts* of all kinds for the State, and our friends say that the whole business of furnishing the State troops, will thus fall into Gov. Matteson[']s hands, and that this necessarily brings the Gov. into business relations with all our friends in the State who will thus be bound to recognize and deal with him."

In October, Edwards defended himself to Lincoln in person and explained his case to Assistant Secretary of War Thomas A. Scott, who told the president that Edwards had been "falsely accused." Lincoln therefore ignored his Springfield friends' protest, but in 1863 he reversed course upon receiving yet more complaints, including one from his friend William Yates, brother of Illinois Governor Richard Yates: "the best interests of the Country Demand" the "immediate removal from Office" of Edwards and others cooperating with him, including William Bailhache, who was an assistant quartermaster with the rank of captain, and Edward L. Baker, Bailhache's coeditor of the Springfield *Illinois State Journal*. (Mrs. Lincoln had facilitated Bailhache's bid for a government post.)

Lincoln's friends Jacob Bunn, Ozias M. Hatch, and Shelby M. Cullom lodged similar protests. "There are men *here* [in Springfield]," Bunn wrote, "having no sympathy with your administration, who have not only been living off of the General Gover[n]ment for the past two years but getting *rich* from the *stealings*; (the sums acquired are too large to have been obtained honestly,) who lose no opportunity to revile and denounce your administration; and whose pecuniary interest is not to put down the rebellion but to prolong it, in order to make *more money*."

Even more compelling was a letter from Lincoln's neighbor and long-time friend and political ally, Jesse K. Dubois, who declared that Edwards and Bailhache "have given all their patronage to the enimies [sic] of your administration," including Dr. Edwin S. Fowler, "and have Contrived to amass fortunes with a rapidity which is a disgrace to the Government and a Scandal to its supporters. They ought to be relieved from duty here and placed where they can do no harm. You cannot afford to keep them here at the risk of alienating the affections of your neighbors and life-long friends." Among those friends were Charles W. Matheny, Pascal P. Enos, Gershom Jayne, William F. Elkin, and John W. Smith, all of whom endorsed Dubois's letter.

To Edward L. Baker, who defended the accused men, Lincoln replied: "The appeal to me in behalf of Mr. Edwards and Mr. Bailhasche, for a hearing, does not meet the case. No formal charges are preferred against them, so far as I know; nor do I expect any will be made; or, if made, will be substantiated. I certainly do not suppose Mr. Edwards has, at this time of his life, given up his old habits, and turned dishonest; and while I have not known Mr. Bailhasche so long, I have no more affirmative [sic] reason to suspect him. The trouble with me is of a different character. Springfield is my home, and there, more than elsewhere, are my life-long friends. These, for now nearly two years, have been harrassing [sic] me because of Mr. E. & Mr. B. I think Mr. E. & Mr. B. without dishonesty on the other hand, could have saved me from this, if they had cared to do so. They have seemed to think that if they could keep their official record dryly correct, to say the least, it was not any difference how much they might provoke my friends, and harrass me. If this is too strong a statement of the case, still the result has been the same to me; and, as a *misfortune* merely, I think I have already borne a fair share of it."

On May 29, 1863, Lincoln asked Jesse K. Dubois and other protestors to suggest men to replace Edwards and Bailhache. A few days later they complied, and on June 22 Lincoln named George R. Weber and James Campbell to the posts held by Edwards and Bailhache, who were allowed to remain in the Quartermaster's Department throughout the war but were transferred from Springfield. Commissary General Joseph Taylor explained to Edwards: "The President does not doubt you in any manner or shape but is embarrassed by circumstances should you remain at Springfield."

Months later, a scandal involving meat rations supplied by Springfield contractors embarrassed Edwards. On December 30, 1863, Orville Browning told him: "I have had repeated conversations with the President in regard to you, in all of which he has expressed himself most kindly, and as having unshaken confidence in your integrity and capacity." General Taylor also "expressed himself in the kindest terms respecting you. You have had a hard time of it, but I trust now you will be let alone, and permitted to discharge your duties in peace. I suggest that you do not talk about this matter.

It is not necessary that the public shall know that either you or the contractors have been subjected to annoyances." In truth, it was Lincoln—more than Edwards or the contractors—who had been "subjected to annoyances." Well might he consider himself "harassed"; the case of Ninian Edwards was indeed a "misfortune" and an embarrassment for him.

Another relative of Mrs. Lincoln—cousin Lockwood Todd—was also appointed a captain and commissary commissioner. In 1861, he had been nominated for the more remunerative post of Drayman of the Port of San Francisco, touching off a furor: California Republicans denounced him as a hardcore Democrat who had campaigned against Lincoln in 1860. The president's friend William Jayne thought it "very strange how as bitter a democrat as Capt Todd can have so much influence over Mr Lincoln." The West Coast protests were so numerous and vehement that the collector of the Port of San Francisco, Ira P. Rankin, withdrew the nomination, which he had originally made as part of an understanding when Lincoln awarded him the juiciest patronage plum in California. Todd appealed to the president, who refused to intervene and instead let the collector's decision stand. In 1864, however, he named Todd to a commissary post after his mother had pled his case.

Ninian Edwards was not the only one of Mrs. Lincoln's brothers-in-law to win a government job; William S. Wallace became an army paymaster. Lincoln liked Wallace, with whom he regularly socialized at his Springfield drug store. As he doled out patronage, the president explained that he appointed Wallace because he "is needy, and looks to me; and I personally owe him much." Mrs. Lincoln boasted that she had fought a "hard battle" to get Wallace appointed and was miffed at her sister Frances (Mrs. Wallace) for her ingratitude. According to Herndon, Lincoln said Wallace was "appointed to a bureau simply to 'keep hell' out his own family!"

In 1849, Lincoln had obtained an appointment for Dr. Wallace as a pension agent in Springfield, causing a rival for that post to observe: "Mrs Lincoln said to some one the other day—that she was now so happy—that she had got Mr. L. to give the Pension Agency to the Doctor & now all of their family difficulties was made up—so you see I was offered up as a sacrifice—a sort of burnt offering—to heal family broils." Apparently Wallace had been frosty toward Lincoln until he won the coveted government post.

Kentuckian Ben Hardin Helm, husband of Mrs. Lincoln's half-sister Emilie, was also offered a position as paymaster in the Union Army, but he turned it down and joined the Confederate Army. Two cousins of Mrs. Lincoln managed to win postmasterships: Lyman Beecher Todd in Lexington, Kentucky and Thomas M. Campbell in Boonville, Missouri. In addition, Charles Stewart Todd, a distant relative of the First Lady, was appointed a tax assessor in Owensboro, Kentucky.

But another of Mrs. Lincoln's cousins, Elizabeth Todd Grimsley, lost her bid for a postmastership, even though the First Lady lobbied vigorously on her behalf. When John Todd Stuart recommended Elizabeth to head the Springfield post office, Lincoln asked: "Will it do for me to go on and justify the declaration that [Senator Lyman] Trumbull and I have divided out all the offices among our relatives?" (The favoritism shown to Mrs. Lincoln's family had created resentment in Illinois, where Ebenezer Peck complained in August 1861 that the president "and his wife have some relatives not yet provided for," and that "until *all* these shall have been provided for, all *newer* friends I suppose must needs wait.")

Other relatives of Mrs. Lincoln also met defeat, including John Blair Smith Todd, whom the president nominated for a brigadier generalship, only to have the Senate reject him.

THE FIRST LADY CAUSES
FURTHER EMBARRASSMENT

In the winter of 1864–1865, Richard H. Wilmer, the pro-Confederate Episcopal Bishop of Alabama, happened to be in Washington and wished to return home. When Mrs. Lincoln urged that he be given a pass, her husband refused, as did Secretary of War Stanton. But she persisted so strongly that Lincoln eventually capitulated. When Wilmer presented that pass, he was arrested by incredulous authorities who mistakenly regarded the document as a forgery. It turns out that the bishop was attempting to smuggle mail into the South. Lincoln abjectly apologized to an infuriated Stanton: "You can never know what I have suffered, or the pressure brought to bear to influence my action."

Another Alabamian in search of a pass embarrassed Lincoln. In late 1863, the First Lady's half-sister, Martha Todd White, who was married to an Alabama doctor, had managed to enter the North; while preparing to return home, she also appealed to Lincoln for a pass. He balked, but Martha White persisted until he finally gave in. He balked once more when she brazenly asked that her luggage be exempt from inspection; she, in turn, once again belabored him, this time with the aid of Kentucky congressman Brutus Clay. When Clay tried to lobby on her behalf, Lincoln snapped: "if Mrs. W. did not leave forthwith she might expect to find herself within twenty four hours in the Old Capitol Prison." Unnerved by this threat, Mrs. White proceeded to Fort Monroe, where she defied Union troops who attempted to inspect her baggage. General Benjamin F. Butler let her continue on her way anyhow, thereby igniting a firestorm in the Northern press. Lincoln had Nicolay look into the matter and compose a defense of the administration for publication in the New York *Tribune*, which had covered the story extensively. The paper retracted its charge of misconduct against Mrs. White, and the controversy, which had commanded the headlines throughout March and April, ended. The scandal had caused Lincoln great anxiety.

Former Congressman David Kilgore of Indiana called Mrs. Lincoln "a corrupt woman who controles her husband." In fact, her voice counted for little except in relatively minor cases, like the men mentioned above and also Amos Tuck. The First Lady pulled strings effectively for that New

Hampshire Republican, who had befriended young Robert Lincoln during his student days at Phillips Exeter Academy (1859–1860). In January 1861, Tuck had visited Springfield, stayed overnight at the Lincoln home, and then escorted Mrs. Lincoln partway on her shopping trip to New York. Tuck won the coveted post of naval officer at the Boston Custom House. (According to Senator Charles Sumner, it was understood in Washington that "Mrs Lincoln appointed a collector [of the Port] for Boston on ac[count] of [her son] 'Bobby.'")

In addition, Mrs. Lincoln and her cousin Lizzie Grimsley successfully pressured Lincoln to appoint Glasgow-born James A. Smith as consul at Dundee, Scotland. He was a Springfield minister who in 1850 had helped the Lincolns cope with the loss of their three-year-old son Eddy. According to Grimsley, she and the First Lady told the president that the "old Doctor was a warm personal friend, had been with us in joy and sorrow, was well-fitted for the post, which was one not much in demand, was an ardent Republican, and he wanted to spend his last days on his 'native heather,' and many words to like effect." Lincoln then arose and laughingly said "send your preacher to the Cabinet Room," from which Smith later "emerged a happy man." The president seemed "well pleased that he could confer the consulship on him," but he made the ladies promise that it would be the final time that they "would 'corner' him."

Mrs. Lincoln pressured cabinet members as well. Among them were Secretary of State Seward, Secretary of the Interior Caleb B. Smith, Treasury Secretary Salmon P. Chase, and Secretary of War Simon Cameron. She vainly asked Seward to appoint a friend as consul at Honolulu and badgered Cameron to award contracts to some of her friends (see Chapter 10). Evidently she clashed early on with Cameron, to whom she wrote on March 29, 1861: "I understand that you *forgive me*, for all *past offenses*, yet I am not Christian enough, to feel the same towards *you*."

She also clashed with Cameron's successor, Edwin M. Stanton. When asking him to find a place for a "half loafer, half gentleman," she justified her request as one appropriate for someone in her position to make: "I thought that as the wife of the President, I was entitled to ask for so small a favor." Stanton replied: "Madam, we are in the midst of a great war for national existence. Our success depends on the people. My first duty is to the people of the United States; my next duty [is] to protect your husband's honor and your own. If I should make such appointments, I should strike at the very root of all confidence in the people in the Government, in your husband, and you and me." She acknowledged that he was right.

This was not the only occasion when Stanton and the First Lady locked horns. According to one of his aides, the war secretary "was often enraged because Mrs. Lincoln sent quantities of flowers from the government greenhouses to the residence of [New York] Congressman Fernando Wood whenever Mr. and Mrs. Wood—both of whom denounced the Secretary and the war incessantly—gave a public reception." The First Lady "retaliated by sending to him [Stanton] books and clippings describing [him as] an exacting and disagreeable person."

Mary Lincoln also lobbied on behalf of David Davis, who sought appointment as a justice of the US Supreme Court. Leonard Swett reported that the First Lady "told me she had been fighting Davis['s] battles" and had opposed Orville Browning's bid for a seat on that high tribunal. She confided to Swett that Browning had become "distressingly loving" as he pressed his case.

Mrs. Lincoln's meddling in patronage distribution harmed her reputation and the president's as well. The influential journalist Murat Halstead wrote that several of Lincoln's "most unfortunate appointments have been made to please his wife who is anxious to be thought the power behind the throne and who is vulgar and pestiferous beyond description."

9

HONEST ABE, DISHONEST MARY: "A NATURAL BORN THIEF"

Mary Lincoln described her husband as "almost a *monomaniac* on the subject of *honesty*" and at the same time also spoke of their "opposite natures." She was, in fact, the opposite of "a monomaniac on the subject of honesty." David Davis called her "a natural born thief," and he knew whereof he spoke, for he served as the administrator of Lincoln's estate and saw proof that she had stolen many items from the White House. Returning to Illinois after the assassination, she had taken with her scores of trunks and boxes containing "a great deal of Government silver, spoons[,] forks etc[.] and a large quantity of linen and stuffs." Ohio Senator Benjamin F. Wade, who served on a committee considering Mrs. Lincoln's appeal for the full $100,000 that her husband would have received in salary if he had served out his second term, told an interviewer: "She took a hundred boxes of something or other—I don't know what—away with her, and the commissioner of public buildings swore there were fifteen other boxes that she wanted to carry off, and he had to interfere to prevent her." At a White House reception on New Year's Day 1866, guests were taken aback by the mansion's decrepit appearance. The New York *World* reported that "no one could look about the house without being almost shocked by the downright shabbiness of the rooms and furniture." The *World* added that "exactly *ninety* boxes were furnished by a certain official for packing up curtains, carpets, vases, pictures, and 'knickknacks' of all sorts, that were carried away not many months ago. The $30,000 appropriated two weeks ago, 'for furnishing the White House,' will scarcely pay the outstanding local bills of the former occupants." When told that such stories about Mrs. Lincoln's looting of the Executive Mansion were exaggerated, David Davis demurred, saying "that the proofs were too many and too strong against her to admit of doubt of her guilt," and "that she carried away, from the White House, many things that were of no value to her after she had taken them, and that she had carried them away only in obedience to her irresistible propensity to steal."

During her husband's presidency, Mrs. Lincoln engaged in other unethical practices, among them influence peddling, falsifying bills, padding payrolls and expense accounts, pinching servants' wages, selling permits to trade, misappropriating funds, selling government property, accepting bribes and kickbacks, and engaging in extortion.

THE CASE OF JOHN WATT

While Mrs. Lincoln regarded the would-be commissioner of public buildings (William S. Wood) as expendable, she did not feel that way about the man whom Wood accused of disloyalty—the White House gardener, John Watt. In collusion with the First Lady, Watt had been cheating the government. According to White House watchman Thomas Stackpole, Watt had "in the beginning of the Administration suggested to Mrs. Lincoln the making of false bills so as to get pay for private expenses out of the public treasury and had aided her in doing so."

Watt had been serving as the White House gardener for nearly a decade, during which he had acquired an unenviable reputation. In Buchanan's administration, Commissioner of Public Buildings John B. Blake had rebuked him for submitting inflated bills.

Early in the Lincoln presidency, Watt's conduct drew even more criticism. In September 1861, Wisconsin congressman John F. Potter, chairman of the House Select Committee on the Loyalty of Government Employees, forwarded to the president testimony about Watt's alleged pro-Confederate sympathies. Two independent witnesses charged that shortly after the Battle of Bull Run, the gardener had declared that the South could not be beaten and that the Union army consisted of human trash.

Mrs. Lincoln emphatically denied those allegations and urged her husband to keep Watt in the White House by nominating him for an army officer's commission. On September 9, Watt was duly appointed first lieutenant in the Sixteenth US Infantry "at Mrs Lincoln's demand." (Maine senator William P. Fessenden and the historian George Bancroft both heard that she "wished a rogue [Watt] who had cheated the government made a lieutenant: the cabinet thrice put the subject aside. One morning in came Lincoln sad and sorrowful: 'Ah,' said he, 'to-day we must settle the case of Lieutenant [Watt]. Mrs. Lincoln has for three nights slept in a separate apartment.'") She pressed Secretary of War Simon Cameron and, according to Charles A. Dana, "after a good deal of bullying on her part & resistance on his, actually gets him [Watt] appointed a lieutenant in the army with orders to report for duty not to the colonel of his regiment, but to the President." The Senate, however, revoked his commission on February 3, 1862, when he was accused of leaking the president's annual message to Congress. He was then dismissed from his White House post (see Chapter 10).

In August 1861, the First Lady tried to charge a White House state dinner for Prince Jerome Napoleon to Watt's account, though it was customary for a president to pay for such dinners out of his own pocket. When she billed the Interior Department $900 for the August 3 banquet, Interior Secretary Caleb B. Smith complained to Secretary of State Seward that Mrs. Lincoln refused to pay the bill, which she insisted was the Interior Department's responsibility. (Watt may have misled her about that matter.) But, as Smith told Seward, the money Congress placed at his disposal was earmarked for maintenance of the White House and its grounds, not for presidential entertaining. To avoid a scandal, Seward proposed that their two departments split the cost evenly. But when Smith reported the bill's amount, Seward was surprised because it was much greater than the sum his department had paid for a dinner he had also given to the prince, even though "I had the same guests at my dinner" and "it was prepared by the same man," Charles Gauthier, a fashionable Washington caterer and restaurateur. So Seward refused to pay any part of the inflated cost, as did both Smith and the First Lady. Finally, Gauthier became importunate, causing Mrs. Lincoln to appeal to Smith once again: "I'll tell you how that little bill can be settled. You see there are three cavalry regiments stationed on our property. Now those horses have left heaps of manure, and it all belongs to us. Now you want manure for the public grounds, particularly those around the White House. Now I will sell it all to you for gardening purpose[s]. You send me the money and I'll pay Gauthier." According to Eunice Tripler, around that time "a great quantity of manure had been delivered at the White House grounds to be spread afterwards upon the grass of the lawns. This Mrs. Lincoln managed to sell and from the proceeds provided for the entertainment which was afterwards known generally as 'the manure dinner.'"

Thurlow Weed alleged that the First Lady instructed Watt to "make out a bill for plants, pots etc. of the required amount, certified it herself and drew the money." This "occasioned scandal."

Yet another version of this story had Mrs. Lincoln trying to persuade Benjamin Brown French to pay the bill. French protested, but she was adamant. So he checked to see if there was any unexpended money in his budget. Discovering that the only funds available were for purchasing manure to fertilize public grounds, he told her that he was reluctant to tap that source. She demanded that he do so, and he did; but Lincoln found out about it, reprimanded him severely, and gave him money from his own pocket to cover the misappropriation. The chairman of a senate investigating committee reported that "a state dinner was paid for out of an appropriation for fertilizers for the grounds connected with the Executive Mansion."

A White House gatekeeper, James H. Upperman, described the gardener's account in which the cost of the dinner was paid for from public funds, not the president's own purse. On October 21, 1861, Upperman complained to Interior Secretary Smith about "sundry petit, but flagrant frauds on the public treasury," the products of "deliberate col[l]usion." According to the gatekeeper, in mid-September Watt had authorized payments for several no-show workers as well as $700 for flowers and $101 for fertilizer. Upperman convincingly described the misappropriations in elaborate detail.

Evidently nervous about Upperman's allegations, Mrs. Lincoln, through Watt, implored Secretary of the Interior Smith to see her husband. On October 26, in reply to a query from Commissioner of Public Buildings French, Lincoln said he would "determine in a few days what he would do." Watt declared that "the arrangement of the accounts was made by [William S.] Wood & that he assured Mrs L[incoln] that the transaction was right & legal and that she had no idea that anything was done which was not authorized by law." Secretary Smith told Seward that he would "be glad to relieve her from the anxiety under which she is suffering."

Smith did so by covering up the scandal. After making inquiries about the $700 flower bill, Smith concluded "that the voucher was correct, and that it had been rightfully paid by Mr. French," and therefore he "pursued the matter no further." He did not interview Upperman or those allegedly involved in the fraud. Gatekeeper Upperman then protested to Solomon Foot, chairman of the Senate Committee on Public Buildings and Grounds. Nothing came of that protest except Upperman's dismissal.

Thurlow Weed reported that the Interior Department and Congress "measurably suppressed" this story out of "respect for Mr. Lincoln." In 1865, Democratic congressman Benjamin M. Boyer of Pennsylvania, a member of the House Ways and Means Committee, confirmed Weed's version of events, adding that Lincoln paid the bill himself and withdrew the government check.

A Senate committee was made aware of the Watt scandal, but Democrat James A. Bayard of Delaware agreed to hush it up, saying: "The thing's a swindle, gentlemen, but this is the wife of our President, the first lady in this land and we only disgrace ourselves by this exposure."

On March 11, 1862, Lincoln asked Comptroller Elisha Whittlesey, known as "the watchdog of the treasury department," to inform him of any suspicious bills emanating from the White House: "once or twice since I have been in this House, accounts have been presented at your bureau that were incorrect. I shall be personally and greatly obliged to you if you will carefully scan every account which comes from here; and if in any there shall appear the least semblance wrong, make it known to me directly."

When Watt later threatened to blackmail Mrs. Lincoln, he received some form of hush money. According to Isaac Newton of the Agriculture Department, Watt "entered into a conspiracy to extort [$]20,000 from the President by using three letters of Mrs. Lincoln." In those missives, the First Lady evidently urged Watt "to commit forgery and perjury for the purpose of defrauding the Government." In 1867, Watt tried unsuccessfully to sell an account of his relations with Mrs. Lincoln that included "a note to Watt signed by Mrs. L (which is genuine) proposing to cover up their schemes etc."

New York Republican leader Simeon Draper cornered Watt and "with much bluster & great oaths" threatened to have him imprisoned. Watt "fell on his literal marrow bones & begged, & gave up the letters & the conspiracy got demoralized & came down, down, to 1500 dollars which was paid, and the whole thing [was] settled." That payment took the form of a sinecure designed to get Watt out of the country. On March 14, 1862, Secretary Smith appointed him a special agent for Isaac Newton's Agriculture Department to purchase seeds in Europe, at an annual salary of $1,500 plus travel costs. (A few days earlier, Thomas Stackpole had warned Senator Orville Browning that "Watt ought to have some appointment which would take him away from Washington," for the gardener "exercised a bad influence over Mrs. Lincoln, and unless he was removed from here [Washington] and a new leaf turned over at the White House, the family there would all be disgraced.")

In 1863, after the government failed to pay him for his European sojourn, Watt sent the president an invoice for $736 [ca. $22,000 in early twenty-first-century dollars] to reimburse him for Mrs. Lincoln's hotels bills, cash advances, and "Commissary stores." Simeon Draper held receipts for these payments and advances. Watt told Simon Cameron, "You know very well what difficulties I had to contend with in regard to Mrs. Lincoln. . . . I paid about $700.00 for Mrs. Lincoln on one trip to Cambridge, Mass."

The Watt affair became the talk of the capital. In February 1862, David Davis wrote his wife: "I got a letter from Washington & the gossip is still about Mrs. Lincoln and the gardener Watt." Newspapers reported that Watt, at the urging of the First Lady, purchased two cows "and charged them to the manure fund—that is, a fund voted in one of the general appropriation bills to provide manure for the public lands." This invoice was rejected, in all likelihood by Interior Secretary Smith.

Smith also challenged other invoices. (In 1862, Mrs. Lincoln lobbied to have him removed from his cabinet post.) According to the New York *World*, when the First Lady ordered $800 worth of china from E. V. Haughwout & Co., she attempted to fold in other purchases—amounting to $1,400—by making the total bill of $2,200 covering the china alone. When Smith questioned that bill, the merchant reportedly admitted that an overcharge was created to disguise the purchase of $1,400 worth of unspecified items. The *World* referred skeptics to the treasury secretary. Haughwout & Co. denied the allegations in a letter to Manton Marble, editor of the *World*. In turn, Marble defended the story and, rather than retracting it, threatened to "expose what I know about Mrs. Lincoln's practices in her New York purchases—her silver service—the champagne[,] manure bills etc. etc. to say nothing of wallpaper, seed commissions, shawls, contracts, etc. etc. etc." The *World* also accused Mary Lincoln of sending discarded White House furniture to Springfield rather than putting it up for auction, as the law required, and also of appropriating $7,000 of public money for her "personal adornment."

Watt asserted that "a bill of $6,000 contracted with Haughwout & Co. for silverware was paid for by a bill charged against gilding gas-fixtures." In 1862, Congress passed a supplemental appropriation of $2,613 to cover expenses involved in plating gas fittings at the White House. On July 30, 1862, Haughwout received $2,343 from the commissioner of public buildings for plating White House cutlery.

Mrs. Lincoln also proposed that a New York merchant supply the Executive Mansion with a chandelier costing $500, charge the government $1000 for it, and thus permit her to disguise $500 worth of jewelry to be secretly included. The merchant declined to participate in such a scheme and apparently lost the sale. According to a Maryland journalist, the First Lady "once bought a lot of china for $1500 in New York & made the seller give her $1500 in cash & sent a bill for $3000. When Lincoln refused to put his signature to the bill prior to sending it to the department to be paid, on the ground that it was exorbitant, [the merchant said,] 'You forget, sir, . . . that I gave Mrs Lincoln $1500.[']"

It was widely rumored that Mrs. Lincoln "appropriated the manure piles which had always been the perquisites of the gardener" and pocketed the funds from their sale. William O. Stoddard, the White House secretary most sympathetic to the First Lady, recalled that a "sudden horror" of future poverty led her "during a few hours of extreme depression" to propose "to sell the very manure in the Executive stables, and to cut off the necessary expenses of the household." Mrs. Lincoln shocked another presidential secretary, John Hay, by trying to raid the $1000 White House stationery fund; Hay thwarted her attempts.

The corrupt actions of Isaac Henderson, George Denison, William Marston, John Watt, Ninian Edwards, and William S. Wood prompted a journalist to ask in 1862: "Does it not seem strange that *so many* doubtful characters contrive to deceive the generous-hearted, confiding President?"

The Watt scandal nearly became an issue in the 1864 election campaign. In February, as Salmon P. Chase and others were maneuvering to win the Republican nomination for president, Agriculture Secretary Isaac Newton told Attorney General Edward Bates "that a secret pamphlet has been gotten up, he thinks, by the machinations of [Interior] Secy. [John Palmer] Usher and Senator [Samuel] Pomeroy levelled agst. Mrs. L. in reference to the infamous Watt scandal. He expects to get a copy tomorrow; and if it turns out to be what he supposes, thinks it will produce an explosion." According to journalist J. K. C. Forrest, "the enemies of Mr. Lincoln, principally represented by the Chase section of the republican party, got hold of the entire [Watt] business" and "threatened to publish it in their organs." Forrest explained the situation to Commissioner of Indian Affairs William P. Dole, who begged him "to go to Mr. Lincoln with him and lay the whole business before him." And so the two men told the story to the president, who was deeply "mortified and humiliated."

Rather than a helpmate to her husband, Mrs. Lincoln was proving to be an embarrassment, for her nagging compelled him "to do things which he knew were out of place in order to keep his wife's fingers out of his hair," as Herndon put it.

MRS. LINCOLN'S
EMOTIONAL FRAGILITY

Herndon could have added that Lincoln placated his wife because he feared she was teetering on the verge a nervous breakdown. In 1862, after the death of their son Willie, he told her that he might have to have her committed to an insane asylum. Once in conversation with Phineas Gurley, pastor of the Washington church where the First Family worshipped, Lincoln indirectly alluded to his willingness to meet the First Lady's unreasonable demands. Dr. Gurley had appealed on behalf of a parishioner seeking a full pardon for his adolescent son whose death sentence Lincoln had already reduced to a prison term. Therefore Dr. Gurley warned against bothering Lincoln with a further plea. The father "replied that he felt so himself but he feared" that his wife "would lose her mind if something were not done." So he submitted his appeal to Lincoln, who responded angrily: "I saved the life of your son after he had been condemned to be shot; and now you come here so soon when you know I am overwhelmed with care and anxiety, asking for his pardon. You should have been content with what I have done. Go; and if you annoy me any more, I shall feel it to be my duty to consider whether I ought not to recall what I have already done." A few days later, Lincoln apologized to the father and pardoned his son. To Dr. Gurley, the president explained that he was induced to change his mind "only by the statement of the father that he feared his wife would lose her mind if something were not done to relieve her." Lincoln then smiled and said: "Ah, Doctor! these wives of ours have the inside track on us, don't they?"

Lincoln also expressed anxiety about his wife's psychological well-being in 1863. While urging Emilie Todd Helm to spend the summer with his family at the Soldiers' Home, he explained: "you and Mary love each other—it is good for her to have you with her—I feel worried about Mary, her nerves have gone to pieces; she cannot hide from me that the strain she has been under has been too much for her mental as well as her physical health. What do you think?"

Mrs. Helm replied that her sister "seems very nervous and excitable and once or twice when I have come into the room suddenly the frightened look in her eyes has appalled me. She seems to fear that other sorrows may be added to those we already have to bear."

In response, Lincoln pleaded: "Stay with her as long as you can." But Mrs. Helm remained only a few days before returning to Kentucky.

When William P. Wood, superintendent of the Old Capitol Prison, informed the president that the First Lady was selling "trading permits, favors and government secrets," Lincoln attributed her behavior to "partial insanity."

Lincoln may well have worried about his wife's mental health long before he became president. In 1844, while stumping for Henry Clay in southwest Indiana (where Lincoln had grown up), he waxed nostalgic; two years later he wrote poetry inspired by childhood memories. One of his poems described Matthew Gentry, a schoolmate who in adolescence had gone insane and tried to kill his parents:

Poor Matthew! Once of genius bright,
A fortune-favored child—-
Now locked for aye, in mental night,
A haggard mad-man wild.
Poor Matthew! I have ne'er forgot,
When first, with maddened will,
Yourself you maimed, your father fought,
And mother strove to kill;
When terror spread, and neighbours ran,
Your dange'rous strength to bind;
And soon, a howling crazy man
Your limbs were fast confined.

Matthew's madness may have unconsciously reminded Lincoln of his wife, "a fortune-favored child" whose uncontrollable temper led her to attack him (whom she called "Father.") When the Lincolns were newly installed in their house at Eighth and Jackson Streets, her rage attacks drove him to seek shelter in his office. (Chapter 6) Such attacks, in the eyes of some (perhaps including Lincoln), "verged on insanity" and were "really a species of madness" (see Chapter 1).

10

LONELY FIRST LADY: HER COTERIE, SHOPPING, AND DEBTS

Preoccupied with affairs of state, Lincoln had little time for his wife, who confided to Joanna Newell in January 1862 that "she often did not see the President for two days [at a time] in the same house." Moreover, as her friend Elizabeth Blair Lee reported in July 1861, Washington's women were "giving Mrs Lincoln the cold shoulder." Earlier that year, when the wife of Michigan senator Zachariah Chandler and some other well-meaning Washington matrons called on the First Lady to advise her about how things were done in the capital, she indignantly rejected their counsel, thus alienating potential friends and allies.

And so the First Lady coped as best she could with the sort of loneliness that she had endured in Springfield. Her principal means of doing so were to assemble a coterie, to travel often, and to shop compulsively.

⤜∾⤛

Mrs. Lincoln had company during the early months of her husband's administration, for several Todds attended the inauguration and stayed on at the White House. Most left soon after the inauguration; by midyear 1861, Elizabeth Edwards had returned to Springfield, and cousin Lizzie Grimsley was eager to follow suit, complaining that "I have overstayed my time so long because Mary has urged and urged and seemed to feel hurt at the idea of my leaving her . . . Mary thinks me very selfish if I speak of going home." Lizzie finally departed for Illinois in August, after accompanying the First Lady on her vacation sojourn at Long Branch, New Jersey, that month.

THE CASE OF HENRY WIKOFF

While at that seaside resort, Mrs. Lincoln's doings were covered for the New York *Herald* by Henry Wikoff, an urbane, sophisticated dandy who came to occupy the center of her Washington salon. According to Henry Villard, Wikoff "showed the utmost assurance in his appeals to the vanity of the mistress of the White House. I myself heard him compliment her upon her looks and dress in so fulsome a way that she ought to have blushed and banished the impertinent fellow from her presence. She accepted Wikoff as a majordomo in general and in special, as a guide in matters of social etiquette, domestic arrangements, and personal requirements, including her toilette, and as always welcome company for visitors in her salon and on her drives."

Wikoff was "exceedingly smart, in the strict sense" and had an "unlimited capacity for elegant leisure." He spent much time in Europe, where he pursued pleasure single-mindedly, hobnobbing with the rich and powerful, and somehow managing to acquire the honorific "Chevelier." Dabbling in the arts as a ballet impresario and in diplomacy as a British spy, he was also a journalist and an off-again, on-again friend of James Gordon Bennett, publisher and editor of the New York *Herald*. Known as a womanizer, an adventurer, "a sort of cosmopolitan knight-errant," and "something of a professional cad," Wikoff achieved notoriety by kidnapping a woman whose fortune he loved. Convicted of abduction, he spent over a year in an Italian jail. In the later 1850s, he worked for Bennett in Washington, acting as a go-between for the editor in his dealings with President Buchanan as well as a freelance diplomatic courier for the administration.

Tall, amiable, and distinguished-looking, Wikoff may have lacked scruples, but he had plenty of charm. Henry Villard called him "an accomplished man of the world, a fine linguist, with a graceful presence, elegant manners, a conscious, condescending way—altogether, just such a man as would be looked upon as a superior being by a woman accustomed only to Western society." John W. Forney thought that one "might travel a long way before meeting a more pleasant companion than the cosmopolite Wikoff." An observer noted that as "a conversationalist the Chevalier was gifted with a retentive memory, and a peculiar charm of manner, which, added to his courtesy and rather formal air, rendered him a delightful companion."

Most people, however, viewed Wikoff as "a political and social intriguer, an unprincipled and shameless adventurer, a man who [was] kicked out of all respectable society wherever he is known," and who possessed "the impudence of the devil." In the fall of 1861, William Howard Russell noted in his diary: "I hear that disgusting fellow Wyckoff [sic] is master of ye situation at ye White House," and ethnologist George Gibbs told a friend that "Mrs L. seems now to be at the head of the State. As the Chevalier Wikoff is an habitue of the White House you need not be surprised at anything." David Davis called Wikoff a "terrible libertine, & no woman ought to tolerate his presence." A journalist reported that "Mrs. Lincoln is making herself both a fool and a nuisance. Chevalier Wikoff is her gallant." An incredulous Connecticut Republican asked rhetorically: "What does Mrs. Lincoln mean by . . . having anything to do with that world-renowned whoremonger and swindler Chevalier Wikoff? Is [Mrs.] Lincoln an old saphead or is she a headstrong fool who thinks she can have a kitchen cabinet? It's a national disgrace." Perhaps reflecting the president's opinion, John Hay called Wikoff an "unclean bird," a "vile creature," a "marked and branded social Pariah, a monstrosity abhorred by men and women," and declared it "an enduring disgrace to American society that it suffers such a thing to be at large."

The eminent journalist and landscape architect Frederick Law Olmsted was scandalized to observe the First Lady and Wikoff alone together atop the White House's south portico, enjoying a band concert. Wikoff, whom Olmsted called "an insufferable beast," sat "right in the center of the portico, the only man seen at the house, & Mrs. L turned constantly and nodded to him, evidently interested in his conversation. If he had been the king he could not have carried it off better." Despite his sophisticated appearance and confident mien, he was in fact "the most perfect picture of stupidity and dullness: a great ass and nothing else."

General John E. Wool found it "certainly strange" that the First Lady would call on Wikoff at the Willard Hotel, "await him in the lobby for a long time, help him don his gloves, and then ride off with him in her carriage." Among other places, Wikoff and the First Lady rode to a theater where William Howard Russell saw them and jotted in his diary: "Mrs. Lincoln in an awful bonnet facing us & Wikoff in attendance. Wicks very good consort."

The public also looked askance at Mrs. Lincoln's friendship with Daniel Sickles, whose reputation was tarnished. In 1859, he had shot and killed his wife's lover in cold blood, then managed to escape punishment by pleading temporary insanity. The New York *Evening Post* indignantly commented at the time: "He is a person of notorious profligacy of life . . . certain disgrace has for years past attended the reputation of being one of his companions." New York attorney George Templeton Strong described Sickles as "one of the bigger bubbles in the scum of the [legal] profession, swollen and windy, and puffed out with fetid gas," an "unmitigated blackguard and profligate," and a "pariah whom to know was discreditable." Another New Yorker, Maria Lydig Daly, thought Mrs. Lincoln "behaves in the most undignified manner possible, associating with Wyckoff [sic] and Sickles, with whom no lady would deign to speak; but she seems to be easily flattered." A Vermont editor called for "the purification of the presidential mansion from the offensive and loathsome presence of such wretches as Wikoff and Sickles." Lincoln "should be made acquainted with the wish of the people that the lepers of society should not be the pets of the White House."

Like his friend Wikoff, Sickles was an adept flatterer, calling regularly at the White House and charming the First Lady. In early 1862, when he was reported to be her "pet beau" and "favored gallant," he was angling for a brigadier general's commission. The following year, when Sickles was named a major general, another officer noted that he "is all powerful at the White House & is the Gallant of Mrs. Lincoln, going there at all times." She reportedly lobbied hard to have Sickles replace General Meade in command of the Army of the Potomac. Colonel Nathan W. Daniels, an abolitionist/spiritualist based in Washington, heard from "responsible and reliable parties" there that Sickles "had presented Mrs President Lincoln a three thousand dollar shawl and that this gift had obtained him the Pro-motion of his Major Generalship." The colonel added that the First Lady was reported "to rule with an iron hand at the white House and has done things that will d[am]n herself and her husband in the eyes of decent people, through all eternity."

The New York *Herald's* premature publication of excerpts from Lincoln's December 1861 annual message to Congress (forerunner of the State of the Union address) created an uproar that led to the dismissal of White House gardener John Watt. Mrs. Lincoln embarrassed the president by accepting a bribe from Wikoff for access to the presidential message. When the House Judiciary Committee grilled him about the leak, he at first refused to answer, whereupon he was promptly clapped into the Old Capitol Prison.

After learning of these developments, Lincoln visited Capitol Hill and "urged the Republicans on the committee to spare him disgrace." He told Chairman John Hickman of Pennsylvania that "he never gave any portion of the Message to anybody except members of the Cabinet" before submitting it to Congress. The committee summoned Sickles, who had been visiting his friend Wikoff in jail. Initially defiant, Sickles backed down when threatened with a contempt-of-Congress citation. He alleged that he had been in contact with John Watt, who showed the document to Wikoff. In turn, Wikoff insisted that he had provided the message to the *Herald* after receiving it from the gardener, who told the incredulous committee that he had been Wikoff's source, implausibly claiming that he had seen a copy of the message lying about in the White House library, had memorized a portion of it, and repeated it verbatim to Wikoff.

In fact, as White House watchman Thomas Stackpole explained, the First Lady was the true culprit. Stackpole revealed to Senator Orville Browning that "the President's message [to Congress] had been furnished to [Henry] Wycoff by her, and not by Watt as is usually supposed—that she got it of [John D.] Defrees, Sup[erintendent] of government printing, and gave it to Wycoff in the library, where he read it—[and] gave it back to her, and she gave it back to Defrees." In 1871, Hiram Ramsdell of the New York *Tribune* reported that Wikoff "bribed Mrs. Lincoln, and she let him read the manuscript while shut up in a closet near Old Abe's room. Wikoff not only read but copied the important . . . parts, and got safely out of the White House with his 'copy' in his pocket."

The president decided to ban Wikoff from the White House when the Reverend Mr. Matthew Hale Smith, a New York correspondent of the Boston *Journal*, warned him of a brewing scandal. Smith later recounted the sordid story: Wikoff had been "very officious in his attention" to the First Lady. "His frequent visits to Washington, and his receptions at the White House, were noticed by the friends of the President." At each of Mrs. Lincoln's formal and informal receptions Wikoff "was an early and constant visitor." Nobody "went so early but this person could be seen cosily seated in a chair as if at home, talking to the ladies of the White House." Wikoff was often "seen riding in the President's coach, with the ladies, through Pennsylvania Avenue. Frequently he was found lounging in the conservatory, or smoking in the grounds, very much at home, and not at all anxious to hide his presence." Wikoff's visits embarrassed the White House staff, and the press began to tut-tut.

Some of Lincoln's friends discovered that Wikoff had been hired by "parties in New York, who were using him as their tool." Those men (the managers of the New York *Herald*) had "furnished him with money and instructions. He was to go to Washington, make himself agreeable to the ladies, insinuate himself into the White House, attend levees, show that he had the power to come and go, and, if possible, open a correspondence with the ladies of the mansion." Once he became known as an insider, he could wield influence that might prove useful to his backers, among them James Gordon Bennett (eager for journalistic scoops) and arms manufacturers (eager for government contracts).

Lincoln's friends "considered that the President should be made acquainted with this plot against his honor" and tasked Matthew Hale Smith with that assignment. Accompanied by an unidentified senator, Smith called at the White House one evening. As he later wrote, Lincoln "took me by the hand, led me into the office of his private secretary, whom he drove out, and locked the door." When Smith showed him documents exposing the fell purpose of Wikoff, the president said: "Give me those papers and sit here till I return." Lincoln "started out of the room with strides that showed an energy of purpose" and confronted Wikoff, who was at that moment downstairs in the White House. The president soon returned, shook Smith's hand, and had Wikoff "driven from the mansion that night."

A Philadelphia newspaper reported that Lincoln "became jealous" of Wikoff and "taxed" his wife. The Chevalier then "volunteered an explanation," telling "the wounded & incensed" president that "he was only teaching the madame a little European Court Etiquette." Wikoff was forbidden to enter the White House, but he continued to meet with the First Lady in the conservatory attached to the mansion. Watt arranged for those meetings in his domain. On January 18, 1862, Joanna Newell reported that during a recent carriage ride, Mrs. Lincoln confided that "she would [have] liked to have had him [Wikoff] ride out with us but could not ever take him in the carriage as the President had requested her not to drive out with him again." Two months later, the First Lady's sister, Elizabeth Edwards, wrote from the White House that the "*Wikoff case*, has added very much to her [Mary's] unhappiness and to Mr. L's also."

In February 1862, a New York journalist reported that Wikoff "plays the toady to Mrs. Bennett, who calls him her 'convenient jackass'—(she swears like a trooper)—and the sycophant to her husband, who denominates him 'my dog Wycoff.' He is the 'peculiar Jenkins' [special gossip correspondent] of the *Herald*, and attends Washington to write up full personal descriptions of balls and parties, weddings and soirees, as well as to 'grease' the itching palms of those about the White House from whom he can surreptitiously obtain gossip, rumors, intelligence of any kind, true or fictitious."

Other palms were also liberally greased, especially those belonging to weapons brokers. Early in the Civil War, contracts with the War Department were negotiated by middlemen, "most of them mere speculators and adventures." Wikoff was one such adventurer. In February 1862, the New York *Times* described him as "a common huckster of war contracts last Summer, under [Secretary of War Simon] Cameron's reign. He was scarcely to be met with, any day, that he did not have a contract to sell that he had obtained from the Secretary of War or some other high Government official. It is supposed that he got them . . . by threatening Cameron and others with the *Herald*'s abuse."

That report was accurate. On September 7, 1861 Wikoff wrote to Cameron denouncing the "obstinate imbecility" of General James Ripley, the army's chief of ordnance: "You cannot be aware that in spite of all your directions I have not obtained a contract for a *single* gun from Gen Ripley," who "has delayed by his dogged obstructions the arming of our troops, at least, three months." Ominously, Wikoff threatened to use his position as a correspondent for the New York *Herald* to embarrass Ripley: "I mean to make all this fully known to the country, which will cry out indignantly for his expulsion from office." Wikoff closed imperiously: "Please order these contracts to be made *forthwith*." Cameron obeyed.

The *Times* noted that Wikoff's relationship with James Gordon Bennett "is evidently intimate, confidential, inseparable. He is known to have used it freely at Washington to obtain not only news but numberless contracts, the profits of which have been shared in this City [New York], the dread of the *Herald's* unscrupulous slander and venom operating upon the fears of the weaklings whom Wikoff selected for his operations. In short, he has filled a department of the *Herald*, never vacant since that paper originated—the bureau for the assessment and collection of blackmail."

Such blackmailing yielded handsome returns. In 1862, the managing editor of the New York *Tribune* stated that Wikoff "made about $20,000 by contracts" which Mrs. Lincoln "knew how to help him to." Evidently the First Lady indicated that she favored Wikoff's attempts to peddle government contracts to men who provided kickbacks. Wikoff probably shared the proceeds with Mrs. Lincoln and James Gordon Bennett.

Evidence supporting that conclusion appears in a note by Cameron explaining that James Gordon Bennett "did write me a letter in behalf of Wykoff" which stated that "this brother-in-law was to be W[ikoff's] partner." That brother-in-law was perhaps Ninian W. Edwards, for Cameron acknowledged that "Mrs. Lincoln was one of the parties whose influence had operated on me."

THE FIRST LADY'S
COTERIE EXPANDS

In addition to Wikoff and Sickles, the First Lady's salon included another shameless flatterer, Nathaniel P. Willis, whose *Home Journal* ran puff pieces about the "joyous *Reine d'Illinois*," praising her "thorough good nature and covert love of fun, which are the leading qualities of our lady President." Such fawning provoked abolitionist Lydia Maria Child to remark that the only thing Mrs. Lincoln "cares for is flattery, and dress, and parties. Willis's *Home Journal* abounds with fulsome compliments about her stylish dressing, her gayeties &c. This is not becoming, when the people are suffering and sacrificing so much." Willis took frequent carriage rides with Mrs. Lincoln, dined with the First Family, and received bouquets and even the promise of a vase that had been presented by the emperor of China. The First Lady did not, however, appreciate his reference to her as a woman with a "motherly expression." In 1861, gently protesting that such language seemed more appropriate to describe an old lady, she misrepresented her age, claiming that she was thirty-six when in fact she was forty-two.

In Mrs. Lincoln's coterie, Henry Wikoff was not the only lobbyist for arms manufacturers. Oliver "Pet" Halsted, a "bright, sociable, agreeable, ne'er-do-well lawyer," joined that select group while she was vacationing at the New Jersey shore in August 1861. Son of a former chancellor of New Jersey, Halsted was a man of "matchless assurance" who "succeeded in making himself a familiar in the councils of men of note." He "penetrated the privacy of President Lincoln's Cabinet and afflicted that patient statesman with piles of documents showing the imbecility of [General George] McClellan and the matchless genius of [General Joseph] Hooker." He "was a florid character, being efflorescent in garb, personal appearance, and general conduct. No public character was so well known in Washington as he." His "was a swagger which was more than magnificent." He "was lavish in his expenditures, and as generous as a prince when he had money." An example of his generosity was the thoroughbred stallion ("Prince Lionel") that he presented to the Lincolns in 1863. Widely known as an accomplished wirepuller whose "financial genius led him to bold flights of lobbying," he was celebrated for his many brilliant "exploits in that fertile field," most notably his help in obtaining "a great wrought-iron gun contract" for a prominent Massachusetts firm.

Halstead joined the First Lady's "kitchen cabinet," serving as a kind of "major-domo" who, along with Wikoff, introduced her into the ways of Washington. In return, he reportedly became "a confidential friend to Mrs. Lincoln, and was admitted to a ready confidence in all important matters in her knowledge." In 1862, he was "hand in glove with the occupants of the President's mansion, handing Mrs. Lincoln out of her carriage, and the like work," which "excited a great deal of public and private comment." Two years later, he urged the president to support a prisoner-of-war exchange program that he favored. (In 1871, the fifty-one-year-old Halsted—then living with his wife and some of their eight children—was murdered at his mistress's apartment by a rival for her affections.)

During Mrs. Lincoln's 1861 summer idyll in New Jersey, she also befriended that state's former governor, William A. Newell, who had served with Lincoln in Congress. A physician as well as a politician, he pioneered plastic surgery and headed the United States Life Saving Service, forerunner of the US Coast Guard. Newell took the First Lady on a tour of life-saving stations along the Atlantic shore and acted as her escort at a ball. He and his wife Joanna joined her salon, winning especial gratitude by helping care for Willie and Tad in early 1862, when both boys were seriously ill.

The New Jerseymen friends were regular guests at the White House. Those two may have been behind a swindle mentioned by journalist Benjamin Perley Poore, who noted that Mrs. Lincoln was "liberally remembered by those who had sold a steamer at an exorbitant price to the Government." In September 1861, she wrote to Navy Secretary Gideon Welles: "Our particular friend Dr. Newell of New Jersey, is making application, for the building of a steamer. The President, is interested that he may succeed in his application, he is esteemed by all who know him, a most estimable gentleman. I enclose his card & we will be under obligation to you, if the contract is awarded, to the men, for whom he applies." In November 1861, Halsted wrote Assistant Navy Secretary Gustavus V. Fox about a steamer he was trying to sell: "As the President is always prompt, & 'well up,' 'as straight as a gun barrel,' understands me fully, and as I have reason to know favors this project, I have no objection to your showing this to him, if you need his direct endorsement, as I am satisfied he will give it to any extent required."

Mrs. Lincoln may have been involved in another scandal involving the navy. Early in the war, Welles authorized his brother-in-law, George D. Morgan, to purchase ships on a commission basis rather than for a flat fee. Under those terms, he bought some ninety vessels. Whereas ship-brokers claimed that they could have done the job for $5,000, Morgan's 1861 commissions totaled over $70,000. He committed no fraud, but it seemed clear that the government had spent far too much for his services. In December 1861, a journalist reported that there "is a rumor that Mrs. Lincoln is concerned in the Morgan speculation, by which a brother-in-law of the secretary of the Navy has made between $90,000 and $100,000 in the space of four or five months. The way I heard the story gives an idea of what is getting to be the popular notion concerning 'Madame President.' Says someone, 'I hear that another member of the cabinet, besides Welles, is involved in that matter,' 'Who,—Cameron?' 'No; higher yet.' 'Seward?' 'No; higher yet.' 'There is no higher.' 'Yes; Mrs. Lincoln!'"

MRS. LINCOLN HOBNOBS WITH
JAMES GORDON BENNETT AND HIS WIFE

Lincoln told a friend that New York *Herald* editor James Gordon Bennett "has made a great deal of money, some say not very properly, now he wants me to make him respectable." That was uphill work, for Bennett and his wife were social pariahs in New York. Many shared the view of Henry Villard, who deplored Bennett's "hard, cold, utterly selfish nature and incapacity to appreciate high and noble aims." Moreover, Bennett's popular newspaper was widely regarded as a scandal sheet. Politically, Bennett desired the president to chart a conservative course and throw Radical cabinet members overboard. Moreover, he sought to gain inside information that would allow him to scoop his rivals. To help Bennett achieve those ends, he dispatched Wikoff to infiltrate the White House inner circle and cultivate the First Lady. Supplementing those efforts, the Bennetts also curried her favor with lavish praise, flowers, and invitations to their palatial New York home.

According to a New York journalist, once Wikoff had secured a foothold at the White House, he "succeeded in persuading Mrs. Lincoln that Mrs. Bennett (whom nobody will associate with here), was a Colossus in crinoline, and that if the sun did not rise and set in the Herald office, it certainly did behind the Bennettian stables, at the Herald villa." (She was, in fact, a multilingual, cultivated, philanthropic woman who had taught piano and elocution before marrying Bennett. Her pariah status was largely attributable to her association with Bennett.) And so the First Lady invited Henrietta Bennett to White House soirees and receptions, prompting Jessie Benton Frémont to observe in December 1861 that the "Herald belongs to Mrs. Lincoln because she visits, [and] invites to the White House, Mrs. Bennett."

Offering a different analysis, a New Yorker thought Henrietta Bennett, not the First Lady, "is the Herald in fact, for she rules her husband with a rod of iron, and orders into and out of the paper what she pleases." Those orders included "'soaping' Mrs. Lincoln *ad nauseam*," which was done largely in Wikoff's dispatches to the *Herald*. Reportedly, Mrs. Bennett "cannot afford to lose her entree to Mrs. Lincoln's White House soirees. She boasts of those entrees too much to throw them away so cavalierly, and she drives down to the *Herald* office every now and then and gives 'that d—d old scoundrel of mine,' as she elegantly terms her husband, 'particular Jessie,' [i.e., bawls him out] right before all his subordinates, whenever he published a paragraph calculated, in her opinion, to damage her back kitchen interests at Washington." (He was indeed old—her senior by a quarter of a century.)

Wikoff's "soaping" dispatches were so shameless that they would have embarrassed most people, but not Mrs. Lincoln. In August 1861, while she was relaxing at Long Branch, New Jersey, Wikoff wrote: "As the wife of Honest Abe Lincoln, of Springfield, she was esteemed as a modest, unassuming, kind-hearted, benevolent, housewifely, matronly little woman—a genuine helpmate to a rising lawyer." In Washington as First Lady, she "took the lead of society with as easy grace as if she had been born to the station of mistress of the White House." In Manhattan, she "visited the most modish stores, and—like the Empress Eugenie, who was as suddenly elevated in rank—displayed such exquisite taste in the selection of the materials she desired, and of the fashion of their make, that all the fashionable ladies of New York were astir with wonder and surprise."

Such "pinchbeck jewelry of Old Bennett's eulogism" offended many, as the Chicago *Tribune* noted: "The sighs and sneers of sensible people all over the land, and the mockery of the comic papers, are the natural consequence." The Philadelphia *Evening Bulletin* deplored the extravagant encomiums bestowed on the First Lady: "Every word of the fulsome praise" that New York journalists "lavish on her looks, her language, her dress, and her manners, is insulting."

The *Herald's* flattering coverage of Mrs. Lincoln helped the paper's Washington correspondent, Simon P. Hanscom, gain easy access to vital news sources. As David W. Bartlett told readers of the Springfield, Massachusetts, *Republican*, "with the Herald's praise of Mrs. Lincoln's beauty and talents, Hanscom finds an easy road into the affections and secrets of the president, and keeps the Herald duly posted."

The *Herald's* editorials echoed Wikoff's flattery of Mrs. Lincoln, who thanked Bennett for the paper's defense of her as an "estimable lady" whose "character and opinions have been so grossly vilified by the *Tribune* and other abolition organs." The *Herald* deemed her "a sensible, unpretending woman," one "of remarkable ability and goodness of heart, and has no superior among the female notabilities of Europe." The paper denounced competing journals for alleging that "the wife of the President had a monomania for display and parade, and was ambitious of political power and influence." (Other papers unfairly criticized the First Lady as a Kentuckian who sympathized with Confederacy, when in fact she firmly supported the Union cause.) Expressing her gratitude, Mrs. Lincoln wrote Bennett: "My own nature is very sensitive; [I] have always tried to secure the best wishes of all, with whom through life, I have been associated; need I repeat to you, my thanks, in my own individual case, when I meet, in the columns of your paper, a kind reply, to some uncalled for attack, upon one so *little desirous* of newspaper notoriety, as my inoffensive self. I trust it may be my good fortune, at some not very distant day, to welcome both Mrs Bennett & yourself to Washington; the President would be equally as much pleased to meet you." Soon thereafter, the Bennetts were invited to a gala party at the White House.

That invitation scandalized some observers. *The American Baptist* was nonplussed: "How Mrs. Lincoln could have invited him [Bennett] to her festivities is a mystery to all who love their country." Philo S. Shelton, a Boston merchant, indignantly remarked that Lincoln "is a *humbug* & his wife worse [—] only think of such men as Wikoff & Gordon Bennett & Mrs. B[ennett] being the special guests of Mrs. Lincoln & of men placed in office thro[ugh] such influences."

According to the New York *Tribune*, Mrs. Lincoln was also carrying on "a correspondence, of a somewhat remarkable character," with Mrs. Bennett. In January 1862, the paper reported that the "subject of the letters varies. Occasionally the fair writers will confine themselves to matters of purely personal interest, to gossip, &c. and often affairs of public interest, receive their attention. Mrs. Lincoln's letters are spoken of, by those who have been favored with an occasional glimpse of their pages, as remarkable for shrewd observation, witty and good-natured satire, and the most genuine spirit of patriotism. Graceful gifts of flowers and other beautiful trifles frequently accompany these most interesting missives; and for some time past Mrs. Bennett has been weekly honored with a superb bouquet from the Presidential conservatory." Henry Wikoff "has several times had the honor of being the bearer of these elegant tokens of friendship."

During Mrs. Lincoln's frequent visits to New York, Henrietta Bennett entertained her royally. In November 1862, a Manhattan journalist reported that the First Lady had been in the city for a week, during which "she dined with Mrs. James Gordon Bennett at the Bennett Palace at Fort Washington. In the evening she visited the Academy of Music and sat in Mrs. Bennett's opera box. Whereat James Gordon [Bennett] was delighted." At the Academy of Music, Mrs. Bennett's "attention to Mrs. Lincoln was marked, and evidently appreciated." The following year, Mrs. Bennett wrote to a Confederate prisoner of war who had asked her to persuade Lincoln to rescind orders preventing POWs from receiving warm clothing: "Yesterday Mrs. Lincoln visited me at Fort Washington. I embraced the opportunity to ask her to use her influence in regard to the request you made me. She assured me she will attend to it immediately on her return to Washington."

In 1862, Mrs. Lincoln again wrote to the politically conservative Bennett after he had urged her to support a reorganization of the president's cabinet. His letter is not extant, but it seems clear that he wanted Treasury Secretary Chase ousted. The First Lady was somewhat reluctant to wade in, for she insisted that she had "a great terror of *strong* minded Ladies." But, she added, "if a word fitly spoken in due season, can be urged, in a time like this, we should not withhold it." She agreed that Radical Republicanism in cabinet councils should be resisted: "Our country requires no ambitious fanatics [a clear allusion to Chase], to guide the Helm."

THE PERIPATETIC FIRST
LADY AND HER DEBTS

To alleviate her loneliness, Mrs. Lincoln often traveled, absenting herself from Washington for a total of more than eight months during her husband's administration (approximately fifteen percent of that time). A favorite destination was New York, where she not only socialized with the Bennetts but also enjoyed shopping.

In later years, Mrs. Lincoln would have been diagnosed as a shopaholic, that is, someone suffering from a personality disorder known formally as oniomania. It afflicts mostly women, especially those with low self-esteem. Encouraged by merchants to spend freely, the First Lady ran up formidable bills. Some of the items that she purchased in the spring of 1864 were described in the press, among them "a splendid set of ear-rings and pin at one of the Broadway jewelry stores, amounting to three thousand dollars."

Mrs. Lincoln was especially fond of A. T. Stewart's huge "marble palace," an upscale department store in Manhattan catering to women. She was snobbish and dressed in a manner she thought appropriate for her perceived social class. In November 1861, a journalist reporting from New York wrote that "Mrs. Lincoln, the 'Queen regnant' of Washington . . . always creates a stir here. She deals at Stewart's, and her purchases are of so gorgeous a nature, that she makes the crowd open their eyes as wide as saucers." She "spends money like the princess we read about in the Arabian Nights, and dresses up to the *comble* [height] of fashion."

At his store, A. T. Stewart waited on her personally, as he did for other important customers. One of the keys to his success was "his personal obsequious attention to women customers." He "never offered to shake hands" with one, "no matter how well he knew the lady, but bowed low, and with becoming gravity and gentle voice inquired her wishes." Accompanied by a clerk, he "then conducted her to the counter where the goods she wanted were kept. As the clerk would take down his goods Stewart had a way of reproving the man thus: 'Not that, Mr. Johnson, not that—you seem to forget whom you are waiting on!' When the lady left, Stewart accompanied her to the door." While shopping there she did not reciprocate the elaborate courtesy of the proprietor and his staff. She would "pull down all the goods

The Lincolns strolling by the White House, drawing by Pierre Morand, 1864. Morand, a French businessman, met Lincoln in Washington during the Civil War and recalled that the president's "features and movements impressed me so vividly, that I made several good sketches of him in various attitudes in June, 1864." There is no photograph of the Lincolns together, for the five-foot-two-inch First Lady did not want to be shown dwarfed by her six-foot-four-inch husband. *From the National Portrait Gallery, Smithsonian Institution, Washington, D.C.*

ABOVE: *Grand reception at the White House, January 1862.* Based on a sketch by the artist Alfred Waud, this hand-colored wood engraving depicts the president and his wife in the east room greeting Treasury Secretary Salmon P. Chase and his daughter Kate. To the left of the president are his secretaries John Hay and John G. Nicolay, as well as his Illinois friend-cum-bodyguard, Col. Ward Hill Lamon. The three officers in the right foreground are Generals William B. Franklin, Samuel Heintzelman, and George McCall. The image appeared in *Harper's Weekly*, January 25, 1862. *From the White House Historical Association.* BELOW: *Mary Lincoln in 1864.* Philadelphia engraver Samuel Sartain used a photograph, now lost, as the basis for this image, which he copyrighted on November 15, 1864. *From the Library of Congress.*

The first known photograph of Lincoln, taken when he was in his mid-thirties by Nicholas H. Shepherd ca. 1846 in Springfield. Robert Todd Lincoln wrote that this "daguerreotype was on the walls of a room in my father's house from my earliest recollection as a companion picture to that of my mother." Growing up in central Illinois, the noted geologist John Wesley Powell observed Lincoln and said "this is Lincoln as I knew him; his sad, dreamy eye, his pensive smile, his sad and delicate face, his pyramidal shoulders, are the characteristics I best remember." *From the Library of Congress, colorized by Jordan J. Lloyd, Dynamichrome, UK.*

The first known photograph of Mary Todd Lincoln, ca. 1846, when she was in her mid-twenties. Taken by Nicholas H. Shepherd in Springfield, it is the pendant to the photo above. *From the Library of Congress, colorized by Gary M. Wilcox of Summersville, WV.*

ABOVE: *Grand Reception of the Notabilities of the Nation, at the White House, March 4, 1865, dedicated to Mrs. Abraham Lincoln by the Publishers of Frank Leslie's* Chimney Corner. This hand-colored lithograph by Henry B. Major and Joseph Knapp, based on a painting by Anton Hohenstein of Philadelphia, was published by Frank Leslie in 1865. It depicts the interior of the east room at the White House during the reception following Lincoln's second inauguration. This image is somewhat fanciful, for the president is shown greeting Mrs. U. S. Grant and her husband, neither of whom was present. On Lincoln's right is Vice President Andrew Johnson and on his left is Mrs. Lincoln. Among those also shown are Senator Charles Sumner, Senator John Sherman, William P. Fessenden, General Winfield Scott Hancock, Horace Greeley, General Benjamin F. Butler, Gideon Welles, William H. Seward, Salmon P. Chase, and Edwin M. Stanton. *From Glasshouse Images / Alamy Stock Photo.*

Mary Lincoln in 1861, by Mathew Brady, colorized by Gary M. Wilcox of Summersville, WV. This is the only known photograph of the First Lady in profile. *From the Library of Congress.*

Mary Lincoln in 1862, detail of a photograph by Mathew Brady, later colorized by Alamy, Brooklyn, NY. It is one of at least nine poses taken by Brady during that sitting. *From Everett Collection Historical / Alamy Stock Photo.*

Mary Lincoln ca. 1861, carte de visite published in 1865 by William H. Mumler and by the New York Photographic Company, photographer unknown. *From the Abraham Lincoln Presidential Library, Springfield.*

Mrs. Lincoln's African American dressmaker and confidante, Elizabeth Keckly, ca. 1861. This image appeared as the frontispiece of her 1868 memoir, *Behind the Scenes, or, Thirty Years a Slave, and Four Years in the White House. Virginia Museum of History & Culture / Alamy Stock Photo.*

Emilie Todd Helm, Mrs. Lincoln's favorite sister. *Undated photo by an unknown photographer. From The Lincoln Financial Foundation Collection, courtesy of the Indiana State Museum and Allen County Public Library.*

Lincoln on February 5, 1865, photograph by Alexander Gardner. He looks older than his fifty-five years, for the war had taken a fierce toll on him. Around the time this was taken, Walt Whitman wrote: "I see the President almost every day. I see very plainly Abraham Lincoln's dark brown face with its deep-cut lines, the eyes always to me with a deep latent sadness in the expression. None of the artists or pictures has caught the deep, though subtle and indirect expression of this man's face. There is something else there. One of the great portrait painters of two or three centuries ago is needed." *From the Library of Congress, colorized by James Nance jimnance4617@icloud.com.*

in the place, bully the clerks, falsify or question their addition, and, in the end, leave without settling her bills."

Stewart also curried Mrs. Lincoln's favor by allowing her to charge purchases and by giving her an expensive lace shawl. A journalist noted disapprovingly: "Mrs. Lincoln, it was well known, had accepted a shawl worth one thousand dollars from A. T. Stewart when he was supplying large amounts of clothing and blankets to the army." In addition to accepting a gift shawl, she also bought some, including "elegant black point lace shawls for $650 each" and a "real camel's hair [shawl] at $1,000." The journalist covering her remarked: "she was dreadfully importuned to enter into extravagances of various kinds; but I heard her, myself, observe at Stewart's that she could not afford it, and was 'determined to be very economical.' One thousand dollars for a shawl was quite as high as her sense of economy would permit her to go in these excessive[ly] hard times!" Eventually, Stewart billed her for these and other items, amounting to ca. $25,000, and threatened to sue if she did not pay up.

Such threats frightened Mrs. Lincoln. In 1864, she expressed to her friend Elizabeth Keckly a fear that the president might lose his reelection bid: "I do not know what would become of us all," she told Keckly. "To me, to him, there is more at stake in this election than he dreams of. I have contracted large debts, of which he knows nothing, and which he will be unable to pay if he is defeated." When a spiritualist predicted Lincoln's defeat, she returned to the White House inconsolable, *crying like a child!*"

To Keckly, the First Lady described her debts: "They consist chiefly of store bills. I owe altogether about twenty-seven thousand dollars; the principal portion at [A. T.] Stewart's, in New York." She also owed the New York jeweler Ball, Black & Company $6,400. In the space of three months, another jeweler sold her four clocks, two diamond and pearl bracelets, and other items totaling $3,200. In March 1865, she spent $2,288 at Galt & Brothers jewelry store in Washington. From various emporia, she purchased expensive china, silver plate, and hundreds of pairs of gloves.

Justifying her purchases, the First Lady explained to Elizabeth Keckly: "Mr. Lincoln has but little idea of the expense of a woman's wardrobe. He glances at my rich dresses, and is happy in the belief that the few hundred dollars that I obtain from him supply all my wants. I must dress in costly materials. The people scrutinize every article that I wear with critical curiosity. The very fact of having grown up in the West, subjects me to more searching observation. To keep up appearances, I must have money—more than Mr. Lincoln can spare for me. He is too honest to make a penny outside of his salary; consequently I had, and still have, no alternative but to run in debt."

Asked if the president was aware of those debts, Mrs. Lincoln exclaimed: "God, no!—I would not have him suspect. If he knew that his wife was involved to the extent that she is, the knowledge would drive him mad. He is so sincere and straightforward himself, that he is shocked by the duplicity of others. He does not know a thing about any debts and I value his happiness, not to speak of my own, too much to allow him to know anything. This is what troubles me so much. If he is re-elected, I can keep him in ignorance of my affairs; but if he is defeated, then the bills will be sent in, and he will know all." She then sobbed hysterically.

Lincoln tried to calm her down, saying: "Mary, I am afraid you will be punished for this overweening anxiety. If I am to be re-elected it will be all right; if not, you must bear the disappointment."

To alleviate her anxiety, the First Lady began to settle some of her debts in March 1864. The following month, she promised A. T. Stewart that she would pay up within a few weeks, saying that she appreciated his "patience" and asked "an especial favor": as someone who had been "a punctual customer & always hoping to be so, a delay of the Settlement of my account with you, until the 1st of June—when I promise, that without fail, *then*, the whole account shall be settled. I deeply regret, that I am so unusually situated & trust hereafter, to settle as I purchase."

In order to meet that deadline, the First Lady may have leaked a state secret to journalist Joseph Howard, who in 1861 had flattered her extravagantly in the columns of the *New York Times* (see Chapter 11). In May 1864, he shocked the nation by supplying some newspapers with a bogus presidential proclamation announcing both a new draft call (for 400,000 men) and a day of fasting and prayer necessitated by recent military setbacks. (That month, Lincoln had in fact written a call for 300,000 men which he intended to issue in July.) After his swift apprehension, Howard said that he concocted the plan to raise the price of gold, in which he had invested heavily. He was to spend months in jail for his indiscretion.

The backstory of this scandal is murky, but it seems likely that Howard learned about Lincoln's intention to issue a new draft call from someone in Washington to whom he may well have paid money to divulge it. On May 18, the false story broke in the two gullible New York papers that he had managed to hoodwink, causing an angry Lincoln to order the arrest of their publishers, editors, and proprietors. On May 20, Democratic Congressman S. S. Cox of Ohio reported to one of those editors that Mrs. Lincoln may have been the source of Howard's tip: "the forged proclamation is based on a *fact*. . . . a proclamation *was written* and similar in impact to the base and damnable forgery for which you are under ban." Cox speculated that "it may come from Mrs. Mary Lincoln."

Cox's guess about the First Lady's culpability is not implausible. As noted above, in 1861 Mrs. Lincoln had sold Henry Wikoff access to at least one presidential document. Like Wikoff, Howard had shamelessly flattered her in a major New York newspaper. A knowledgeable reporter for another important New York paper described her in March 1864 as an insider who "sold state secrets" and was "one of the *leaky vessels* from which contraband army news, gets afloat." (Years later, Carl Schurz recalled that "it was commonly believed that she sold war secrets for large sums of money.") Moreover, she desperately needed cash to pay one of her major creditors by June 1.

In October 1864, the First Lady reportedly paid off some more debts. A New York paper alleged that the "numerous creditors of Mr. Lincoln, Mrs. Lincoln, and all the little Lincolns, were both astonished and gladdened last week by a notification that their bills would be cashed if presented at the desk of Messrs. A. T. Stewart and Co." Those bills totaled around $20,000 "and have been standing since the beginning of Uncle Abe's term of office." Approximately $12,000 reportedly was paid, covering "every variety of liability—gloves, clothing, etc."

Most likely she was able to pay the greater part of those bills because she had accepted a bribe of $20,000 from Simeon Draper, a New York real estate developer, merchant, and auctioneer, whom a contemporary described as "an active politician, very popular with his fellow workers in the Republican organization, and prominent in the movements of the party." In 1856, Henry Villard heard Draper, then serving as chairman of the State Republican Central Committee, speak: "I remember well the admiration I felt every time I saw his commanding figure and heard his stentorian voice." On September 7, 1864, Lincoln named Draper to replace Hiram Barney as collector of customs in New York. The collectorship was a lucrative post, with an annual salary of $6,340 and supplemental "pickings and fees" amounting to about $20,000 a year. Shortly after becoming the collector, he also won another remunerative job: cotton agent in New York, whose duties included auctioning the cotton seized at Savannah in December 1864. Mrs. Lincoln facilitated his good fortune; according to David Davis, "Draper had paid her $20,000 for his appointment as cotton agent in the city of New York."

By various fraudulent means, Draper reaped immense profits. An 1867 congressional report noted that at the time he assumed the position of cotton agent, Draper "was known to be a bankrupt. It is a well-known fact that he settled his debts and died [in 1866] leaving property estimated at millions." Upon hearing of Draper's appointment, Gideon Welles wrote that he "sickened" at "the idea of sending such a man [to Savannah] on such a mission," which he accurately predicted "will be a swindle." The navy secretary felt sure that a "ring will be formed for the purchase of the cotton, regardless of public or private rights."

Draper traveled to Savannah to oversee the auction of cotton there, arriving on January 11, 1865. The following month, he reportedly had already received $50,000 in fees. Seven months later, he begged Treasury Secretary William P. Fessenden, who had fired him as collector of the port of New York, to allow him to stay on as the custom house official in charge of auctioning property seized in the South. Draper had agreed to help Mrs. Lincoln pay a large bill for furs, but after Lincoln's death he reneged.

In 1866, Mrs. Lincoln denied that she ever had much to do with Draper: "It has been *three* years since I have laid eyes on S. Draper & never saw him—but two or three times, in my life[.] I never saw one of his family, in my life—I never received a line from him or a cent in my life." But in January 1865, she urged him to reinstate one Mr. Martin to a clerkship in the New York Custom House and also asked him to find a place for one Joseph Hertford, either in New York or Savannah.

Draper may not have been Mrs. Lincoln's sole rescuer. Friends reportedly paid some of her bills. In 1867, Isaac Newton told John Hay: "that lady has set here on this here sofy & shed tears by the pint a begging me to pay her debts which was unbeknown to the President. There was one big bill for furs which give her a sight of trouble—she got it paid at last by some of her friends."

Desperate for money to pay her remaining creditors, Mrs. Lincoln in December 1864 fired the "good & kind," well-liked White House doorman, Edward McManus, who had apparently alienated the First Lady by spreading what she termed "vile falsehoods" about her. In his place she hired one Cornelius O'Leary, with whom she colluded in a corrupt money-making scheme. He told people who wished to have someone released from a prisoner-of-war camp that he could expedite their appeal for a fee. All the money he thus obtained was shared with the First Lady. When a Democratic newspaper exposed this scheme, Lincoln promptly fired O'Leary.

Although some of her outstanding bills were paid in 1864, the First Lady continued to incur so many debts that, according to Keckly, she "owed, at the time of the President's death, different store bills amounting to seventy thousand dollars," about which Lincoln "knew nothing." In Keckly's view, "the only happy feature of his assassination was that he died in ignorance of them. Had he known to what extent his wife was involved, the fact would have embittered the only pleasant moments of his life."

To help Lincoln win reelection, his wife had inveigled lobbyists, politicos, contractors, and office holders into giving her money. She confided to Keckly: "In a political canvass it is policy to cultivate every element of strength. These men have influence, and we require influence to reelect Mr. Lincoln. I will be clever to them until after the election, and then, if we remain at the White House, I will drop every one of them, and let them know very plainly that I only made tools of them. They are an unprincipled set, and I don't mind a little double-dealing with them." When asked if the president knew about such cynical schemes, she exclaimed: "God! No; he would never sanction such a proceeding, so I keep him in the dark, and will tell him of it when all is over. He is too honest to take proper care of his own interests, so I feel it to be my duty to electioneer for him."

According to Keckly, the First Lady "sometimes feared that the politicians would get hold of the particulars of her debts, and use them in the Presidential campaign against her husband; and when this thought occurred to her, she was almost crazy with anxiety and fear. When in one of these excited moods, she would fiercely exclaim: 'The Republican politicians must pay my debts. Hundreds of them are getting immensely rich off the patronage of my husband, and it is but fair that they should help me out of my embarrassment. I will make a demand of them, and when I tell them the facts they cannot refuse to advance whatever money I require.'"

In 1864, Democrats did in fact make the First Lady's conduct a campaign issue. Some Democratic newspapers published an exposé of the First Lady's imperious and tightfisted ways. They reported that in 1862, a dentist called at the White House to remove a tooth. After completing the job, he asked for $2.50, prompting Mrs. Lincoln to insist that she had never paid more than 50¢ for such services. The dentist said that he did not make house calls for such a small fee and would charge nothing. Intervening to resolve the dispute, Lincoln paid him $2.50.

The First Lady allegedly treated hoteliers, theater proprietors, and merchants in a similar fashion. At a Boston hotel she "had a most wordy discussion with the head bookkeeper, a scene appropriate rather to the Fulton [Fish] Market than to the best chambers of the best hostelry." In Washington, she was "in the habit of ordering a row of the best seats at Grover's or Ford's [theatres] and sweeping out of them without any gratuity." When she requested one of those establishments to reserve a pair of private boxes, the theater's treasurer asked for money. Told that "Mrs. Lincoln never pays anything," he replied: "Then, d[am]n me, if she can have any box in this theater." In New York, she offended dry goods dealers, who regarded her as "very mean."

Also offended were some Union troops, who disapproved of the First Lady's spendthrift ways. "I can hardly wish that Mrs. Lincoln should occupy the White House for four years longer," wrote a lieutenant who supported the president's reelection. "Her want of sympathy with the loyal ladies of the North—our mothers and sisters, who to their arduous labors in behalf of our soldiers in the field and in the hospitals, have added dispensing with expensive luxuries [so] that our National finances may be thereby improved, is not at all to her credit."

Following Lincoln's assassination, his widow carried out her threat to extort money from Republican officeholders. That ugly blackmail attempt became public knowledge two years after the war, when she tried to sell some of her old clothes. She had long been contemplating that fundraising strategy. Elizabeth Keckly recalled that the First Lady had "said to me at different times, in the years of 1863 and '4, that her expensive dresses might prove of great assistance to her some day." Mrs. Lincoln explained that her husband "is so generous that he will not save anything from his salary, and I expect that we will leave the White House poorer than when we came into it." (That fear was unjustified; Lincoln in fact had saved most of his presidential salary.) If she found herself in need of money, she said, "I will have no further need for an expensive wardrobe, and it will be [a wise] policy to sell it off."

In 1865, she tried to hawk a few of her costly garments. She also sold some of her husband's clothing. Shortly after the assassination, a Washington restaurateur, John Hammack, paid her $84 for several of Lincoln's shirts. This embarrassing transaction was widely reported. According to William P. Wood, the First Lady colluded with Thomas Stackpole, a White House watchman and a "subtle[,] partisan, Yankee Democrat" who "had an eye to business and was anxious to make an extra dollar whenever occasion offered." He managed to gain the confidence of Mrs. Lincoln and used her to obtain trading permits, which he sold to his friend Hammack, "a Virginia-bred Democrat and rabid secessionist." Hammack then peddled them to eager buyers. Wood recollected that while he was telling Lincoln about these shady dealings, the president "exhibited more feeling than I had believed he possessed."

In 1867, assuming "an attitude of threat very strongly savoring of extortion," she wrote to men who had won lucrative contracts or appointments to high office during her husband's administration, asking them to buy her cast-off finery, which she put up for sale in New York. If those men failed to comply, her broker would threaten to expose them by publishing her letters. Among those whom Mrs. Lincoln intended to shake down was Abram Wakeman, a politico appointed in 1864 as surveyor of the port of New York. (Chapter 8)

When the public learned of this scheme, Mrs. Lincoln was widely denounced. One paper described her as "a termagant . . . shaking her clenched fist at the country and forgetful of her dead husband and all manner of propriety, demanding gold as the price of silence and pay what is her due because she was the wife of a President." The editor found it difficult to "imagine a more shocking exhibition, or one more calculated to put one to the blush in her behalf." Another newspaper thought her extortionate acts consistent with her earlier behavior: "Her conduct throughout the administration of her husband was mortifying to all who respected him . . . She was always trying to meddle in public affairs, and now she will have it known to the whole world that she accepted costly presents from corrupt contractors." Thurlow Weed remarked "that no President's wife ever before accumulated such valuable effects, and those accumulations are suggestive of 'fat contracts and corrupt disposal of patronage.'" Donn Piatt asked: "Mrs. Lincoln was not only as unprincipled and avaricious as the late sale indicated, but she was, and is, exceedingly ignorant and stupid; and yet how are we to account for the control she exercised over the domestic life and public affairs of the lamented president?"

The "Old Clothes Scandal," as it came to be called, made Mrs. Lincoln look especially bad, for the press had reported that Lincoln's estate was worth $110,000, and yet she considered herself poor. In 1867, her son Robert lamented to his fiancée: "My mother is on one subject not mentally responsible . . . [I]t is very hard to deal with one who is sane on all subjects but one. You could hardly believe it possible, but my mother protests to me that she is in actual want and nothing I can do or say will convince her to the contrary."

When Frederick Douglass and another prominent black leader, Henry Highland Garnet (along with other African Americans), offered to raise money for Mrs. Lincoln, she turned them down. Later on, according to Elizabeth Keckly, she "consented to receive contributions from my people, but as the services of Messrs. Douglass, Garnet, and others had been refused when first offered, they declined to take an active part in the scheme; so nothing was ever done."

MRS. LINCOLN OVERSPENDS ON WHITE HOUSE "FLUB DUBS"

Upon moving into the White House in 1861, Mrs. Lincoln "felt it was a degradation to have to submit to such abominable furniture." To replace it, hang new curtains, cover the floors with new carpets, repaint and repaper the walls, and restock the china cabinet, she overspent the $20,000 which Congress had appropriated for that purpose, as well as a $6,000 supplementary appropriation. In September 1861, after she had ordered expensive china, carpets, curtains, and the like, Commissioner Public Buildings Benjamin Brown French advised her that funds were unavailable to pay for $3,500 worth of wallpaper purchased in Paris on her instructions. So if the redecorating was to be completed, Congress must pass another supplemental appropriation. The following month, French complained about "the interviews I have with the 'Republican Queen'—who plagues me half to death with wants with which it is impossible to comply, for she has an eye to the dollars!"

Four days later, in a panic, Mrs. Lincoln appealed to Commissioner French: "Major, I have sent for you to get me out of trouble,—if you will do it. I never will get into such a difficulty again." She acknowledged that one contractor's bill exceeded the original appropriation by $6,700. "Mr. Lincoln will not approve it," she predicted. "I want you to see him and tell him that it is common to overrun appropriations—tell him how *much* it costs to refurnish, he does not know much about it, he says he will pay it out of his own pocket." With tears in her eyes, she pled for help: "Major, he cannot afford that, he ought not to do it. Major, you must get me out of this difficulty, it is the last, I will always be governed by you, henceforth, I will not spend a cent without consulting you. Now do go to Mr. Lincoln and try to persuade him to approve the bill. Do, Major, for my sake, *but* do not let him know that you have seen me." She handed the commissioner an invoice with her annotation, dated December 13: "This bill is correct. Mr Lincoln will please have it settled—this closes the house furnishing." (After describing this scene to his sister-in-law, French added that the First Lady "is a very imprudent woman in many things.")

In obedience to her pleas, French, whose position as commissioner of public buildings made him practically a member of the White Household, explained to Lincoln that "a Mr. Carryl has presented a bill of some $7,000 over the appropriation, for furnishing this house, and, before I can ask for an appropriation to pay it, it must have your approval."

The president, "a little excited," exclaimed: "It never can have my approval—I'll pay for it out of my own pocket first—it would stink in the nostrils of the American people to have it said that the President of the United States had approved a bill overrunning an appropriation of $20,000 for *flub dubs* for this damned old house, when the poor freezing soldiers cannot have blankets! Who is that Carryl, and how came he to be employed[?]"

French replied: "I do not know, sir—the first I ever heard of him he brought me a large bill for room [wall] paper."

Lincoln was especially shocked by the cost of a "Rich, Elegant Carpet made to order" that his wife had purchased. "I would like to know where a carpet worth $2,000 can be put," he queried.

"In the East Room," French suggested.

Lincoln, who was "inexorable" in his resistance to the plea for a special appropriation, deemed the carpet "a monstrous extravagance," adding: "Well I suppose Mrs. Lincoln *must* bear the blame, let her bear it, I swear I won't! . . . It was all wrong to spend one cent at such a time, and I never ought to have had a cent expended, the house was furnished well enough, better than any one we ever lived in, and if I had not been overwhelmed with other business I would not have had any of the appropriation expended, but what could I do? I could not attend to everything." He concluded "by swearing that he *never* would approve that bill" and that rather than sign such legislation "he would pay it out of his own pocket!"

In the spring of 1862, French told his son that Mrs. Lincoln "is a little troublesome, & I can tell you some rather funny things relative to my experience with the worthy President and his Lady. Abraham is my *beau ideal* of an honest man, and Mrs. L. is—not my *beau ideal* pendant to that picture. You have heard the song I presume 'Oh Kitty Clover *she troubles me*

so, Oh—oh—oh—oh—oh–oh.' Substitute Mrs. L- for Kitty & I can sing
it from my heart!" Similarly, he confided to his brother: "The President is
the very soul of honesty, honor & openness of heart. Mrs. Lincoln is—Mrs.
Lincoln & no body else, & like no other human being I ever saw. She is not
easy to get along with, though I succeed pretty well with her. If ever I see you
again, I will amuse you with yesterday's [March 22] experience. I dare not
put it on paper—even to you." He added: "We rather wish Mrs. President
was—a more prudent lady." In 1864, he complained that "Mrs. Lincoln is
boring [i.e., pestering] me daily to obtain an appropriation for fitting up a
new house for her and the President at the Soldiers' Home and I, in turn,
am boring the Committee on Ways and Means. If Thaddeus [Stevens], the
worthy old chairman did not *joke me off*, I think I should get it."

After Lincoln's death, French wrote about the dealings he had had with
the First Lady: "I always felt as if the eyes of a hyena were upon me, & that the
animal was ready, if I made a single mismove, to pounce upon me!" He
called her a "bundle of vanity and folly" and wrote poetry about her regal
ways:

> [She] moved in all the insolence of pride
> as if the world beneath her feet she trod;
> Her vulgar bearing, jewels could not hide,
> And gold's base glitter was her only god!

In February 1862, Congress appropriated $14,000 for White House
"extras," despite the opposition of some Republicans, including senators
Lyman Trumbull, Morton Wilkinson, and James Grimes. Democratic
senator James Nesmith thought the White House "was sufficiently gorgeous for a prince" when Buchanan left it and Nesmith was scandalized
that Mrs. Lincoln had overspent the $20,000 appropriation by thousands
which Congress was asked to pay "while our troops are suffering for the
necessities of life." The Oregon senator wrote his wife that the "old Spanish

proverb which says, 'put a beggar on horseback and he will ride to the D[evi]l' was never better illustrated."

Republican senator James R. Doolittle of Wisconsin explained that he and other lawmakers "were placed in this fix[:] either the President must pay this money out of his own pocket or we must appropriate it to cover deficiencies." According to Doolittle, Senator James A. Pearce of Maryland "very delicately passed the matter on in the Senate and we voted it somewhat upon the principle that it is not gentlemanly to overhaul a lady's wardrobe." The lawmakers also believed that "it would not be just to compel the President to pay" for the act of his "silly" and "vainglorious" wife. It was, Doolittle lamented, "exceedingly mortifying."

PENNY-PINCHING
PENURIOUSNESS

Mrs. Lincoln was both a spendthrift and a pinch-penny; while she overspent on refurbishing the White House, she economized tightly on its day-to-day operations. In early March 1861, Charles Francis Adams Jr. attended a reception at which her cost-cutting ways were discussed: "All manner of stories about her were flying around; she wanted to do the right thing, but, not knowing how, was too weak and proud to ask; she was going to put the White House on an economical basis, and, to that end, was about to dismiss 'the help,' as she called the servants; some of whom, it was asserted, had already left because 'they must live with gentlefolks.'" One servant allegedly quit because Mrs. Lincoln had set her to work "making drawers out of the linen sheets of the establishment," a chore that "wounded her feelings so much that she soon 'gave notice.'" When she later spoke to friends about her White House duties, she revealed "that the extraordinary length of the drawers" left no doubt in her mind "as to the person who was to have the comfort of wearing them."

That servant's discontent was not unique. Mrs. Lincoln reportedly "was never considered an extravagant woman, but on the contrary, very penurious, so much so that her servants talked of it on the street." In 1861, when the First Lady hired Alexander Williamson to tutor Willie and Tad, she haggled over his compensation, and the two could not agree on terms; ultimately William-son's wife took over and negotiated a salary for him with the First Lady. (After the president's death, Mrs. Lincoln used Williamson for over two-and-a-half years as an agent to raise money for her, in which capacity "she treated him little better than an errand boy" and "paid him little or nothing.")

Some believed that Mrs. Lincoln was "close" with money because she wished to preserve her husband's salary "as much as possible to build them a house after [his] term at Washington expires." According to the editor of the Washington *Constitution*, she told the White House "major domo" that she and her husband "were poor and hoped to save twelve thousand dollars every year from their [$25,000] salary." When someone appealed to her on behalf of a White House staffer who wished to be retained, Mrs. Lincoln explained that "she had brought her own girl. She must economize." Mary Boykin Chesnut, who assumed that Mrs. Lincoln intended to pocket the employee's salary, indignantly remarked: "It is an infamy to economize the public money, to put it in one's private purse" and thus to "put the nation to an open shame. One would suppose this money was given them as a reward of merit for getting a plurality of votes." In 1861, William Howard Russell heard that Mrs. Lincoln "beat down a poor widow" by paying her 14¢ instead of 20¢ for cloth "after immense chaffing." Russell commented: "Mrs. L's meanness is beyond belief." When she hired a dressmaker, the First Lady insisted that her charges must be cheap: "I cannot afford to be extravagant. We are just from the West, and are poor." (As Benjamin Brown French observed, Mrs. Lincoln "does love money—aye, better than I do, and a great deal better than her honored spouse.")

In an unprecedented move, Mrs. Lincoln sold the milk of White House cows. In 1883, a "White House domestic" explained that demand for

Executive Mansion dairy products "has been the same for years but in my recollection [it] was never turned to profit except in Mrs. Lincoln's time." She "was very fond of her cows, took a particular pride in their affairs and begrudged any one outside the household a drop of milk or a pound of butter." She therefore resented the wives of cabinet members and military officers who "were continually sending to her for milk and butter, offering all manner of excuses and couching their requests in the most flattering terms." For a time, Mrs. Lincoln honored those requests, but eventually considered it "either necessary to stop the outside donations altogether or to open up a dairy business generally." So she "sat down one day and addressed notes to each of her most persistent applicants, informing them of the annoyance that they had caused, and added that in order to continue to oblige them it had become necessary to purchase two more cows and to employ additional help to assist in their keeping; if they wished to continue to receive their daily allowances from the executive dairy, they would be expected to pay for it at the regular market rates." Mary Clemmer Ames remarked that if the milk had "been sent to the hospitals," the First Lady "would have received golden praise. But the whole city felt scandalized to have it haggled over and peddled from the back door of the White House."

In the spring of 1863, the feminist/abolitionist Elizabeth Cady Stanton visited Washington and reported that people were saying "Abraham's shriveled appearance & poor health is owing to being underfed. Madame is an economist & the supplies at the White House are limited. In front of the Mansion she has fenced off a place where she pastures her cow, thus she sacrifices taste to thrift."

As another economy move, the First Lady reduced the quality of state dinners. According to a pastry chef at the White House, Mrs. Lincoln "anxiously inquired as to the cost of state dinners." When told $10 a plate, not including wine, "she was so astonished she held up her hands and said: 'Oh, that will never do. We must have cheaper dinners than that or not any dinner at all.'" She then "sat down and figured on a piece of paper a little while and finally said in a gentle but decisive way, 'Hereafter the state dinners must not exceed $3 a plate, and that figure is to include the wines as well.'"

Mrs. Lincoln soon dismissed the pastry chef and ultimately did away with state dinners altogether. According to Mary Clemmer Ames, those dinners "could have been dispensed with, without a word of blame, had their cost been consecrated to the soldiers' service; but when it was made apparent that they were omitted from personal penuriousness and a desire to devote their cost to personal gratification, the public censure knew no bounds."

Mrs. Lincoln also cut back on food and drink at Executive Mansion receptions, much to the annoyance of Michigan senator Zachariah Chandler, who told his wife: "If she will prepare refreshments I have no objection to a dress parade, but to fix up for nothing is in my judgment a humbug." He groused that "of all Stupid things White House receptions are the most so."

In 1864, Mrs. Lincoln bridled at similar criticism appearing in the New York *World.* To Abram Wakeman she wrote: "With such an establishment [as the White House] to keep up, you may imagine we have not enriched ourselves. In truth, I have had to endeavor to be as economical as possible; more so than I have ever been before in my life. It would have been a great delight to me to have had the means to entertain, generally as should be done at the Executive Mansion, it would have been my pride and pleasure, so when the World dares to insinuate aught against us, the public should take them in hand."

Mrs. Lincoln's niggardly ways did not endear her to White House coachman and doorkeeper Edward Burke, who lent her $50 that she failed to repay. Nor did they please Mary Ann Cuthbert, whose $600 annual salary as White House stewardess was pinched by the First Lady, leaving Mrs. Cuthbert "pennyless." Similarly, after Mrs. Lincoln had fired the White House steward, Richard Goodchild, in 1861, she replaced him with Jane Watt, wife of the corrupt gardener John Watt, and appropriated her salary.

By conducting herself in an undignified manner, the First Lady further justified her husband's fear that she would "bring him into disgrace." As Mary Clemmer Ames recalled, Mrs. Lincoln "brought shame upon the President's House, by petty economies, which had never disgraced it before."

11

UNPOPULAR FIRST LADY

E arly in her husband's administration, Mrs. Lincoln had received extensive and generally favorable press coverage. But her elaborate receptions, her lavish spending on herself and the White House, her shady coterie, her meddling in patronage distribution, her extensive traveling, her imperious manner, and her seeming indifference to the gravity of the times undermined her popularity. By 1865, it was reported that "Mrs. Lincoln is not popular either with men or women; and, of the latter she probably has fewer genuine friends than any lady that has filled her station before her. Parasites in crinoline attend her; but she is not loved by her friends; and she is hardly respected by females in society near enough her own grade to know all about her."

UNPOPULARITY IN SPRINGFIELD

Mrs. Lincoln had been unpopular in Illinois. In 1860, David Davis observed that the "people of Springfield do not love Lincoln's wife, as they do him."

A case in point was Albert Hale, pastor of the Second Presbyterian Church, who told a friend that while Lincoln enjoyed the local reputation as a "man of uncorrupted if not incorruptible integrity," he could not "speak as highly of his wife, as of Lincoln."

Mrs. Lincoln's local unpopularity may help explain why she did not want to go back to Springfield after her husband's presidency ended. When late in the Civil War, John Todd Stuart asked Lincoln if he intended to return to the Illinois capital, he replied: "Mary does not expect ever to go back and don't want to go—but I do—I expect to go back and make my home in Springfield for the rest of my life."

Shortly after Lincoln's death, the Reverend Dr. Phineas Gurley, minister at the Presbyterian church in Washington where the Lincolns worshiped, reported from Springfield that everyone there "loved Mr. Lincoln, but as for Mrs. L., I cannot say as much. Hard things are said of her by all classes of people, and when I got to know how she was regarded by her old neighbors and even by her relatives in S[pringfield], I did not wonder that she had decided to make her future home in Chicago. . . . The ladies of Springfield say that Mr. Lincoln's death hurt her ambition more than her affections—a hard speech, but many people think so who do not say so." Similarly, Lincoln's friend H. P. H. Bromwell wrote from Springfield about Mrs. Lincoln: "She has no friends here." In June 1865, a visitor to the Illinois capital echoed that judgment: "I have not heard one person speak well of Mrs. Lincoln since I came here."

In 1866, Mrs. Lincoln implausibly wrote that her husband "positively assured me—he would not return" to Springfield and that "he would not carry me back there again." But, as the editors of her collected letters delicately observed: "She was not above stretching or abandoning the truth to serve her own purposes, however obscure" and "was prone to complicated and less-than-straightforward ways of expressing herself." At that time, she was insisting that American philanthropists and taxpayers provide her enough money to live at Chicago "very genteelly" in "an elegant brick house" befitting her station as a "lady who has enjoyed distinction" and "the cherished wife of the man, to whom the nation owes so deep a debt of gratitude."

UNPOPULARITY IN WASHINGTON

In Washington, Mrs. Lincoln's popularity began to deteriorate quickly. Reporter J. K. C. Forrest recalled the dinner party at which he first met her: "I was not favorably impressed with Mrs. Lincoln" because she "appeared to be filled with the idea of her own importance and to be resolved that she would work the exalted position in which she unexpectedly found herself at that time as far as possible for her own personal benefit and behoof." In May 1861, a New York paper asked rhetorically how "unbecoming does it seem for Mrs. President Lincoln to be daily dashing through the lines of soldiers on the [Pennsylvania] Avenue, with her driver and postilion in livery, in a glaringly labelled carriage [with the interlocked initials *AL*], to denote who is the passer," on shopping expeditions in "a time of mourning like this"? Others complained about the way she rode about the capital "in her gaudy coach." In June 1861, Murat Halstead of the Cincinnati *Commercial* called her "a fool—the laughing stock of the town, her vulgarity only the more conspicuous in consequence of her fine carriage and horses and servants in livery and [her] fine dresses, and her damnable airs." In August 1861, the district attorney for New York County was upset with Mrs. Lincoln because just when "the country was in the throes of revolutionary travail she was coolly buying china and dresses." A Republican leader in Maryland "one day mentioned to Mr. Lincoln that Mrs. Lincoln was being criticized by the women of the U.S. [for] being in New York and leading a gay life while so many of the people were in mourning."

In the fall of 1861, Joseph A. Scoville told readers of the London *Standard* that "her Majesty Mrs. Lincoln is doing much to make King Abraham unpopular. Her conduct is described as that of an uneducated female without good sense, who has been unluckily elevated into a sphere for which she cannot fit herself." The First Lady was "making a *Judy* [i.e., a fool, an ass] of herself." In October, the eminent ethnologist, geologist, and naturalist George Gibbs reported from Washington that she "is a byword among the officials here for ignorance, vulgarity and meanness." In December, Senator William Pitt Fessenden of Maine echoed Scoville and Gibbs: Mrs. Lincoln "by common consent, is making both herself & her husband very ridiculous."

The following year, a New York gentleman reported that because of her indiscretions, "Mrs. Lincoln is seen in society at the North to be the worst enemy" of her husband, and a Vermont newspaper concluded that "Mrs. Lincoln is not equal to her place, has not steadiness and stability of character sufficient to keep her from being made the dupe of lying flattery and cunning intrigue." Mary Clemmer Ames surmised that Mrs. Lincoln was "unconsciously elated, carried away with the sudden honors of her new condition," and was "unsuspectingly pleased with the delicate, dangerous flatteries of brilliant yet unprincipled intriguers." In early 1863, commenting on the public's then-current distrust of the Lincoln administration, Mrs. Lincoln's friend Jane Grey Swisshelm wrote that one cause "has been the unpopularity of the Lady of the White House," who has "selected her friends amongst persons of flippant character."

Mrs. Lincoln was widely denounced for indulging in extravagance and frivolity while taxes soared. Upon reading about her shopping trips, the prominent abolitionist Lydia Maria Child exclaimed: "So *this* is what the people are taxed for! to deck out this vulgar doll with foreign frippery." When a delegation from the Ladies League of Washington asked her to forgo costly imported fashions and adornments, Mrs. Lincoln reportedly "gave a point blank negative" and "rather took the matter in high dudgeon, and was not at all pleased with the ladies who made the unwelcome proposition." Alluding to the First Lady, Jane Grey Swisshelm told readers of the Chicago *Journal* that there "is no doubt that in her lavish and expensive style of dress, she believes, from some cause, that she is thus maintaining the dignity of the nation in the eyes of the representatives of foreign countries."

One day in 1862, the First Lady received eighteen hostile letters. Mary Clemmer Ames described some of those missives: "Letters of rebuke, of expostulation, of anathema even, addressed to her, personally, came in to her from every direction. Not a day that did not bring her many such communications, denouncing her mode of life, her conduct, and calling upon her to fulfil the obligations, and meet the opportunities of her high station." When such critical letters reached the White House, "she considered herself an injured individual, the honored object of envy, jealousy and spite, and a martyr to her high position." While Mrs. Ames acknowledged that some of those letters were doubtless "unjust" and "unkind," she nonetheless thought that it never occurred to the First Lady "that any part of the provocation was on her side, and after a few tastes of their bitter draughts she ceased to open them." To deal with such correspondence, she instructed William O. Stoddard (known as "Mrs. Lincoln's secretary") to screen it, passing along only those items that he believed she would like to peruse.

In 1882, Mrs. Ames wrote that Mary Lincoln lacked the personal warmth and empathy that might have made her more popular: "Her sympathies, strong and steadfast, running in deep but narrow channels, did not flow over or out to masses or to classes. 'People in general' were not of large or close account to her. The outraying kindness of heart and of speech which bound thousands in real affection to Mrs. [Lucy] Hayes [First Lady from 1877 to 1881] was wholly wanting in Mrs. Lincoln, save to those whom she personally knew and liked." Comparing her with a different First Lady, A. Oakey Hall remembered that soon after her husband's inauguration, it "became obvious to all that Mrs. Lincoln would never shine as a hostess in Washington society. She lacked presence, spontaneity, and all the magnetic and intellectual qualities which made Dolley Madison so popular."

In February 1862, the Methodist Episcopal *Ladies Repository* lamented that one "of the saddest evidences of our social demoralization as a people, and the depth and extent of that demoralization, is seen in the utter unconsciousness of the ruin and misery of this country which prevails in Washington. That unconsciousness seems to environ the White House. No woman ever had a better opportunity to show how much a patriot mother could do for their country than Mrs. Lincoln. It is sad that the golden opportunity is thrown away."

The First Lady affected a regal manner that did not endear her to the public. A Springfield woman termed her "haughty." Benjamin Brown French, who often introduced her at White House receptions, referred to her as "The American Queen" and deplored her tendency "to put on the airs of an Empress." (Others who worked closely with her in the White House had even more unflattering sobriquets for the First Lady. The two main White House secretaries referred to her as "the Hell Cat" and "her Satanic Majesty," and the presidential physician, Dr. Robert K. Stone, varying the image slightly, called her "a perfect devil.") The Indianapolis *Journal* remarked that she had "been spoiled by the gross flatteries of the fools about the White House, and thinks she must conduct herself like a European Queen." If Lincoln "hasn't sense enough, or control enough, over his foolish wife," then it was up to members of Congress "to exert that control themselves over him and his wife both." Other papers referred to the First Lady as "our parvenu queen" who had "no conception of dignity" but "all the peevish assurance of a baseless parvenu." David Davis deplored the "*queenly*" way in which she traveled. Mrs. Lincoln's imperious manner and grandiosity led other people to label her "the Queen Regnant of the Union," "our rosy Empress," "her royal majesty," "the American Empress," and the "*Reine d'Illinois.*" Even her close friend Mercy Levering Conkling referred to her as the "*royal highness.*"

In 1864 a Radical Republican, Karl Heinzen, criticized the military detail stationed outside the White House: "Two cavalrymen hold continual guard at the gate and two infantrymen at the entrance to the door. Mrs. Lincoln, they say, wants it so, and to please her, the republican President must make lackeys of a dozen republican citizens every day."

A satirical newspaper piece criticized the First Lady for being "stuck up," for accepting inappropriate gifts, and for wasting taxpayer dollars on fancy china. A resident of Crawfordsville, Indiana, noted that everybody there thought her "decidedly a snob" and regretted that the country had "a presidentess with so little of the lady."

Mrs. Lincoln behaved imperiously when shopping. A case in point was Genin's fashionable hat shop in New York. While in her carriage, the First Lady called to a clerk conversing with a friend by the front door. He ignored her, and when informed that Mrs. Lincoln was summoning him, he "replied somewhat indifferently, that he did not care," and that he acknowledged no "difference between Mrs. Lincoln and the wife of a mechanic. If she will come into the store, I will attend to her, but I am not employed to wait on people in the street." In December 1864, Horatio Nelson Taft observed the First Lady shopping at a Washington emporium: "Here is the carriage of Mrs[.] Lincoln before a dry goods Store[;] her footman has gone into the Store. The Clerk is just going out to the carriage (where Mrs[.] L is waiting) with some pieces of goods for her to choose from. I should rather think that she would have a better chance at the goods if she was to go into the Store but then she *might* get jostled and gazed at and that too would be doing just as the common people do. The footman holds the carriage door open. The driver sits on the box and hold[s] the horses. Mrs[.] L. thumbs the goods and asks a great many questions."

Taft's daughter Julia was shocked by the First Lady's exaggerated sense of entitlement. "It was an outstanding characteristic of Mary Todd Lincoln that she wanted what she wanted when she wanted it and no substitute!" Julia commented after relating a story about Mrs. Lincoln's request that Julia's mother surrender her favorite bonnet so that its strings could be used to decorate headgear coveted by the First Lady.

That sense of entitlement amused Mrs. Lincoln's fellow spiritualist, the poet John Pierpont, who one day in the White House heard her ask, as she admired Francis B. Carpenter's huge painting, "The First Reading of the Emancipation Proclamation of President Lincoln": "What puzzles me is, what on earth we are ever going to do with it?" Evidently she had "a vague idea that it must somehow be got" into her modest house in Springfield.

The First Lady spoke and acted indiscreetly, ignoring the advice of her husband, who she said, "always enjoined upon me to be quiet." The journalist J. K. C. Forrest, who covered Washington during the war, recalled that Mrs. Lincoln "never for a moment hesitated to express an opinion on any leading topic of the day or any public character. At times these opinions were biting." A Chicago woman, a lifelong friend of the Lincolns, described the First Lady as "an injudicious talker. I was with her once on Pennsylvania avenue, when a New York politician was in the carriage with us. The man immediately began talking politics and soon brought the conversation around to one of the cabinet officers [Interior Secretary Caleb B. Smith]. Mrs. Lincoln said, 'I do wish we could get rid of him. I have been trying to get Mr. Lincoln to make him a judge in the court of claims' (then being organized). Even to my inexperienced eyes the politician had gotten what he wanted and soon got out of the carriage." She added: "I shall always believe that even then Mrs. Lincoln's mind was slightly affected or else she was a woman in whom judgment was totally wanting." Similarly, the First Lady and Carl Schurz traveled together from City Point, Virginia to Washington in early April 1865. En route, she overwhelmed Schurz "with a flood of gossip about the various members of the cabinet and leading men in Congress who in some way had incurred her displeasure." Schurz found the "gossip so reckless" that he "was not only embarrassed as to what to say in reply, but actually began to fear for the soundness of her mind." He told his wife, "I learned more state secrets in a few hours than I could otherwise in a year." In 1863, Pennsylvania Congressman James H. Campbell conversed with Mrs. Lincoln and was surprised by her "bitter prejudices." Two years earlier, a woman who had attended a White House levee wrote that if she had been the First Lady, "I wouldn't have talked quite so freely in a promiscuous crowd about my husband's affairs."

Mrs. Lincoln's conduct at those White House receptions at first received positive reviews, including one by Joseph Howard of the New York *Times*: "She stood near her husband, with dignity and ease. Self-possession, under such circumstances, one would not naturally expect, but it was there. Had the mistress of the White House been born and bred at Washington, accustomed from childhood to the surroundings of the most prominent positions, she could not have exhibited, outwardly, less embarrassment or more entire 'savior faire.'"

(Howard had lavished similar praise on her the previous month, protesting against "unscrupulous newspaper men" who accused Mrs. Lincoln of being "ungenial and unrefined." On the contrary, Howard described her glowingly as a woman with a "large and well developed" head, an "eye clear and intelligent," a mouth "large, well shaped, and capable of great expression," and a chin "that rounds gracefully." Her "form inclines to stoutness but is well-fashioned and comely, while her hands and feet are really beautiful, indicating, as does the well shaped ear, that she has come from a race of people who were well born." Her "carriage is good, her manners are pleasant, her greetings are affable, and, without doubt, her intentions are correct." She "goes to the White House, versed in the goodly knowledge of housewifery and substantial living, rather than skilled in the cunning tricks of politics." She enters upon her duties as First Lady with a "sound substratum of common sense," "natural tact," the "esteem of all who knew her at her old home," as well as "the best wishes of every decent woman in the land.")

Gustavus Fox reported that at a White House reception in March 1861, Mrs. Lincoln was "Lady Like, converses easily, dresses well and has the Kentucky pronunciation," and John W. Forney wrote that she was, "as all exclaim, an affable, good-looking little lady." Commissioner of Public Buildings Benjamin Brown French noted that at one reception she "greeted every guest with such cheerful good will and kindness as to do infinite credit to her position and her heart."

But her method of greeting guests did not impress all those guests favorably.

A British journalist found her query about his health disconcerting. At an 1864 levee, the First Lady asked him: "Do you keep your health, sir?"

He replied that he enjoyed tolerably good health.

"How long have you been in this country, sir?"

He said seven months. As he recalled, Mrs. Lincoln "then asked 'how I liked the country.' I replied diplomatically, that it was very large and very beautiful. Now ensued a deep, and to me, embarrassing silence. At last she spoke again, and once more in the interrogatory form: 'And do you keep your health, sir?'"

Other White House visitors found the First Lady's conversation less than stimulating. Even her good friend and admirer, the Radical journalist Jane Grey Swisshelm, thought Mrs. Lincoln was "not very 'quick witted.'" An Indiana matron wrote in 1864 that Mrs. Lincoln "is not what can be called an intellectual woman, and in many things has no doubt acted injudiciously."

Some people were disconcerted by the First Lady's frequent use of "sir" and "ma'am" in conversation. Mrs. William H. Emory was scandalized by her "bad manners" and propensity to say "'yes *ma'am*,' and 'no *ma'am*' like a servant-woman." The historian and diplomat John Lothrop Motley thought the First Lady "is rather nice-looking, youngish, with very round white arms, well dressed, and chatty enough, and if she would not, like all the South and West, say 'Sir' to you every instant, as if you were a royal personage, she would be quite agreeable." William Howard Russell noted that she "is profuse in the introduction of the word 'sir' in every sentence."

MRS. LINCOLN'S
APPEARANCE CRITICIZED

Most observers shared the opinion of journalist Sara Jane Lippincott, who wrote that the First Lady "was not handsome." William Howard Russell confided to his diary that the "impression of homeliness produced by Mrs. Lincoln on first sight, is not diminished by closer acquaintance." Eunice Tripler was more blunt, calling Mrs. Lincoln "an ugly little woman." Elizabeth Blair Lee, "one of the few ladies with whom Mrs. Lincoln was on intimate terms in Washington," said that Elizabeth Todd Edwards was ten times better looking than her sister Mary.

The First Lady's nose was described as "rather *retroussé*," "not Grecian," and "pugnosed"; her mouth as "only an opening without any graceful, soft, light outlines"; her lips as "exceedingly thin," "pinched," and "compressed"; her features as "plain," "hard," "coarse," and "wooden"; her face as "snubby," "sharp," "mean," and "vulgar"; her complexion as "sallow," "mottled," and "mealy"; her figure "fat," "fattish," "plump," "round favored," "quite fleshy," "stocky," "decidedly stout," and "like an old dray horse." In 1865, a French aristocrat, Adolphe Pineton (Marquis Chambrun) paid her a backhanded compliment: "she must have been pretty when young."

Mrs. Lincoln's sartorial taste failed to please many. In 1867, the Cincinnati *Commercial* observed that during the Civil War, the "gaudy bad taste with which she dressed, and the constant effort to make a show of herself disgusted all observers." Abolitionist Lydia Maria Child thought the First Lady looked "more like a dowdy washerwoman" than the "representative of fashion." Another abolitionist, Wendell Phillips, echoed that sentiment: "Mrs. Lincoln is vulgar, and wants to be fashionable!" Attorney Richard Henry Dana of Massachusetts, who attended some White House receptions, described Mrs. Lincoln as a "short, fat," "cross, suspicious, under-bred" woman who "looks like the housekeeper of the establishment, & a notable, prying, & not good tempered housekeeper," with a "not good-tempered look." In 1863, an English lady visiting Washington deemed Mrs. Lincoln "a short, stout, commonplace-looking woman." In 1861, William Howard Russell wrote: "Poor Mrs. Lincoln [—] a more preposterous looking female I never saw." The following year, he wrote that the First Lady at her gala White House party resembled "a damned old Irish or Scotch (or English) washerwoman dressed out for a Sunday at Highbury Barn" (a lower class "pleasure garden" frequented by prostitutes and male cross-dressers). A senatorial guest at that event reported that the "weak minded Mrs Lincoln had her bosom on exhibition and a flower pot on her head, while there was a train of silk or satin drag[g]ing on the floor behind her of several yards in length." He "could not help regretting that she had degenerated from the industrious and unpretending woman that she was in the days when she used to cook Old Abe[']s dinner, and milk the cows with her own hands." Now, he acidly observed, her "only ambition seems to be to exhibit her own milking apparatus to the public eye." In 1864, an attendee at a White House reception noted that Mrs. Lincoln "wore a *very* low-necked dress, reminding me of the 'French fool' fashion." Similarly, Prince Jerome Napoleon, the honored guest at an 1861 White House state dinner, confided to his diary: "Mrs. Lincoln was dressed in the French style without any taste; she has the manner of a petit bourgeois and wears fake jewelry."

Alexander K. McClure recalled that Mrs. Lincoln "was vain, passionately fond of dress and wore her dresses shorter at the top and longer at the train than even fashion demanded. She had great pride in her elegant neck and bust, and grieved the president greatly by her constant display of her person and her fine clothes." Observing her in an especially low-cut dress with an unusually long train, Lincoln told his wife: "Mother, it is my opinion, if some of that tail was nearer the head, it would be in better style." A correspondent of the Springfield, Massachusetts, *Republican* reported that Mrs. Lincoln had "a beautiful bust, which was largely shown to admiring gaze" at an 1864 White House reception. Mary Clemmer Ames informed readers of that newspaper that the "very dumpy" First Lady "stuns me with her low-necked dresses and the flower-beds which she carries on the top of her head." A Democratic newspaper described her as an "uninteresting woman in white robes, and wearing a band of white flowers about her forehead, like some over-grown Ophelia."

Occasionally Lincoln would veto his wife's fashion choices. At a White House reception, one woman was astounded to observe the First Lady wearing headgear unlike any that Ophelia might have donned: "a genuine crown" that "was made of gilt, but looked precisely like those which are found on the heads of those distinguished women about whom we read in Agnes Strickland's *Lives of the Queens of England*. The stones or gems were wanting, but the tinsel and gilt were all there." The president "ridiculed it so severely that its debut and withdrawal all took place the same night."

Critics judged Mrs. Lincoln's wardrobe inappropriate for someone her age. While en route to Washington in February 1861, she attended a reception in Albany, where a legislator noted that "Mrs. Lincoln, although nearly forty [actually forty-two], was dressed like a girl of eighteen with little loops over her shoulders, her arms bare." That December, a New York matron remarked that the First Lady "is not a young woman by any means, but dresses like one." Another observer recalled that Mrs. Lincoln "regarded herself as a youthful woman, and appeared at her first reception in gay raiment, which might have been more appropriate at the time of her marriage nearly twenty years before."

Other women thought the First Lady had dressed improperly at the funeral of Colonel Edward D. Baker, where she appeared in a lilac outfit that shocked members of her circle. Thinking that she should be told that more sober garb was appropriate on such solemn occasions, they asked one of her best friends to convey that message, which Mrs. Lincoln did not appreciate. "I am so glad you have come," the First Lady told that friend. "I am just as mad as I can be. Mrs. Crittenden has just been here to remonstrate with me for wearing my lilac suit to Colonel Baker's funeral. I wonder if the women of Washington expect me to muffle myself up in mourning for every soldier killed in this great war?"

"But Mrs. Lincoln," came the reply, "do you not think black more suitable to wear at a funeral because there is a great war in the nation?"

"No, I don't. I want the women to mind their own business; I intend to wear what I please."

MRS. LINCOLN'S CONTROVERSIAL
WHITE HOUSE PARTY IN FEBRUARY 1862

Nothing did more to erode the First Lady's popularity than her decision to throw an elaborate party in early February 1862, when her sons Willie and Tad lay sick abed and the Union armies seemed unable to win a victory. Instead of a traditional open house, she decided to invite a select group. Previously, the only White House events closed to the public were state dinners, and many critics objected to the exclusiveness of the party, which seemed like a throwback to the quasi-aristocratic "drawing rooms" of Martha Washington and a repudiation of the more democratic practice introduced by Thomas Jefferson. Referring to the invitations that guests had to present at the door, Lincoln disapprovingly remarked: "I don't fancy this pass business." He emphatically forbade dancing at the event.

Some newspaper editors waxed indignant because their reporters were not invited. When two New York congressmen, flatterers of Mrs. Lincoln, asked that an exception be made for the New York *Herald* and the *Spirit of the Times*, the president's secretaries feared that she would accommodate them, thus provoking other journalists to denounce such favoritism. John G. Nicolay, in charge of White House social arrangements, appealed to his assistant, William O. Stoddard: "I can't do anything! It will make all sorts of trouble. 'She' is determined to have her own way. You will have to see to this. 'She' wouldn't listen to me." The tactful Stoddard managed to persuade the First Lady to reject the appeal of the two politicos, much to their dismay.

Less than a week before the party, Mrs. Lincoln asked Commissioner of Public Buildings Benjamin Brown French to take charge of the arrangements, replacing Nicolay. "That good lady, who is not popular, but 'more sinned against than sinning,' is hand and glove with me, and seems to expect me to get her out of every difficulty," French told his son. "She implores me, & I try my best to respond to her implorations."

The First Lady decided to break with tradition in order to rebut critics who complained that recent White House entertainments did not live up to the high standard set by Southern leaders' wives. She evidently considered it "her duty to show those haughty secessionist dames" who once ruled Washington society "that there is sufficient of fashion and respectability among the ladies of loyal families in and about Washington to constitute a court that will easily cast into the shade that of their bogus President [i.e., Jefferson Davis]."

Mrs. Lincoln's party was widely viewed as a major social blunder. The *National Anti-Slavery Standard* remarked that she "has selected this darkest hour of the Republic for fiddling and dancing at the Presidential mansion. It is fit and proper that the most favored of her guests should be Mr. and Mrs. James Gordon Bennett. So we go. If we cannot fight, let us show the world that we can dance." The Cleveland *Herald* remarked that a party at the White House, "with opera music, champagne punch in Japanese bowls, and a supper costing thousands of dollars, superintended by a caterer imported from New York for that special occasion, is about as appropriate as games, feasts and gallopades at a funeral." Echoing that sentiment, Massachusetts congressman Henry L. Dawes observed of Mrs. Lincoln: "Poor woman. She seems to act as if she expected to be the last President's wife and was disposed to make the most of it. Trifling at the White House in these times seems as inappropriate as jollity at a funeral." Dawes warned the president that nothing could "break down his administration so rapidly as this dancing-party given at the time when the nation is in the agonies of civil war. With equal propriety might a man make a ball with a corpse in his house!" Ohio senator Ben Wade asked rhetorically: "Are the President and Mrs. Lincoln aware there is a Civil War? If they are not, Mr. and Mrs. Wade are and for that reason decline to participate in feasting and dancing." George H. Boker, an ardent Republican poet, wrote a scathing set of verses, "The Queen Must Dance." A Massachusetts paper declared that it was "bad enough for Mrs. Lincoln to make an ostentatious display of her gayety at fashionable watering places last summer," which was "generally borne in silence." But the "recent scenes of rout and revelry at the White House" were intolerable. "How forcibly and unpleasantly it calls to mind the fiddling of Nero at the burning of Rome!" Winding up his criticism, the editor alluded to other figures in ancient history: "Shade of Belshazzar—ashes of Nineveh—golden calf of Aaron—come forth, ye are wanted in Washington."

Some women deplored the bad example set by the First Lady. A New York matron made that point bluntly: "It is humiliating to all American women who have to economize and struggle and part with their husbands, sons, and brothers in these sad times, to see this creature sitting in the highest place as a specimen of American womanhood." In Washington, young Maria M. C. Hall longed for a role model "to set the women of America an example of economy, prudence, patriotism, and nobleness!" Mrs. Lincoln, she thought, was "not a woman of sufficient dignity of character to fill the post at the White House in any time, but now how much more do we expect to see her filling the place with a bearing worthy of at least a patriotic wife." The president she considered "every inch a man—every inch but one—that is where he lets his wife rule him. 'Abe' has a weak point." To some, that weak point called to mind a Biblical story: "Sampson was shorn of his strength by a woman of the Philistines. The White House may have its Delilah; who can tell?"

Midwest papers were especially critical of the First Lady's party. The Cincinnati *Commercial* thought it "unfortunate that Mrs. Lincoln has so poor an understanding of the true dignity of her position, and the duties devolving upon her. It is not becoming her to be assuming the airs of a fine lady and attempting to shine as the bright star of 'the Republican court,' as shameless and designing flatterers call the White House circle." The editors disapproved of her "rich dresses and glittering equipage, her adornment of the President's House with costly upholstery," and her penchant for "crowding it with gay assemblages." The *Gazette* of the Queen City asserted that to the public "the occasion seems too serious, the national peril too imminent, the distress of the country too great, and the condition of the nation too humiliating, to inaugurate a carnival at the Government mansion." The Indianapolis *Journal* protested: "With an empty treasury and a failing credit, a war raging all around us, and foreign nations threatening to interfere, such displays as that at the White House are a disgrace to the President." A leading Christian Evangelical newspaper in Ohio regretted that the First Lady lost an opportunity to win public favor: "If Mrs. Lincoln had put herself at the head of the Soldiers' Aid Society—had she said, 'The nation is in distress, and my time, my heart and my money are sacred to the cause of my country—hundreds of dollars, yea, millions, if need be, for our country's life, but not one cent for ball or supper till the rebellion is crushed'—she would have made her name immortal. She has missed her hour for such an immortality."

CRITICISM OF MRS. LINCOLN'S "EXCESSIVE GRIEF"

Public criticism continued unabated even when Mrs. Lincoln was grief-stricken following the death her favorite son, Willie, two weeks after the controversial White House party. Like her husband, she was wracked with grief, lamenting to Congressman Elihu Washburne that the White House seemed "like a tomb and that she could not bear to be in it." Willie, she said, "was the favorite child, so good, so obedient, so promising."

"She mourned according to her nature," Mary Clemmer Ames wrote. "She shut herself in with her grief, and demanded of God why he had afflicted *her*! Nobody suffered as she suffered."

At that time, Mrs. Lincoln was unable to care for her youngest son, Tad, who ran a dangerous fever when Willie became fatally sick. Providing immediate help was a twenty-five-year-old hospital volunteer, Maria M. C. Hall, detailed to the White House by the head nurse of the Union Army. On February 21, 1862, the day after Willie died, Hall reported to the bedroom of the First Lady, whom she observed closely over the following week. "I doubt not I saw the best there is in her," she told a friend, but that best was none too good: Mrs. Lincoln "is very impulsive and totally undisciplined" and "has no self-control." After a "passionate outburst of grief for her child she would soon be talking gaily and cheerfully on some quite different topic. Not with me but I heard her talking with Mrs. [Orville] Browning from Illinois, an old friend." Weeping uncontrollably, Mary Lincoln now and then entered Tad's room, where he told her: "I wish you would not come in here. You make me cry." Such erratic behavior suggested that Mrs. Lincoln teetered on the verge of a nervous breakdown, something her concerned husband feared.

Maria Hall was replaced by an army nurse, Rebecca Pomroy, who grew close to the Lincolns. She wrote a friend: "Nothing is the matter with Mrs. Lincoln but deep sorrow, such as others have felt, and being a fashionable woman of the world, the blow falls hard, but it was intended to soften her and make her realize her position in the eyes of the world but more especially her obligations to that being who has crowned her with loving mercy."

Also helping to care for Tad after his brother's death was Mrs. Lincoln's sister Elizabeth Edwards, who hastened from Springfield to Washington upon hearing the sad news. A week after her arrival, Mrs. Edwards wrote that the First Lady "has been but little with him [Tad], being utterly unable to control her feelings." Mrs. Lincoln become so upset that she had to be sedated. The following month, Elizabeth Edwards added that her sister was "nervous and dependent upon the companionship of someone," and "feels since her trouble that she cannot again be alone." For weeks that companionship was provided by Elizabeth Edwards, who reported that "my presence here, has tended very much to soothe, the excessive grief" of her sister. Such "excessive grief" caused Elizabeth to tell her daughter Julia: "Your Aunt Mary's manner is very distressed, and subdued"; Willie's death "is a serious crush to her *unexampled frivolity*, such language, sounds harsh, but the *excessive indulgence*, that has been revealed to me, fully justifies it." Elizabeth hoped Mary would now forego "*pleasures*" but was not optimistic: "Such is her nature, that I cannot realize that she will forgo *them* all, or even long, under existing circumstances." She "confines herself to her room, feeling very sad and at times, gives way to violent grief. She is so constituted, and the surrounding circumstances will present, a long indulgence of such gloom."

It was indeed long. Custom dictated that parents formally mourn the loss of a child for a year, but her mourning significantly exceeded that span. It was so prolonged that Washingtonians came to resent the First Lady's grieving. Immediately after Willie's death, she forbade the Marine Band to perform its popular weekly concerts on the White House's South Lawn. The prohibition remained in effect month after month, causing public discontent. When Gideon Welles suggested that the concerts be performed in Lafayette Park across the street from the White House's north entrance, the First Lady rejected that compromise. Employing the "royal we," she wrote: "It is our especial desire that the Band, does not play in these grounds, this summer. We expect our wishes to be complied with."

Elizabeth Keckly recalled that after Willie died, his mother "could not bear the sight of anything he loved, not even a flower. Costly bouquets were presented to her, but she turned from them with a shudder, and either placed them in a room where she could not see them, or threw them out of the window. She gave all of Willie's toys—everything connected with him—away, as she said she could not look upon them without thinking of her poor dead boy, and to think of him, in his white shroud and cold grave, was maddening." Keckly said that never in her life had she seen "a more peculiarly constituted woman."

When Elizabeth Edwards expressed a desire to return to Springfield, the president tearfully urged her to remain: "you have Such a power & control Such an influence over Mary—Come do Stay and Console me." He feared that his wife might have to be sent to a mental hospital.

After two months in Washington, Elizabeth Edwards became restless, as she told her daughter: "I am staying here, much against my inclination, having as Mr & Mrs Lincoln think, no pressing duty at home, whereas they feel that I can do much to mitigate their trials." So Edwards tried to persuade their sister Frances Todd Wallace to help out by sending her young daughter Mary to provide company for the First Lady; a "companion is absolutely necessary," for Mrs. Lincoln "is at times very gloomy." But Frances balked, evidently fearing that her daughter would not be treated well. In addition, she had recently had a falling-out with Mrs. Lincoln. Elizabeth urged Frances to forget the past and help their grieving sister. When that suggestion proved unavailing, Mrs. Edwards tried to persuade her daughter Julia to do some lobbying: "Tell your Aunt Frances not to hesitate, [for] it would be construed as unkindness, should she oppose [her daughter] Mary's coming." After that tactic also failed, Elizabeth gave up and returned to Springfield.

Once Mrs. Edwards left, and it was understood that no replacement would be coming from Illinois, Lincoln appealed to Rebecca Pomroy, the professional nurse who had helped care for Tad. The president arranged to have her transferred from a Washington military hospital to the White House in order to comfort his wife. In her diary, Pomroy noted: "Mrs. Lincoln is very anxious for me to stay here all summer; but if I cannot, always to come here for rest." The pious nurse derived much solace from the Bible and thought that "Mrs. Lincoln needs the comfort of it too. She said she is tired of being a slave to the world and 'would live on bread and water if she could feel as happy as I do.' We have frequent conversations on these things, and my heart yearns to see her seeking comfort in something besides these unstable pleasures." After she returned to her nursing post, Rebecca Pomroy wrote: "Mrs. Lincoln is very anxious that I should leave the hospital and make my home with her, but I do not know what a day may bring forth, and I do not encourage her in the least. I am happy here in doing my duty by those brave men, and would not change places with Mrs. Lincoln for all her honors. She suffers from depression of spirits, but I do think if she would only come here and look at the poor soldiers occasionally it would be better for her."

With Pomroy back at the military hospital, the First Lady turned for companionship to her African American dressmaker Elizabeth Keckly, whose only son had been killed in battle the previous year. Keckly recalled that the First Lady's "grief was inconsolable"; she often said that Willie, "if spared by Providence, would be the hope and stay of her old age." Because Keckly had stoically accepted her own son's death, she was taken aback by the First Lady's excessive grieving. The modiste, however, tried hard to comfort Mrs. Lincoln and encouraged her to consult spiritualists.

Willie's death made his mother especially fearful that something untoward might happen to her remaining sons, Robert and Tad. Many people wondered why Robert, then a student at Harvard, had not joined the army. In fact, he wanted to, but his mother objected. In 1863, Emilie Todd Helm, who was alarmed to find her sister Mary "so nervous and wrought up," told the president that his wife was under "a terrible strain and her smiles seem forced. She is frightened about Robert going into the army." Mrs. Helm recorded in her diary a conversation she overheard between the president and the First Lady:

"Of course, Mr. Lincoln, I know that Robert's plea to go into the army is manly and noble and I want him to go, but oh! I am so frightened he may never come back to us!"

Lincoln replied: "Many a poor mother, Mary, has had to make this sacrifice and has had to give up every son she had—and lost them all."

"'Don't I know that only too well?' cried Mary; 'before this war is ended I may be like my poor mother in Kentucky, with not a prop left in her old age.'" In the closing months of the war, Lincoln arranged to have Robert join General Grant's staff in a position that would likely keep him out of harm's way.

Referring to Willie's death, Elizabeth Edwards wrote her daughter: "What effect, this severe chastisement may have upon her [Mary], time only, will show us." David Davis feared that such chastisement would not "be a lesson" to the First Lady, though he hoped that it "may change her notions of life." It did not.

In May 1862, Charles A. Dana observed that the president "is the most popular man & the most confided in, since Washington. Since the death of his boy led Mrs Abe into retirement, there has been nothing to diminish the public trust and attachment."

MRS. LINCOLN
AND SPIRITUALISM

The death of Willie impelled Mary Lincoln to heed Elizabeth Keckly's advice to consult spiritualists. In addition to Keckly, Isaac Newton of the Agriculture Department encouraged the First Lady's interest in that fad. He would busily talk to her about the subject and escort her "with his old time chivalry and grace" to visit spiritualist mediums.

Newton, the enabler who helped Mrs. Lincoln cover up some of her misdeeds, was a jolly, gossipy sexagenarian farmer and restaurateur from Philadelphia. In 1860, soon after winning the Republican presidential nomination, Lincoln chose him to help deliver the Quaker vote in Pennsylvania and elsewhere. The two men corresponded briefly during the campaign, after which Newton came to Washington in search of a job. There he cultivated Mrs. Lincoln, providing her with fresh produce, much to her delight.

She then urged her husband to give Newton a cushy government post. And so, in August 1861, the president nominated him as chief clerk in the Patent Office's Division of Agriculture, an agency regarded by some as "a perfect Augean stable of corruption and shameless ignorance."

During his tenure at the Patent Office, Newton continued cultivating Mrs. Lincoln, "to whom he paid assiduous and successful suit by the daily presentation of all the delicacies of the season which could be procured in the markets of Washington, Baltimore, Philadelphia, and New York." When members of Congress urged Lincoln to fire Newton, he reportedly said: "I didn't appoint Newton and therefore can't remove him. Mrs. Lincoln appointed him. She has the sole power of removal in his case. You may go see her, if you please, and if she removes him, remove him it shall be, but as long as he continues to send her fresh butter and vegetables, and strawberries out of season, I don't think she will remove him."

To curry favor with the First Lady, Newton did more than provide berries and butter; he also filled her in on the latest gossip, which he shared freely with others as well. In 1862, Attorney General Edward Bates recorded in his diary: "Certainly friend Newton does hear more gossip than anyone I know."

In the spring of 1862, Lincoln nominated Newton to head the recently established Agriculture Department over the protests of the Patent Office staffers, who told the president that "we consider him entirely incompetent and without qualifications for that position. He is totally deficient in Scientific Knowledge of the various subjects which are left to his Control; he has no acquaintance with even the simple elementary principles of Botany Geology or Chemistry and but a limited Knowledge of the English language, not speaking or writing it correctly. His Knowledge of accounts is not sufficient to prevent errors of his own or to detect them in others."

Agricultural journals were equally indignant. The *Ohio Farmer* dismissed Newton as "utterly incompetent" and lamented that "instead of one of the best and ablest men in the nation, he is one of the weakest, most illiterate, and ignorant." The paper described Newton as "a great lubbery old quaker, who has been known as the keeper of an ice cream saloon and truck stop." There was "not a Secretary of a County Agricultural Society in Ohio, who is so great a dunce." Moreover, he "doesn't even know by name the sciences that belong to his department." Newton's appointment "is a great outrage on the farmers of the country." The *Rural New Yorker* complained that he was so ill-educated that he misspelled words like "lettis, shoogar, inons (onions) and sausgee (sausage)." Prominent journalists called him "an ignorant, credulous old gentleman, quite rotund about the waistband," an "amiable old blockhead," a "Philadelphia market gardener," an "ice cream vender and keeper of a low restaurant," and an "artless old muff."

To reward an Indiana Republican for services to the party, congressional Republicans recommended three Hoosiers as candidates to head the new department. Lincoln, however, ignored their suggestions and chose Newton instead, despite a storm of criticism. The Senate confirmed him even though the Patent Committee declined to report his nomination favorably. Ohio senator John Sherman, whose horses and cattle Newton kept and groomed for free, thwarted many attempts to have him removed. "Certain it is," reported the Milwaukee *News*, "that in the face of his known nepotism, lechery, venality, and extraordinary illiteracy, he was continued in his responsible post in defiance of the serious and indignant protests of nearly all of the agricultural organizations in the country."

The Agriculture Department was apparently created at the instigation of a cabal of shady characters who colluded with the First Lady to raid the public treasury and create patronage opportunities. According to Mrs. Lincoln's journalist friend Emily Briggs, some "crafty men put their heads together and decided to call into being a 'Bureau of Agriculture'" whose "different departments were to be 'run,' each one by its particular head, independent of the other," constituting "a cluster of little kingdoms with a nominal head that should be empty of ideas, possessing only one requisite, that of managing Mrs. Lincoln and the appropriation of the public funds."

Those "shrewd men made the good old Quaker Newton believe that he was among the greatest men of the universe," while his department heads "were scattering the worthless seeds broadcast over the country and making up those absurd reports which have brought ridicule on one of the most important branches of the public service."

Newton remained commissioner of the agriculture department until his death in 1867. During his tenure, "Sir Isaac" became an object of ridicule, widely renowned for his malapropisms and ignorance. At Mrs. Lincoln's request, he appointed the young spiritualist Nettie Colburn to a post in the seed room in his department, sewing small seed bags, labor which Colburn derided as a form of make-work.

The First Lady became the easy prey of charlatans who claimed that they could put her in communication with Willie's spirit. On New Year's Eve 1862, she and Newton rode to the Georgetown home of Cranstoun Laurie and his wife Margaret, a prominent spiritualist who, the First Lady said, "made wonderful revelations to her about her little son Willie."

The spiritualist fad had become quite popular during the Civil War. Mrs. Lincoln was a true believer who visited mediums in Washington and invited some of them to the White House. The president did not share her enthusiasm. Ward Hill Lamon often heard Lincoln say "that drinking spirits was like spiritualism to him, he wanted to steer clear of both evils; by frequent indulgence he might acquire a dangerous taste for the spirits and land in a drunkard's grave; by frequent thought of spiritualism he might become a confirmed believer in it and land in a lunatic asylum." Similarly, Lincoln assured Phineas D. Gurley, minister of the Presbyterian church in Washington where the First Family worshipped, that he was no spiritualist. Gurley recalled that the president "was greatly annoyed by the report that he was interested in spiritualism. He told me he thought the report originated from the fact that a medium had chanced to call on Mrs. Lincoln. 'A simple faith in God is good enough for me, and beyond that I do not concern myself very much,' he added."

When Mrs. Lincoln began attending spiritualist séances, the president consulted with the secretary of the Smithsonian Institution, Joseph Henry, who became skeptical after a medium gave an unconvincing demonstration at his office. Another skeptic whose doubts were strengthened by such a demonstration was the journalist Noah Brooks, a good friend of the Lincolns. The First Lady invited him to attend a séance presided over by Charles Colchester, who, according to a Cincinnati newspaper, was "regarded as the leader of Spiritualism in America, and, as a consequence, his votaries, believers, and visitors are counted by the hundreds."

Brooks declined, but because his curiosity had been aroused, he did accept a friend's proposal to attend one of Colchester's séances. In a darkened room, Brooks and the other guests (who had paid a $1 admission fee) joined hands as they sat around a table upon which rested various musical instruments. When those instruments began to play, ostensibly by themselves, the suspicious Brooks broke free from the grip of his seatmates, reached out in the darkness toward the sound of a beating drum, and grabbed something that turned out to be the arm of Colchester, who struck him. When the gas-lights were turned on, the participants beheld the medium with a drumstick and bells in hand, embraced by Brooks, whose forehead was covered in blood. Colchester stormed out, telling his host that he had been so insulted that he would not reappear that evening. The mountebank promptly wrote a note to Mrs. Lincoln in which (according to Brooks) he asked her to "procure for him from the War Department a pass to New York, and intimated that in case she refused he might have some unpleasant things to say to her." It is not clear just which "unpleasant things" Colchester referred to.

The First Lady, "somewhat discomposed" by that blackmail threat, summoned Brooks to the White House and handed him Colchester's note. Brooks devised a scheme to expose the charlatan: she should invite him to visit the Executive Mansion, which he would do, expecting to receive the desired pass, but would instead be confronted by Brooks. She liked that plan, and the following day Colchester called on her by invitation. After introducing him to Brooks, she withdrew, whereupon the journalist lifted the hair covering his head wound and asked: "Do you recognize this?" Colchester mumbled something about being insulted, whereupon Brooks declared: "You know that I know you are a swindler and a humbug. Get out of this house and out of this city at once. If you are in Washington to-morrow afternoon at this time, you will be in the old Capitol prison."

Lincoln may have attended séances to humor his credulous wife or to satisfy his curiosity about the phenomenon, though the evidence is inconclusive. Nettie Colburn claimed many years later that the president attended her sessions, but her testimony is suspect. The First Lady was so impressed with Colburn, who was lecturing around the country, that (as mentioned above) she persuaded Commissioner Newton to appoint Nettie and a fellow spiritualist to positions in his department. Mrs. Lincoln also arranged to have Nettie Colburn's brother, a soldier who was struck ill, granted a furlough. Colburn recalled that Mrs. Lincoln "was ever kind and gracious to me; yet I could never feel for her that perfect respect and reverence that I desired to entertain regarding the chief lady of the land," for "she was lacking in the general control, demeanor, and suavity of manner which we naturally expect from one in [a] high and exalted position."

The First Lady did not always use an intercessor to commune with the departed Willie. In late 1863, when her favorite sister Emilie Todd Helm visited the White House, Mrs. Lincoln told her: "one may not be wholly without comfort when our loved ones leave us. When my noble little Willie was first taken from me, I felt that I had fallen into a deep pit of gloom and despair without a ray of light anywhere. If I had not felt the spur of necessity urging me to cheer Mr. Lincoln, whose grief was as great as my own, I could never have smiled again, and if Willie did not come to comfort me I would still be drowned in tears, and while I long inexpressibly to touch him, to hold him in my arms, and still grieve that he has no future in this world that I might watch with a proud mother's heart—he lives, Emilie!"

MRS. LINCOLN'S
HOSPITAL VISITS

After Willie's death, his mother found solace not only in spiritualism but also in visits to military hospitals. It is not clear just when the First Lady began visiting sick and wounded soldiers, but it seems that before Willie died, she did not undertake such missions of mercy. An admirer of hers, the painter Alban Jasper Conant, recalled that neither she nor the wife of Attorney General Edward Bates "visited the hospitals, a fact which I heard criticized occasionally." Conant was recollecting his time at the capital in 1861 and 1862, so it is likely that Mrs. Lincoln began visiting hospitals after he left town.

Other evidence suggests she did not often visit hospitals before 1863. In August 1862, patients at Finley Hospital (located at Camp Sprague) wrote a public letter expressing some surprise at press accounts indicating that "Mrs. Lincoln has been quietly engaged for some weeks past in a systematic visitation of the hospitals of the city and vicinity." While they did not wish to dispute that report, nonetheless "we, the sick and wounded soldiers occupying several wards in this hospital from two to six weeks past, have not, as yet, had a sight of Mrs. Lincoln." Nor, apparently, had they heard tell of any such visits. If there is any hospital she would be likely to visit, surely it would have been Rebecca Pomroy's, but that nurse indicated that the First Lady had not done so.

Another of Mrs. Lincoln's admirers, Jane Grey Swisshelm, offered two reasons to explain why the First Lady did not regularly visit hospitals. First, she did not want to be in the way. According to Swisshelm, women volunteering to visit hospitals "were generally considered a nuisance by those who were the legally appointed caretakers of the sick and wounded soldiers." When the First Lady did visit hospitals now and then, her gesture "was often treated by surgeons as an impertinent meddling." So she felt dutybound *not* to make hospital visits. Because "her example would be so likely to be followed by other women," it was "easy to understand that she might have been, and no doubt was, made to feel that sick soldiers were better without her attentions." Second, she was too busy meeting the obligations of her official station: "To the place of lady of the White House there are prescribed duties attached, almost as onerous as those of the President, and those who grumbled about Mrs. Lincoln not being in a hospital, would have grumbled still more if she had not been in another place when custom gave them reason to expect to see her there."

There were, in fact, many grumblers. After the war, Mary Clemmer Ames summarized their opinion: "While her sister-women scraped lint, sewed bandages, and put on nurses' caps and gave their all to country and to death, the wife of the President spent her time in rolling to and fro between Washington and New York, intent on extravagant purchases for herself and the White House."

Though the First Lady's visits may have been few, she confided to a friend "that but for these humane employments, her heart would have broken when she lost her child." In June 1862, the press reported that she "has at length sufficiently recovered from her recent severe family bereavement to venture forth and resume her mission of mercy. She visits the hospitals, brings kind gifts and kinder words to our sick and wounded soldiers, and is everywhere welcomed as the fit wife of our beloved President." The following year, the Boston *Journal* praised "her kindness of manner, her goodness of heart, and the generous devotion with which she has tenderly cared for the sick and wounded soldiers."

Lincoln may have encouraged his wife to visit hospitals, at least for the sake of appearances, because she was being criticized for not doing so, as Alban Conant noted. Soon after the First Battle of Bull Run, a leading New York Republican was upset with the First Lady because "now that wounded men pant for Florence Nightingales in Washington *she* is relaxing at Long Branch from—the cares of state." In 1862, an Indiana paper remarked that if Mrs. Lincoln would "visit the sick soldiers who have sacrificed home and happiness to defend the Capital of the nation and the White House against a hostile enemy," she "would then be entitled to the homage and respect of the nation; would become an example to be patterned after by the opulent everywhere, and would cease to be an object of reproach and disgust to all high-minded, democratic, American men and women."

Worried about criticism of the First Lady's shopping expeditions and vacations, Francis Corkran, a prominent Maryland Republican, called on the president in 1863 and observed "that it would be well to have Mrs. Lincoln to return to the White House, and to visit the soldiers in the hospitals, distributing flowers and fruit to the soldiers with her own hands." (From July 20 to September 28, 1863, she was away from the capital, spending much time in New York but also traveling to Massachusetts, New Hampshire, Vermont, and West Point.) According to Corkran's daughter, her father volunteered to supply grapes from his arbor for that purpose. In late September 1863, Lincoln wrote him: "Mrs. L. is now at home & would be pleased to see you any time. If the grape time has not passed away, she would be pleased to join in the enterprize you mentioned." The following month, she did in fact distribute grapes at military hospitals.

Sometimes the president accompanied his wife on hospital visits, though he was more likely to have a cabinet secretary or member of Congress as a companion. The First Lady would occasionally go alone or with Tad. It is difficult to say how often, for the press carried few accounts of such activity. In her surviving correspondence, she referred to such visits only once—in the spring of 1863. She could have won more favor if she had called at hospitals regularly, especially if those occasions had been publicized. William O. Stoddard lamented that reporters seldom joined the First Lady on her hospital excursions: "If she were worldly wise she would carry newspaper correspondents, from two to five, of both sexes, every time she went, and she would have them take shorthand notes of what she says to the sick soldiers and of what the sick soldiers say to her." Alexander Williamson, who tutored Willie and Tad at the White House, similarly observed: "Mrs. Lincoln made no effort to win popular favor." In fact, as the Albany *Evening Journal* remarked in 1869, "Mrs. Lincoln seems determined to separate herself from the sympathies of the people."

A hospital visit she would *not* have wanted publicized was one that she and her husband made to the Virginia front in 1865. There she was observed by a nurse, Sarah Palmer. Just before calling at nurse Palmer's hospital, the First Lady toured one at Point of Rocks, whose officer in charge recalled that she was "richly dressed in black silk" and "was rather large, stout and dignified in appearance. She had been escorted through several of the hospital wards by some of the officers' wives." A few days later, she toured the City Point hospital complex, where nurse Palmer recorded in her diary: "One lady in rich garb sauntered through our worn walks, leaning on the arm of a Congressman, noting what we lacked in our appointments. My bed-tick dress made a sorry contrast to her costly-attired figure, but I looked at my hands, which were not afraid to touch the dirty blouse of a wounded soldier, and wondered if her jeweled fingers would shrink from the contact." Mrs. Lincoln remarked: "There should be a greenhouse yonder," indicating a nearby spot. When someone objected that it would cost too much, she "said disdainfully, 'What of the expense?'" That question shocked nurse Palmer, who wrote: "there were men who had not had a change of clothing in weeks, and to whom the smallest dainty from the cookhouse was sweeter than [anything that] could be concentrated from all the greenhouses in America." The nurse returned to her tent, "sick of folly—sick of fashion—sick of that spectacle of my sex which trailed costly silks and laces in the dry dust." She lamented that "wealth and position transform people into other beings" who sometimes become "insensible to the miseries of poor humanity."

MRS. LINCOLN AND THE CABINET

In addition to messages from Willie's spirit, the First Lady also received political commentary through spiritualist mediums. At Mrs. Laurie's

Georgetown home on New Year's Eve 1862, the spirits announced "that the cabinet were all enemies of the President, working for themselves, and that they would have to be dismissed." Two weeks later, Mrs. Lincoln proclaimed loudly in a social setting that "that there was not a member of the Cabinet" except Postmaster General Montgomery Blair "who did not stab her husband & the Country daily." She qualified her observation by admitting that "she did not know anything about Politics—but her instincts told her that much." In addition to her instincts, the spirits channeled by Mrs. Laurie provided that insight. (Responding to such outbursts from his wife, Lincoln told her: "If I listened to you, I should soon be without a Cabinet.")

The cabinet members whom Mrs. Lincoln most disliked were Secretary of State Seward and Treasury Secretary Chase. Fearing that they would encroach on her husband's turf, she "used often to remark to him, 'These men should realize, Mr. Lincoln, that you are the President,' or 'Don't forget that you are President,' to which Mr. Lincoln would smile and say, 'Never fear, Mary, there is no doubt who is President.'"

When she told him that Seward was unprincipled, he demurred:

"Mother, you are mistaken; your prejudices are so violent that you do not stop to reason. Seward is an able man, and the country as well as myself can trust him."

She replied: "Father, you are too honest for this world! You should have been born a saint. You will generally find it a safe rule to distrust a disappointed, ambitious politician. It makes me mad to see you sit still and let that hypocrite, Seward, twine you around his finger as if you were a skein of thread." She thought that Seward was "capable of *any meanness*," among them spreading unfavorable gossip about her. Elizabeth Keckly reported that the First Lady "rarely lost an opportunity to say an unkind word" about Seward. In early 1863, when Radicals were attacking Seward, she egged them on, remarking "that unless Seward was dismissed, the country would be ruined within three months." She invited Radical Senators Zachariah Chandler and Benjamin F. Wade to confer with her about Seward. In 1865,

Chandler spoke at length to the First Lady and reported that she "hates him [Seward] worse than ever & says the feeling is mutual."

Unlike her husband, Mrs. Lincoln was a good hater. In discussing the possibility of capturing Jefferson Davis, she exclaimed: "Don't let him escape. He must be hanged." The president replied calmly: "Let us judge not that we be not judged." According to a soldier commanding a unit guarding the First Family, Mrs. Lincoln was "one of the best rebel-haters that I met during my stay in Washington."

The First Lady treated Seward and his family rudely when they paid her a courtesy call in September 1861. A White House doorkeeper, Edward McManus, ushered the Sewards into the Blue Room, where they took a seat while he announced their arrival. After a long absence, he returned and told them: "Mrs. Lincoln begged to be excused —she was *very* much engaged." Young Fanny Seward, who thought that this was "the only time on record that she ever refused to see company in the evening," wrote in her diary: "The truth of Mrs. L's engagement was probably that she did not want to see Mother—else why not give general directions to the door keeper to let no one in? It was certainly very rude to have us all seated first." Fanny was probably mistaken, for in all likelihood Mrs. Lincoln desired to snub Seward himself rather than his wife.

Mrs. Lincoln so detested the secretary of state that once she told the White House coachman "in the most emphatic way: 'I won't drive past Seward's house. I won't do it.'" Her husband then "calmly ordered the coachman to drive down a different street than the one he had previously named."

Attorney General Bates heard that there was "a formidable clique organized against Mr. Seward," which, "fearing his adroitness, worked very privily against him." Critics of the secretary of state wanted "to compel his retirement and put Senator [Ira] Harris in his place. It is said that some of them have approached Mrs. Lincoln and not without success, making her believe that Mr. Seward is laboring with persistent effort, to override the Prest. and make himself the chief man of the adm[inistratio]n. They do tell me that she is made fully to believe *that*." Accordingly, she "insulted Seward one day," telling him: "It is Said you are the Power behind the Throne—I'll show you that Mr L[incoln] is President yet." In 1862, Harriet Beecher Stowe called on the First Lady, who "denounced McClellan with a will (Seward also.)"

Mrs. Lincoln was equally contemptuous of Salmon Chase, whose appointment as treasury secretary she had opposed. When he won confirmation, Horace Greeley ascribed his success to the "clear-headed sagacity of Old Abe himself, powerfully backed by Hamlin, who is a jewel. All the Kitchen Cabinet [including Mrs. Lincoln] were dead against him." According to Elizabeth Keckly, Mrs. Lincoln thought (quite reasonably) that Chase was "a selfish politician" and warned her husband "not to trust him too far." Her "hostility to Mr. Chase was very bitter."

One day she said: "Father, I do wish that you would inquire a little into the motives of Chase."

"Mother," he replied, "you are too suspicious. I give you credit for sagacity, but you are disposed to magnify trifles. Chase is a patriot, and one of my best friends."

"Yes, one of your best friends because it is in his interest to be so. He is anything for Chase. If he thought he could make anything by it, he would betray you to-morrow."

"I fear that you are prejudiced against the man, mother. I know that you do him injustice."

"Mr. Lincoln, you are either blind or will not see. I am not the only one that has warned you against him."

"True, I receive letters daily from all parts of the country, telling me not to trust Chase; but then these letters are written by the political enemies of the Secretary, and it would be unjust and foolish to pay any attention to them."

"Very well, you will find out some day, if you live long enough, that I have read the man correctly. I only hope that your eyes may not be opened to the truth when it is too late."

In 1864, when Lincoln had to choose a successor to Chief Justice Roger B. Taney, the First Lady implored Francis P. Blair Sr. to help thwart Chase's candidacy. The former treasury secretary and his allies, she told Blair, "are besieging my Husband for the Chief-Justiceship[.] I wish you could prevent them."

When his wife denounced military officers, Lincoln responded: "Well, mother, supposing that we give you command of the army. No doubt you would do much better than any general that has been tried."

In response to her criticism of others, Lincoln would often tell her: "Do good to those who hate you and turn their ill will to friendship."

In February 1864, Francis Lieber predicted to a leading Republican senator that "Mrs. Lincoln has not done much good to the president, and she will hear of it, I am afraid, in the forthcoming presidential struggle." Indeed, the Democrats made the First Lady's behavior a campaign issue that fall, criticizing her unethical, imperious, and tightfisted ways. Rather than a political asset, Mary Lincoln proved to be a liability to her husband.

Summarizing these various reactions to what defensive biographer Ruth Painter Randall called "Mary's bundle of defects," the journalist Laura Redden Searing concluded that Mrs. Lincoln was unfortunate to find herself "in a situation for which her natural want of tact, and her deficiencies in the sense of the fitness of things, and her blundering outspokenness, and impolitic disregard of diplomatic considerations unfitted her."

Another Washington correspondent, Mary Clemmer Ames, offered a similar explanation to the readers of the Springfield, Massachusetts, *Republican*: "Mrs. Lincoln seemed to have nothing to do but to 'shop,' and the reports of her lavish bargains, in the newspapers, were vulgar and sensational in the extreme." Mrs. Ames concluded that "no other woman of America had ever been vouchsafed so full an opportunity for personal benevolence and philanthropy to her own countrymen. To no other American woman had ever come an equal chance to set a lofty example of self-abnegation to all her country-women. But just as if there were no national peril, no monstrous national debt, no rivers of blood flowing, she seemed chiefly intent upon pleasure, personal flattery and adulation; upon extravagant dress and ceaseless self-gratification. Vain, seeking admiration, the men who fed her weakness for their own political ends were sure of her favor. Thus, while daily disgracing the State by her own example, she still sought to meddle in its affairs." Mrs. Lincoln "was incapable of lofty, impersonal impulse. She was self-centered, and never in any experience rose above herself." Yet another journalist, Sara Jane Lippincott (who used the *nom de plume* Grace Greenwood), lamented that Mrs. Lincoln "certainly lacked worldly wisdom, tact and judgment—fatal lackings in her case." Other women concurred, among them Mary S. Logan, who wrote: "Loftiness of soul, consecrated purpose, broad and profound sympathy, self-sacrificing endeavor—all these, unhappily, were wanting in the character of the Mistress of the White House."

Henry C. Whitney offered a sad commentary on Mrs. Lincoln's unpopularity: "She desired to occupy an exalted position—to be paid court to, to be feted, flattered, admired, stared at, waited on, talked to and about, to be the center of attraction, to make a display, and to wield power. Such things were well known and observed of all men; she not only took no pains to conceal, but she gloried in such vain performances; and she was judged chiefly by those facts apparent to the world, and unsparingly condemned."

12

THE FIRST LADY AND
AFRICAN AMERICANS

Some of Mrs. Lincoln's biographers have deemed her an "ardent abolitionist," but her treatment of African Americans belies that characterization. One of those biographers lamented that while "Lincoln's friendship" with blacks "has been well fixed in the public mind," it was not so well known that "his wife was at one with him in this matter." In fact, she was not.

⌘

At White House receptions, Mrs. Lincoln, unlike her husband, was reluctant to admit black guests. In February 1864, Major Alexander T. Augusta, the African American director of the Freedmen's Hospital—along with his assistant surgeon and protégé, Dr. Anderson R. Abbott (also black)—attended such a reception, where Lincoln received them "kindly" and showed them "marked attention." Dr. Abbott recalled that the official greeter, Benjamin Brown French, welcomed both physicians with "with all the urbanity imaginable" and conducted them to the president. While they exchanged greetings, Lincoln's son Robert, who had been standing nearby alongside of his mother, approached and, as Dr. Abbott remembered, "asked a question very hastily, the purport of which I took to be, 'Are you going to allow this invasion?' referring, doubtless, to our presence there!" (Robert was almost certainly acting at the behest of his mother.) Lincoln responded: "Why not?" Without further ado, Robert retreated to the First Lady's side.

On January 2, 1865, the Washington *Chronicle,* widely viewed as an organ of the Lincoln administration, announced that "all the people present" in the District of Columbia, "of every creed, clime, color and sex, are invited by the President to call upon him" at the New Year's reception that day. African Americans were admitted only briefly, however. According to a Democratic newspaper, a large crowd gathered near the portico of the White House, including several hundred well-dressed blacks. Among them were some clergy and a few soldiers, as well as "the *bon ton* of negro society in Washington." When the front door opened, members of both races surged forward, much to the astonishment of the whites, who had expected the blacks to wait until the white guests had left. Alerted by jeers and curses, police quickly moved to stop the African Americans, who nonetheless persisted in their attempts. Despite the constabulary's best efforts, at least twenty blacks managed to gain entry.

The Lincolns greeted some of their black guests, but not many. According to one press account, when "a colored woman presented herself, Mr. Lincoln shook hands with her, and Mrs. Lincoln gave the invariable bow; on the passage of the second one Mrs. Lincoln looked aghast; and when the third colored woman appeared, Mrs. Lincoln sent word to the door that no more colored persons would be admitted to mingle with the whites. But if they would come at the conclusion of the levee, they should receive the same admittance." Quite a number did so.

The well-known African American abolitionist, Sojourner Truth, tried to meet Mrs. Lincoln but was denied admission to the First Lady's reception on February 25, 1865. A white woman present at that event described how the famous black grandmother "went with Capt. [George] Carse" but "the policemen wd. not allow her to go in to see the President. When I went in she was sitting in the Anteroom waiting for the Capt. to come out. When I said it was too bad, she said 'never mind honey. I don't mind it.' It did not occur to me until too late that I should have gone directly in & told the President. I would like to know what he wd. have said. I cannot think it was done by his orders."

On February 27, when a British journalist told Lincoln that Sojourner Truth had been denied admittance to a White House reception two days earlier, the president "expressed his sorrow, and said he had often seen her, that it should not occur again, and that she should see him the first opportunity: a promise which he kept by sending for her a few days afterward." Although an English paper alleged that "the President has received her several times to a private interview," there is evidence of only one such occasion—on October 29, 1864. Sojourner Truth described it to a friend: "It was about 8 o'clock in the morning when I called on the President," accompanied by the abolitionist Lucy N. Colman. "On entering his reception room, we found about a dozen persons waiting to see him; amongst them two colored women, some white women also." Lincoln "showed as much respect and kindness to the colored persons present as to the whites." When Sojourner Truth praised him as "the best President who has ever taken the seat," he demurred, modestly speculating that his predecessors would have done just as he had done if their circumstances had resembled his. She added that she "never was treated by any one with more kindness and cordiality" than "by that great and good man." As she was about to leave, Lincoln shook her hand

and said he "would be pleased" to have her call again. She felt as if she had been "in the presence of a friend."

A Washington correspondent reported that on March 4, 1865, at the reception following Lincoln's inauguration, "Mrs. Lincoln was very indignant at the intrusion of a number of negroes" and "gave directions to admit no more, and eject those who were admitted." (Among those turned away was Frederick Douglass, who famously managed to gain admission despite her efforts.) That story prompted the Columbus *Ohio Statesman* to remark: "Mr. and Mrs. Lincoln are tenants at the White House upon the strength of the negro's popularity, and now they turn around and exclude him from its precincts."

The First Lady's reluctance to admit African Americans to White House receptions was in keeping with her views on slavery and race. Soon after the election of 1856, during which Lincoln labored tirelessly on behalf of the Republicans' first presidential candidate, John C. Frémont, who ran on a strong antislavery platform, Mrs. Lincoln confided to her Kentucky-based sister Emilie Todd Helm that if she could have voted that year, she would not have supported Frémont but rather Millard Fillmore, standard bearer of the anti-Catholic, anti-immigrant American Party (the Know Nothings): "My weak woman's heart was too Southern in feeling, to sympathize with any but Fillmore, I have always been a great admirer of his, he . . . feels the necessity of keeping foreigners, within bounds. If some of you Kentuckians, had to deal with the 'wild Irish,' as we housekeepers [in Illinois] are sometimes called upon to do, the south would certainly elect Mr Fillmore next time."

Other than that letter, Mrs. Lincoln wrote little about slavery and race, though her views may be inferred from her behavior and the reports of others. She gave a hint of her feelings about racial equality when she indignantly criticized Stephen A. Douglas for his attacks on Lincoln during their 1858 Illinois senatorial contest. She told her sister Emilie: "How foolish for Douglas to think that because you demand justice for the negro you are in favor of abolition or that you would ever, in any event, countenance social equality with a race so far inferior to your own." The expression "a race so far inferior to your own" indicates that she shared the belief, widely held among whites, that blacks were "far inferior" to them.

Mrs. Lincoln also seems to have shared the notion popular among whites that African Americans (whom she referred to as "darkies") were lazy; she wrote a letter of recommendation for a black woman who, she said, "although colored, is very industrious."

During the Civil War, Mrs. Lincoln evidently did not change her mind about slavery and blacks, even though the abolitionist-feminist Jane Grey Swisshelm claimed that she was "more radically opposed to slavery" than her husband, whom the First Lady allegedly urged to support emancipation "as a matter of right, long before he saw it as a matter of necessity." Historian Mark Neely has persuasively argued that Mrs. Swisshelm's assertion "was almost certainly wrong," though "it has had remarkable staying power and has been given considerable prominence by those modern writers bent on reviving Mary Lincoln's reputation." The "fact of the matter is that Mary's political views were so shallow and her political instincts so worthless that she had no discernable *political* influence on her husband."

Moreover, no evidence supports Mrs. Lincoln's 1867 statement that "I never failed to urge my husband to be an *extreme* Republican." As historian Brian Dirck noted, it is "impossible to know what she shared with her husband in terms of their respective perceptions of African Americans and slavery. . . . There is no reliable record of any conversations concerning the peculiar institution that may have passed between them."

And yet there is some testimony about a conversation the First Couple had regarding emancipation. Their son Robert reportedly said that his mother "was very much opposed to the signing of the Emancipation Proclamation." As the president made a fair copy of that historic document, she interrupted him, "inquiring in her sharp way, 'Well, what do you intend?'" He allegedly replied: "I am a man under orders, I cannot do otherwise."

That seems plausible in light of a contemporary press account. In November 1862, a Philadelphia journalist reported that the First Lady had consistently advised her husband not to issue an emancipation decree: "It is not generally known that it was Mrs. Lincoln's influence which . . . kept the President straight on the constitutional questions involved in the slavery business. This distinguished lady, as I well know, has not the slightest doubt that slavery in slave States is protected by the constitution." She "does not hesitate to say, in a frank and open way, that she hopes never to see the day when Abraham Lincoln will occupy the same platform with Jefferson Davis, and break up the constitution to destroy slavery."

This jibes with the First Lady's few surviving comments about public affairs. At Baltimore in February 1861, she told her hosts that "being a Kentuckian," she "was sometimes too conservative for some of Mr. Lincoln's friends." Soon thereafter in Washington, she made "no secret of her conservative opinions." To the historian George Bancroft, she confided that she was "a conservative." After chatting with the First Lady in 1863, Pennsylvania Congressman James H. Campbell described her as "an ordinary woman with strong likes, and dislikes, and with bitter prejudices. She prides herself on being a 'little Southern'" and "hates the angular Yankees."

To be sure, in 1866 Mrs. Lincoln did sing the praises of emancipation in a letter to Charles Sumner, the Senate's foremost Radical. Nothing in the historical record, however, indicates that she strongly favored the Emancipation Proclamation *before* she wrote that. Only after the war did she laud it to that abolitionist senator who flattered her and championed her effort to win a government pension.

Mrs. Swisshelm asserted that Mary Lincoln's "sympathies were with the radical Abolitionists from the first to the last of the War of the Rebellion," but Sumner was the only one of that faction whom she befriended. No other leading Radical attended her soirees, formed part of her coterie, or corresponded with her. Moreover, she was close to none of the more Radical cabinet members or their wives; in fact, she disparaged "some two or three" cabinet secretaries whom she called "ambitious fanatics" (a dig at Chase) and contemptuously referred to Seward as an "Abolition sneak." The cabinet member she seems to have liked best was the most conservative one, Montgomery Blair. The political wives whom she befriended were married to conservatives like Navy Secretary Gideon Welles and Connecticut Senator James Dixon. Moreover, abolitionist newspapers were critical of her, whereas her staunchest press supporter was the conservative New York *Herald*, with whose proprietor/editor and his wife she was friendly. She had no such relationship with Radical editors.

Mrs. Lincoln's most intimate friend and confidante in Washington was her dressmaker, Elizabeth Keckly, a former slave who had worked for prominent families in the capital. According to Jennifer Fleischner, during Mary's childhood, the formidable slave known as Mammy Sally was her "maternal haven, her most consistent adult caretaker. Sally had nursed her before her mother's death [when Mary was six] and remained loyal in her affections after her mother died, and her relatively uninterrupted presence would have consoled a little girl in the midst of the emotional chaos in which she seems to have lived." Some of the deep affection that she felt for Mammy Sally appears to have predisposed Mrs. Lincoln to make her African American seamstress a confidante. With Mrs. Keckly, the First Lady shared secrets that would prove embarrassing when revealed in the dressmaker's 1868 memoir, *Behind the Scenes, or, Thirty Years a Slave and Four Years in the White House.* According to Rosetta Welles, another black woman employed at the White House, Elizabeth Keckly "was the only person in Washington who could get along with Mrs. Lincoln when she became mad with anybody for talking about her and criticizing her husband." In 1862, Mrs. Keckly founded the Relief Association for the Contrabands in the District of Columbia, to which the First Lady, to her credit, contributed $200, fifteen boxes of clothing, and $10 worth of groceries. (The $200 came not from her own family's pocket but from a $1,000 fund established by a philanthropist.)

In general, however, the relationship between the two women was that of a mistress-and-servant, which—no matter how close—was not one of true social equality. As Donna McCreary, who has spent years studying and writing about Mrs. Lincoln, noted: "Many of the letters Mary wrote to Keckly have the tone of something written to an employee, not a dear friend." The abolitionist Lucy Colman noted disapprovingly that Mrs. Keckly "always dressed her (Mrs. Lincoln) for the receptions, but was never permitted to go into the house as a caller." At times, the First Lady sharply reprimanded her modiste: "you have disappointed me—deceived me," she complained when a dress was not finished on time. Mrs. Keckly tried to explain, but she was told once again: "you have bitterly disappointed me." (The First Lady similarly rebuked a milliner: "I am surprised to find that you have sent me no flowers - the bonnet is perfectly useless. . . . I did not suppose you would treat me thus.") After the publication of Elizabeth Keckly's *Behind the Scenes*, Mrs. Lincoln cut off all contact with her dressmaker, ending their seven-year-long relationship.

Mrs. Lincoln had a contentious relationship with the White House staff, whom she referred to as "menials." A historian of the Executive Mansion noted that the "queenly reserve she affected was quickly recognized by the servants as an effort to disguise her insecurities. She could seldom hold her tongue, and entered readily into open conflicts." A case in point was her strained relations with a White House laundress, not to mention her dealings with servants in Springfield (Chapter 5). African American staff members in the White House recalled that the First Lady was agreeable "when she was not sick with the dreadful headaches she used to have and was not worried about the war and things in general." (She often had headaches and "worried about the war and things in general.") One of those servants, Rosetta Welles, said that Mrs. Lincoln related to black employees, who constituted a minority of the White House staff, with some difficulty; she "had her ways, but nobody minded her, for she would never hurt a flea, and her bark was worse than her bite." She evidently did a lot of barking;

according to historians of the daily life of First Families, "White House servants who could not abide her outbursts quit." The role of steward was held by five different people during Lincoln's administration.

Perhaps Rosetta Welles was alluding to the First Lady's mercurial nature, which caused a sympathetic White House secretary, William O. Stoddard, to wonder "why a lady who could one day be so kindly, so considerate, so generous, could, upon another day, appear so unreasonable, so irritable, so despondent, so even niggardly, and so prone to see the dark, the wrong side of men and women and events."

Historian Brian Dirck has suggested that "Mary Lincoln wrought a little revolution in the way black people were treated at the White House." Just as her husband "granted unprecedented access to African American leaders like Sojourner Truth and Frederick Douglass," so allegedly "Mary did much the same, and with far less fanfare." Her purportedly revolutionary step was to invite "an African American teacher for an afternoon tea at the White House."

But the story of that supposed *tête-à-tête* is dubious. It first appeared in Ishbel Ross's 1953 popular biography of Kate Chase Sprague, which contains no footnotes, so the source of the author's information cannot be checked. This tale was repeated in Catherine Clinton's 2009 biography of Mrs. Lincoln, which merely cites Ross's undocumented book. A biographer of Mrs. Sprague plausibly observed that "there is good reason to doubt this story." Ishbel Ross did not include that episode in her later, defensive biography of Mary Lincoln. The teacher who reportedly took tea at the White House, "Rebecca Orville," is unknown to history. Her name appears neither in searchable newspapers and public records of the time nor in subsequent historical works. The school where she supposedly taught is unnamed. Moreover, it seems out of character for Mrs. Lincoln to treat a black person as a social equal.

If the First Lady really had invited a black person to tea, it would indeed have constituted "a little revolution in the way black people were treated at the White House," for neither she nor her husband hosted an African American at a private social occasion like a tea or a meal. But in the late summer of 1864, Lincoln did invite Frederick Douglass to tea at the Soldiers' Home, where the First Family resided during the warmer months. Because of a prior engagement, Douglass regretfully declined.

Douglass did meet with Lincoln thrice at the White House, and he recalled that each time the president received him cordially and respectfully. Partly as a result of those visits, Douglass termed Lincoln "emphatically the black man's president: the first to show any respect for their rights as men" and "the first American President who . . . rose above the prejudice of his times, and country."

As the evidence adduced above indicates, his wife had not risen "above the prejudice of her times and country."

13

THE FIRST LADY HUMILIATES LINCOLN

A s noted in chapter 4, Mrs. Lincoln early in her marriage "seemed to take a special delight in contradicting her husband, and humiliating him on every occasion." She continued to humiliate him during his presidency, though not on every occasion.

◆

A striking example occurred on February 22, 1864, at the opening of a charity fair in Washington to benefit the Christian Commission. Lincoln's Illinois friend, General Richard J. Oglesby, had persuaded him to attend the event only after assuring the president that he would not have to speak. When the official ceremony ended, "there was a universal clapping of hands for the President to come forward." It was "so long and so earnest that several gentlemen on the stage went to him to persuade him to gratify the general desire." He hesitated "some moments before he would allow himself to be moved at all, and when he did rise and come forward, it was evidently with very great reluctance." The president "was looking extremely pale and worn, but smiled good-naturedly" and delivered a few extemporaneous remarks. He said "that he thought the Committee who had invited him to be present had practiced a little fraud upon him, as no intimation had been given that he would be expected to say a word. He was unprepared for a speech, and felt that after the eloquent address [by Lucius Chittenden] and poem [written and delivered by Benjamin Brown French] to which the audience had listened, any attempt of his would be a failure; besides, from the position he occupied everything that he said necessarily went into print, therefore, it was advisable that he should say nothing foolish. It was very difficult to say sensible things. In speaking without preparation he might make some bad mistake, which, if published, would do both the nation and himself harm. Therefore, he would only say that he thanked the managers of the fair for the persevering manner in which they had prosecuted the enterprise for so good an object, and with this expression of his gratitude, he hoped they would accept his apology and excuse him from speaking.'"

Afterward, while the First Couple and General Oglesby were awaiting their carriage, Mrs. Lincoln told her husband: "That was the worst speech I ever listened to in my life. How any man could get up and deliver such remarks to an audience is more than I can understand. I wanted the earth to sink and let me go through." The president made no reply, and the trio returned to the White House in silence.

Oregon senator George H. Williams recalled a similar outburst. Williams had met Lincoln in 1847 when they both served as delegates to a Rivers and Harbor Convention at Chicago. Williams moved to Washington in 1864 as a senator-elect and renewed his acquaintance. As he recalled, Lincoln "was very cordial in his greeting, and I had the pleasure of meeting and riding out with him and Mrs. Lincoln on several occasions." On one of them, Williams was "treated the entire ride with upbraiding and a tirade from Mrs. Lincoln," throughout which the president sat "with tired, worn, patient face, saying not a word."

The most humiliating episodes of this sort occurred as a result of Mrs. Lincoln's inordinate jealousy. According to Mary Clemmer Ames, the First Lady "could not bear a rival, and was never known to invite as a continuous guest at the White House any woman younger or fairer than herself." The journalist J. K. C. Forrest reported that early in her husband's administration, Mrs. Lincoln had admitted to her circle Julia Edwards Baker and Mrs. Donn Piatt, both of whom were quite beautiful. The First Lady, however, quickly expelled them because she had "become jealous of their good looks and of their monopoly of the admiration of the masculine portion of the court, a part of which Mrs. L[incoln] thought ought to have been bestowed on herself." Forrest commented: "This was one of the many trials of this description with which the president, overborne as he was by others of this description, was compelled to [undergo.]" Elizabeth Keckly, who described Mrs. Lincoln as "extremely jealous," noted that "if a lady desired to court her displeasure, she could select no surer way to do it than to pay marked attention to the President. These little jealous freaks often were a source of perplexity to Mr. Lincoln." Keckly recalled that once, as the Lincolns prepared for a reception, the president asked his wife:

"Well, mother, who must I talk with to-night—shall it be Mrs. [Adele] D[ouglas]?"

"That deceitful woman! No, you shall not listen to her flattery."

"Well, then, what do you say to Miss [Kate] C[hase]? She is too young and handsome to practise deceit."

"Young and handsome, you call her! You should not judge beauty for me. No, she is in league with Mrs. D., and you shall not talk with her."

"Well, mother, I must talk with some one. Is there any one that you do not object to?"

"I don't know as it is necessary that you should talk to anybody in particular. You know well enough, Mr. Lincoln, that I do not approve of your flirtations with silly women, just as if you were a beardless boy, fresh from school."

"But, mother, I insist that I must talk with somebody. I can't stand around like a simpleton, and say nothing. If you will not tell me who I may talk with, please tell me who I may *not* talk with."

"There is Mrs. D. and Miss C. in particular. I detest them both. Mrs. B. also will come around you, but you need not listen to her flattery. These are the ones in particular."

"Very well, mother; now that we have settled the question to your satisfaction, we will go down-stairs."

The First Lady objected to the custom dictating that at White House receptions the president should promenade with some woman other than his spouse: "Now it occurs to me that this custom is an absurd one," she told Keckly. "On such occasions our guests recognize the position of the President as first of all; consequently, he takes the lead in everything; well, now, if they recognize his position they should also recognize mine. I am his wife, and should lead with him. And yet he offers his arm to any other lady in the room, making her first with him and placing me second. The custom is an absurd one, and I mean to abolish it. The dignity that I owe to my position, as Mrs. President, demands that I should not hesitate any longer to act."

The "Miss C" with whom the First Lady did not want her husband to converse was Treasury Secretary Chase's beautiful young daughter Kate, who vied with the First Lady for the leadership of Washington society. Adolphe Pineton noted that Kate Chase "has a reputation for wit and beauty which the Washington ladies are rather impatient of." Unlike her husband, Mrs. Lincoln refused to attend the gala wedding of Kate Chase to Rhode Island senator William Sprague, a major social event. A visitor in Washington at the time reported that Mrs. Lincoln and the president argued about the matter, "and the music of her voice penetrated the utmost end of the house."

At an earlier White House event, the First Lady reportedly told Kate Chase that she "hoped she would call again soon." To this invitation, Chase "haughtily replied that she had generally been at home, and that if Mrs. Lincoln had wished to see her she could most probably have done so by returning her previous call."

In January 1864, the First Lady refused to add the names of Secretary Chase, his daughter, and her spouse to the guest list for a cabinet dinner. When Lincoln overruled that decision, there "soon arose such a rampage as the House hasn't seen for a year," according to John G. Nicolay. Mrs. Lincoln's rage made another White House secretary, William O. Stoddard, cower "at the volume of the storm." Nicolay too was buffeted by it; as he told John Hay, "after having compelled Her S[atanic] Majesty to invite the Spragues I was taboo, and she made up her mind resolutely not to have me at the dinner." She persisted in keeping Nicolay on the sidelines, he reported, "till the afternoon of the dinner when Edward [McManus] came up to tell me that she had backed down, requested my presence and assistance—apologizing, and explaining that the affair had worried her so [much] she hadn't slept for a night or two. I think she has felt happier since she cast out that devil of stubbornness."

Journalists played up the rivalry between Kate Chase and Mrs. Lincoln. In 1863, the Dayton, Ohio, *Empire* reported that the "Lincoln-Chase contest [for the 1864 Republican presidential nomination] has extended into the women's department. Mrs. Lincoln has got a new French rig with all the posies, costing $4000. Miss Kate Chase 'sees her and goes one better,' by ordering a nice little $6000 arrangement, including a $3000 love of a shawl."

One day Mrs. Lincoln grew enraged at a tall, beautiful Connecticut woman who visited the White House to press a claim. There the caller fell to her knees, hugged the president's legs, and was pleading her case when the First Lady entered and "jumped at conclusions. 'Out of the room, you baggage,' she cried, and going into the hall she shouted to Edward, one of the household servants, 'Put this woman out and never admit her again.'" Lincoln told Congressman Henry C. Deming of Hartford: "Send that long-legged woman back to Connecticut and keep her there."

At one White House levee, a woman known for her beauty chatted with the president during a brief pause in the reception ceremony. The First Lady observed her "with no amiable eye" and instructed a servant to "go tell that woman to stop talking to Mr. Lincoln, and that if she didn't know her place, she'd better learn it." Upon receiving this message, the woman replied in a voice loud enough for Mrs. Lincoln to hear: "Tell your mistress that I shall talk to the president as long as courtesy allows. Tell her, too, that I not only know my place, but hers, and that as long as I keep mine I will make her keep hers."

In the spring of 1863, Mrs. Lincoln grew jealous of officers' wives when the First Couple visited the Army of the Potomac, then commanded by Joseph Hooker. Lincoln called at the headquarters of General Daniel Sickles's Third Corps near Falmouth, Virginia. There he found himself besieged by a few spouses of officers, among them the beautiful eighteen-year-old wife of a Prussian prince, Colonel Felix Constantin Alexander Johann Nepomuk of Salm-Salm. The princess recalled that General Sickles "proposed to appoint for the time of the [presidential] visit some ladies of honour to attend on Mrs. Lincoln. This plan was, however, not to the liking of the American ladies, each of whom thought herself quite as sovereign as the wife of the President." Evidently sensing the coolness of those women, Mrs. Lincoln remained at headquarters while her husband attended Sickles's collation.

Upon the president's arrival, Princess Salm Salm asked Sickles *sotto voce*: "General, he is a dear, good man, we want to kiss him; would it do any harm?"

Sickles replied: "Not a bit of harm. I am only sorry not to be in his place."

According to Mrs. Daniel Butterfield, wife of General Hooker's chief of staff, the princess glanced "toward the ladies following in her train," who "quickly surrounded Mr. Lincoln, embracing and kissing him with eagerness and fervor." Surprised by this friendly onslaught, Lincoln "could not have been more helpless, or more confused, yet he smiled and laughed, and seemed warmly touched by this public expression of hearty, sincere admiration and sympathy."

According to Sickles, when Tad informed his mother of this episode, she "was quite furious about it, and she gave the President a curtain lecture [i.e., a bawling out] which lasted throughout most of the night, and which was easily heard by the officers nearby guarding the tent."

"No matter how strongly he protested his innocence, his good wife could not be quieted," Mrs. Butterfield reported.

"But, mother, hear me," Lincoln pleaded.

"Don't mother me," she replied angrily, "and as for General Sickles, he will hear what I think of him and his lady guests. It was well for him that I was not there at the time."

All the next day, Mrs. Lincoln "would have nothing to say" to Sickles. The president "noticed her freezing coldness whenever Sickles was present, and did all he could to relieve the embarrassment."

Also eager to relieve the embarrassment was General Hooker, who assigned Sickles to accompany the First Couple back to Washington. En route, as Sickles recalled, everything "went well until supper was announced. Seated at the table in a private cabin, face to face with Mrs. Lincoln, I at once saw how much I was out of favor. I was not recognized. The president tried his best to put his good wife in a better temper, but in vain; she evaded every overture, even the amusing anecdotes he related with characteristic tact and humor. Not a smile softened her stern features. At last Lincoln turned to me, exclaiming:

"Sickles, I never knew you were such a pious man until I came down this week to see the army."

"I am quite sure, Mr. President, I do not merit the reputation, if I have gained it."

"Oh, yes, they tell me you are the greatest Psalmist in the army. They say you are more than a Psalmist—they say you are a Salm-Salmist."

"That was more than Mrs. Lincoln could resist," Sickles recalled. "She joined in the hearty laugh" and "peace was restored."

This contretemps foreshadowed a more volcanic eruption of jealous rage that occurred in 1865 at City Point, Virginia, where the Army of the Potomac was then based. Feeling sorry for the careworn president, General Grant invited him to visit the front. Lincoln accepted and had Assistant Secretary of the Navy Gustavus Fox make the necessary arrangements. Fox asked Captain John S. Barnes, commander of the USS *Bat*, a swift blockade enforcer, if his vessel would be suitable for the president. When Barnes replied that it could be made so, Fox escorted him to the White House for instructions. "I'm only a fresh-water sailor and I guess I have to trust you salt-water folks when afloat," Lincoln said, adding that he "wanted no luxuries but only plain, simple food and ordinary comfort."

Next day, however, Lincoln told Captain Barnes that more deluxe accommodations were necessary, for the First Lady had decided to join him and would be accompanied by a maidservant. Barnes recalled that as Lincoln explained the need to revise the earlier plans, he had "a certain look of embarrassment and a look of sadness which struck me forcibly and rather embarrassed me. He appeared tired and worried." (Mrs. Lincoln insisted on joining her husband, "much against the very apparent wishes of the President," according to Barnes, who spoke with both the Lincolns.) After Barnes told Fox that the *Bat* was unsuitable for female passengers, they chartered the *River Queen*, a side-wheeled passenger ship, despite Barnes's fear "that the President was incurring great risk in making the journey on an unarmed, fragile river-boat, so easily assailed and so vulnerable." Confederates had recently sunk the *River Queen's* sister ship with a bomb resembling a lump of coal. Fox told Barnes how much he regretted "that the determination of Mrs. Lincoln to accompany the President had made the *Bat* an impossible home for him and his family party."

On March 23, Lincoln, along with his wife and their son Tad, boarded the *River Queen* and set sail for City Point, escorted by the *Bat*. The next evening, they reached their destination, where they were greeted by Grant and his wife. The general and the president then retired to discuss military affairs.

A journalist reported that the First Lady received Mrs. Grant "coldly" and "rather haughtily." The general's wife offended her hostess by sitting down next to her, prompting Mrs. Lincoln to exclaim: "How dare you be seated until I invite you!"

Captain Barnes gave a fuller version of this episode, though he placed it a few days later aboard a boat taking the presidential party on a sightseeing excursion: "I witnessed the interview between these two women, and saw that it was exciting; Mrs. Lincoln talking excitedly; Mrs. Grant gradually but in a low, gentle voice and quiet dignified manner, becoming for her, emphatic. As she joined Mrs. Lincoln she sat upon one of the stools, Mrs. Lincoln standing; whereupon Mrs. Lincoln accused her of want of etiquette, in sitting in the presence of the President's wife, without being invited—that such action was not respectful—contrary to White House usage, that if Mrs. Grant ever came to Washington she would learn what etiquette demanded. Mrs. Grant, who repeated to me the conversation, replied that if Mrs. Lincoln was the wife of the President, she was the wife of the General in Command of the armies of the United States, who could be President of the United States if he wished, and that she would sit down anywhere if she thought it more agreeable than to stand in any one's presence. Whereupon Mrs. Lincoln asserted that she had observed Mrs. Grant and me 'laughing at her.'"

The First Lady would soon react with equal indignation to other perceived affronts. One day, Mrs. Grant sent the president a bouquet, which made Mrs. Lincoln "furiously angry, and a lively scene ensued." Her sense of entitlement led the First Lady to insist that the *River Queen* be berthed next to the dock, even though Grant's headquarters boat, the *Carrie Martin*, had been assigned that position. Those two vessels had been placed side by side, but Mrs. Lincoln refused to traverse "Mrs. Grant's boat" in order to reach the dock. So, according to Captain Barnes, "several times the *Martin* was pushed out and the *Queen* in, requiring some work and creating confusion, despite Mr. Lincoln's expostulations."

Sylvanus Cadwallader, a journalist whose wife was friendly with Mrs. Grant, recalled that the First Lady "seemed insanely jealous of every person, and everything, which drew him [the president] away from her and monopolized his attention for an hour." She often dispatched Tad to summon his father back to the *River Queen*. One day the youngster, after an unsuccessful attempt to deliver such a message, interrupted Lincoln as he was engaged in an animated conversation: "Come, come, come now, mama says you must come instantly." Lincoln's face fell, he hesitated briefly, then stood up and asked rhetorically: "My God, will that woman never understand me?" He "meekly, and sadly" returned to the *River Queen* with his son.

On March 26, Lincoln rode with Grant and General E. O. C. Ord to review Ord's troops. The First Lady and Mrs. Grant, accompanied by the commanding general's aides Adam Badeau and Horace Porter, followed them in a field ambulance, which had insufficient room for Mrs. Ord, "a remarkably handsome woman, and a most accomplished equestrienne." So she rode alongside their vehicle, escorted by Captain Barnes. When the president learned that Ord's men had long been awaiting his arrival, he urged his party (including Mrs. Ord and Barnes) to hasten forward, leaving the party in the ambulance to catch up later.

Meanwhile, as Major Badeau conversed with the First Lady and Mrs. Grant, he accurately predicted that a battle would soon take place, for Grant had ordered to the rear the wives of all other officers, he said, except Mrs. Charles Griffin. (She was "one of the best known and most elegant women in Washington," widely "celebrated in the national capital for her beauty.") Badeau explained that the twenty-seven-year-old former Sarah "Sallie" Carroll, a member of the illustrious Carroll family of Maryland, had received special permission from the president.

The news about Mrs. Griffin angered the First Lady. "What do you mean by that, sir?" she asked Major Badeau indignantly. "Do you mean to say that she saw the President alone? Do you know that I never allow the President to see any woman alone? Let me out of this carriage at once. I will ask the President if he saw that woman alone." Mrs. Grant tried to come to the aid of poor Badeau, who hesitated when the First Lady told him to order a halt. Impatient with his delay, she seized the driver, but Mrs. Grant and Colonel Porter cajoled her into staying in the vehicle until they reached their destination.

During a brief pause, General George G. Meade, unaware of the tense situation, temporarily replaced Badeau and Porter as the women's escort. Upon returning to the ambulance, the First Lady glared at Badeau and remarked: "General Meade is a gentleman, sir. He says it was not the President who gave Mrs. Griffin the permit, but the Secretary of War."

During that delay, Mrs. Ord and Barnes forged ahead. She, like Mrs. Griffin, had permission to remain at the front. On her high-spirited mount she rode alongside Lincoln while the First Lady's ambulance wended its way toward the reviewing site. Badeau recalled that as "soon as Mrs. Lincoln discovered this her rage was beyond all bounds. 'What does the woman mean,' she exclaimed, 'by riding by the side of the President? and ahead of me? Does she suppose that *he* wants *her* by the side of *him*?' She was in a frenzy of excitement, and language and action both became more extravagant every moment."

The First Lady grew still more angry when Mrs. Grant tried once again to calm her down. Rhetorically she asked: "I suppose you think you'll get to the White House yourself, don't you?" Julia Grant replied that she was content with her present situation. "Oh!" exclaimed Mrs. Lincoln, "you had better take it if you can get it. 'Tis very nice."

Making this awkward situation still worse, an officer drew up beside the ambulance and innocently observed: "The President's horse is very gallant, Mrs. Lincoln; he insists on riding by the side of Mrs. Ord."

"What do you mean by that, sir?" Mrs. Lincoln asked heatedly. The abashed officer promptly slunk away. When the ambulance finally reached Ord's headquarters, that general's wife rode up to greet it.

As Badeau recalled, the First Lady "positively insulted" Mrs. Ord, "called her vile names in the presence of a crowd of officers, and asked what she meant by following the President. The poor woman burst into tears and inquired what she had done, but Mrs. Lincoln refused to be appeased, and stormed till she was tired. Mrs. Grant still tried to stand by her friend, and everybody was shocked and horrified."

Captain Barnes had a similar recollection: Mrs. Ord, whom he had been escorting, "asked me whether it was proper for her to accompany the reviewing party. I didn't know, but one of the staff said 'of course, come along!' and we fell in to the rear. Half way down Mrs. Ord exclaimed: 'Oh, Captain, there come Mrs. Lincoln and Mrs. Grant; I think I had better join them,' and running out of the crowd, we galloped over to the side of the ambulance, where Mrs. Ord attempted to express regret at their delay. I saw there was trouble. Porter and Badeau were glum. Mrs. Lincoln was simply furious with anger; Mrs. Grant silent and unhappy. I will not repeat Mrs. Lincoln's remarks, levelled at Mrs. Ord and at me. They can only be attributed to an unbalanced mind. Mrs. Ord was petrified, only uttering painfully, 'Oh, Mrs. Lincoln, what have I done?', and as Mrs. Lincoln said she would have me dismissed from the Navy, we both backed out of hearing absolutely dumb with astonishment. There were other victims of her displeasure after the review ended. Mrs. Ord joined the General, and I made my way back to City Point on horseback, sore and discomforted, Mr. and Mrs. Lincoln returning to the *River Queen*."

At supper that night, "Mrs. Lincoln berated General Ord to the President, and urged that he should be removed. He was unfit for his place, she said, to say nothing of his wife."

Around 11 P.M., the First Lady demanded that her husband summon Barnes, who was fast asleep. Upon receiving the message, the captain arose and hastened to the president, who, he recalled, "seemed weary and greatly distressed, with an expression of sadness that seemed the accentuation of the shadow of melancholy which at times so marked his features." Mrs. Lincoln, who did most of the talking, "objected very strenuously to the presence of other ladies at the review that day, and had thought that Mrs. Ord had been too prominent in it, that the troops were led to think that she was the wife of the President, who had distinguished her with too much attention." Lincoln "very gently suggested that he had hardly remarked the presence of the lady, but Mrs. Lincoln was hardly to be pacified and appealed to me to support her views." Barnes, who could scarcely be expected to mediate the dispute, tried to remain neutral by simply recounting what he had seen.

In another version of his reminiscences, Barnes wrote: "Mr. Lincoln was the saddest man I ever saw. The conversation which ensued will not bear repeating. The general purport was that Mrs. Ord had, to Mrs. Lincoln's mind, very improperly conducted herself on the review, had made herself too conspicuous, had tried to pass herself off as the wife of the President. Mr. Lincoln said he hardly noticed her presence, a remark not received kindly. Mrs. Lincoln appealed to me to corroborate her impressions. The interview lasted some twenty minutes, with all shades of argument and assertions. It was extremely painful to the President, and I think I discovered the cause of that vein of sadness which so often was observed in the expression of the features of this gentlest and most affectionate man. I asked permission to retire, backed out, the President bidding me good night sadly."

According to Badeau, Mrs. Lincoln over the next few days "repeatedly attacked her husband in the presence of officers because of Mrs. Griffin and Mrs. Ord." The contretemps dismayed Badeau, who wrote: "I never suffered greater humiliation and pain . . . than when I saw the Head of State, the man who carried all the cares of the nation at such a crisis—subjected to this inexpressible public mortification." Lincoln "bore it as Christ might have done; with an expression of pain and sadness that cut one to the heart, but with supreme calmness and dignity." With "old-time plainness" he called his wife "mother." He also "pleaded with eyes and tones, and endeavored to explain or palliate the offenses of others, till she turned on him like a tigress; and then he walked away, hiding that noble, ugly face that we might not catch the full expression of its misery."

Captain Barnes echoed Badeau: "I was not the only one who had come under Mrs. Lincoln's displeasure, and her mental condition was a matter of discussion; the general conclusion being that her mind was unbalanced. She was at no time well, the mental strain upon her was excessive, evidenced by hysteria, misapprehensions, extreme sensitiveness as to supposed slights or want of politeness or consideration on the part of others about her. I had great sympathy for her and greater for Mr. Lincoln, who I know felt great anxiety for her. His manner towards her was always marked by the most affectionate solicitude, that no one seeing them together could fail to be impressed by it, and on his account made every allowance for the frequent eccentricities marking her intercourse with the distinguished officers and civilians who every day visited the President."

At a subsequent dinner party, Elizabeth Keckly heard a young captain, "by way of pleasantry," tell Mrs. Lincoln: "you should have seen the President the other day, on his triumphal entry into Richmond. He was the cynosure of all eyes. The ladies kissed their hands to him, and greeted him with the waving of handkerchiefs. He is quite a hero when surrounded by pretty young ladies." That officer "suddenly paused with a look of embarrassment. Mrs. Lincoln turned to him with flashing eyes, with the remark that his familiarity was offensive to her. Quite a scene followed, and I do not think that the Captain who incurred Mrs. Lincoln's displeasure will ever forget that memorable evening." (Mary Harlan similarly recalled that at a dinner party a little later, a young officer described an episode that took place on the president's tour of Richmond: all doors were closed to Lincoln save one, which "was opened furtively and a fair hand extended a bunch of flowers, which he took." Mrs. Lincoln "made manifest her dislike of the story, much to the narrator's chagrin.")

Over the next several days, the First Lady repeatedly snubbed Julia Grant. Though the general's boat was adjacent to the Lincolns', Mrs. Grant was frozen out of their circle. As she later wrote, "I saw very little of the presidential party now, as Mrs. Lincoln had a good deal of company and seemed to have forgotten us. I felt this deeply and could not understand it, as my regard for the family was not only that of respect but affection." She was particularly hurt by her failure to receive an invitation to accompany the presidential entourage on excursions to Richmond and Petersburg.

On April 1, Mrs. Lincoln returned to Washington, escorted by General Carl Schurz. In the manuscript version of his autobiography, he stated that he had "misgivings" about accepting the invitation to accompany her: "I had not come into contact with Mrs. Lincoln frequently, but whenever I did, she had treated me with friendly politeness. She had even on some occasions spoken to me about others with a sort of confidential and not at all conventional freedom of tongue, which had embarrassed me not a little. But now, when I was substantially her sole social companion on that steamboat, with no means of escape, she overwhelmed me with a flood of gossip about the various members of the cabinet and leading men in Congress who in some way had incurred her displeasure—gossip so reckless, that I was not only embarrassed as to what to say in reply, but actually began to fear for the soundness of her mind." The trip lasted twenty-four hours. "While this giddy talk was rattling on almost without interruption from City Point to Washington, save sleeping time, I had the pathetic figure of tender-hearted Abraham Lincoln constantly before my eyes as he was sorely harassed not only by public care but also secretly by domestic torment." Elsewhere, Schurz allegedly "set down verbatim a conversation on her part so vulgar and venomous that it can be fairly described as outrageous."

Five days later, Mrs. Lincoln returned to the front, where she once again indulged in hysterics. Disappointed that she had been unable to accompany her husband on his entry into Richmond two days earlier, the First Lady was anxious to tour the Confederate capital, which she did on April 6. The following day, when she expressed a wish to visit Petersburg, Lincoln reluctantly agreed to join her. Once again, she behaved badly. Just as she had snapped at Mrs. Grant for an act of *lèse-majesté* by sitting down in her presence without permission, she now berated Mrs. James Harlan for a similar *faux pas*. Worse still, she erupted in anger at Admiral David D. Porter for including his wife as well as Mrs. Harlan and other women in the party. According to Porter, she threw herself on the ground and tore her hair. Later she upbraided him in a "very sharp letter." Laconically, Porter observed that the First Lady had "an extremely jealous disposition."

On April 9, Mrs. Lincoln did not calm down during the return trip to Washington. Thomas Stackpole, the White House steward who accompanied the Lincolns on their trip back to the capital, reported that she struck her husband in the face, damned him, and cursed him (see Chapter 5).

On April 11, the First Lady once again embarrassed her husband, this time as he attempted to deliver an important speech. A huge crowd had gathered beneath a White House window to hear what the president had to say in the wake of Robert E. Lee's surrender two days earlier. As he delivered his remarks, Mrs. Lincoln stood with friends before a nearby open window, chatting "with almost boisterous animation, until the noise quite drowned the voice of the speaker." Initially the crowd tolerated such rude behavior, but eventually some of its members began to shush the First Lady and her companions so emphatically that Lincoln feared "some word of his own had called for the unwonted demonstration." But he quickly realized that "no disrespect to him was intended." With "an expression of pain and mortification which came over his face as if such strokes were not new, he resumed his reading."

Mrs. Lincoln's rudeness to Julia Grant and her outrageous treatment of General Ord's wife would have an unfortunate effect soon thereafter, when the Lincolns and the Grants were scheduled to attend a performance of *Our American Cousin* at Ford's Theatre. Mrs. Grant discouraged her husband from accepting the invitation to join the First Couple because, as she told a friend, she "objected strenuously to accompanying Mrs. Lincoln." When Edwin Stanton's wife Ellen learned that Julia Grant had declined to attend, she told her that she too would refuse: "I will not sit without you in the box with Mrs. Lincoln!"

Grant needed no persuasion, for he himself had just experienced a disagreeable encounter with Mrs. Lincoln, who held him in contempt. The previous evening, Lincoln had felt too unwell with a headache to join the First Lady for a carriage ride and admire the brilliant illuminations lit to celebrate Lee's surrender. In his stead, Grant, at the president's request, had agreed to escort Mrs. Lincoln. As she and the general stepped into their carriage, a crowd outside the White House shouted "Grant!" several times. Deeply offended, the First Lady instructed the coachman to let her out. She changed her mind, however, when the crowd also cheered for Lincoln. This sequence recurred again and again as the carriage rolled along the streets of the capital. Mrs. Lincoln evidently thought it inappropriate for people to cheer Grant before they had cheered her and her husband. To avoid upsetting Mrs. Lincoln yet again, Grant readily agreed with his wife to skip the theater date and instead to leave abruptly for New Jersey, where their children were staying.

If Grant had attended Ford's Theatre on the night of April 14, it is entirely possible that John Wilkes Booth would have failed to carry out his murderous plan. The general would probably have been accompanied by a security detail far more efficient than Lincoln's. At the very least, his ever-present cipher-and-telegraph officer, Captain Samuel Beckwith (known as "Grant's Shadow") would have been posted outside the presidential box; he probably would have been less willing to admit Booth than was Charles

Forbes, the White House footman and messenger who did allow the assassin to enter the box. Moreover, Grant's own self-protective instincts, honed by long battlefield experience, would have made it unlikely that Booth would have succeeded.

But he did.

CONCLUSION

Mary Lincoln had long been a trial to her spouse. How often she berated him in private is unknown, but since she felt few compunctions about doing so in public, it seems likely that she often did so when they were alone.

J. K. C. Forrest recalled that it "was an open secret at Washington" that throughout Lincoln's presidency the First Lady "was a source of great and perpetual anxiety and annoyance" to her husband. "The sufferings of the man on account of her eccentricities—to designate them by no stronger appellation—were literally such as would crush a man of less elastic moral and physical constitution. The most charitable conclusion is that the lady was mentally unbalanced and thus at times was not responsible for her acts."

Similarly, Alexander McClure stated that Lincoln "had a crazy wife when he entered the presidency, and many as were his sorrows because of the war and bloody struggle for the preservation of the union, the crowning sorrow to one of his domestic taste and love of home and family, was the dark shadow that Mrs. Lincoln cast upon his life." Lincoln's friends "all knew the situation, and her failings were overlooked, although few, if any, of Mr. Lincoln's close political friends entertained the respect for Mrs. Lincoln that should have been accorded the Mistress of the White House."

One of those political friends was Carl Schurz, who spent time with Mrs. Lincoln during the Civil War and heard testimony before the US Senate Committee on Pensions when she applied for relief in 1869 and 1870. (Many witnesses told that committee that she "had been a curse to her husband." A report from that committee, recommending against the proposal to grant Mrs. Lincoln a pension, stated: "There are some other facts bearing on this subject which it is probably not needful to refer to, but which are generally known, and the evidence to part of which is in possession of the committee.") Schurz wrote of Lincoln: "it was no secret to those who knew the family well, that his domestic life was full of trials. The erratic temper of his wife not seldom put the gentleness of his nature to the severest tests; and these troubles and struggles, which accompanied him through all the vicissitudes of his life from the modest home in Springfield to the White House at Washington, adding untold private heartburnings to his public cares, and sometimes precipitating upon him incredible embarrassments in the discharge of his public duties, form one of the most pathetic features of his career." Schurz, who voted in favor of the bill granting Mary Lincoln a pension, put it even more strongly in an interview, calling the president's marriage "the greatest tragedy of Mr. Lincoln's existence."

Lincoln once gave his wife a copy of *The Elements of Character*, an 1854 book by Mary G. Chandler in which he had underlined a passage indicating that marriage could deteriorate from "the highest happiness that can exist on earth" to "a fountain of misery, of a quality absolutely infernal." The Lincolns' marriage was such a fountain of misery, yet from it flowed incalculable good for the nation. Lincoln may not have had such a successful presidency, during which he showed a preternatural ability to deal with difficult people, if he had not had so much practice at home. As Henry C. Whitney wrote: Lincoln possessed "an equanimity and patience, which captivated the masses, while it tired out petulant grumblers, like [Horace] Greeley,

[Wendell] Phillips, etc.; which enabled him to force unwelcome policies on his Cabinet, on Congress and on the nation; which allowed him to bear his 'faculties with meekness,' and finally to restore peace to his bleeding country, and give physical freedom to the blacks and political freedom to the whites." Whitney speculated that if Lincoln had not undergone the harsh "domestic discipline" he experienced at the hands of his difficult wife, he might well have failed as president. "The nation is largely indebted to Mary Todd Lincoln for its autonomy," Whitney concluded.

Equally important, Lincoln may never have become president if his wife had not turbocharged the restless engine of his ambition (see Chapter 5). As Herndon put it, Mary Todd was "a stimulant to Lincoln in a good sense: she was always urging him to look up—struggle—conquer and go up to fame by becoming a big man: she coveted place—position—power—wanted to lead society and to be worshipt by man and woman: she was ambitious and helped Lincoln along in her own providential way, while she crushed his spirit in another way."

By war's end, Lincoln's spirit was indeed so crushed that he may have longed for death, as Elizabeth Keckly speculated: "I know, and I know it well, that so unhappy was that great man, so tired of life and its burdens, that if he could have expressed an opinion concerning the work of the assassin, he would have said: 'I am glad that it is all over.' He was always ready for death, and I knew him so well that I have always felt that death was welcome to him when it came." As early as February 1863, when Benjamin Brown French suggested to Lincoln that "he would feel glad when he could get some rest," he "replied that it was a pretty hard life for him." He could not find the rest that might make him feel glad; to his journalist friend Noah Brooks he confided that "nothing could touch the tired spot within, which was all tired."

With "a pathos which language cannot describe," Lincoln told another good friend, Isaac N. Arnold: "I feel as though I shall never be glad anymore." During his presidency, Arnold noted, Lincoln "had no respite, no holidays. When others fled away from the heat and dust of the capital, he remained. He would not leave the helm until all danger was passed, and the good ship of state had weathered the storm." Arnold enumerated a few of the sources of Lincoln's fathomless sorrow: "Anxiety, responsibility, care, thought, disasters, defeat, [and] the injustice of friends, wore upon his giant frame." To that list Arnold might well have added yet another item: Lincoln's woe-filled marriage to a woman who publicly humiliated him, physically abused him, criticized him sharply, disgraced him with her unethical conduct, and made his domestic life what William Herndon termed "a burning, scorching hell."

APPENDIX

AN APPRAISAL OF
THE LITERATURE ON
THE LINCOLNS' MARRIAGE

T he most extensive annotated bibliography of writings on Mary Todd Lincoln and her marriage is *Mary Lincoln for the Ages* (2019), by Jason Emerson, who has written and edited several important books about Mrs. Lincoln as well as a biography of her son, Robert.

Arguably the most controversial treatment of the Lincoln marriage appeared in William H. Herndon's 1889 biography, *Herndon's Lincoln: The True Story of a Great Life*, actually written by Jesse W. Weik, based on the reminiscences of Herndon himself and of the many people whom Herndon consulted. Herndon told Weik that in "her domestic troubles I have always sympathized with Mrs. Lincoln. The world does not know what she bore, or how ill-adapted she was to bear it." Nonetheless, the book paints a most unflattering portrait of Mrs. Lincoln, based largely on the testimony of numerous informants with whom Herndon had corresponded or spoken. Two excellent Lincoln scholars, Douglas L. Wilson and Rodney O. Davis, have published a thoroughly annotated version of the biography and of the massive archive of research materials on which it rests (Herndon's Record); in addition they have edited Herndon's letters about Lincoln.

Early in the twentieth century, some Lincoln biographers—including William E. Barton, Ida M. Tarbell, and Carl Sandburg—objected in passing to Herndon's portrayal of the marriage, but not till midcentury did *Herndon's Lincoln* come under systematic attack, led by Ruth Painter Randall, wife of the foremost Lincoln scholar of the day, James G. Randall. Assisting her were two of her husband's graduate students, David Donald and Wayne Temple. Ruth Painter Randall wished to prove that the only woman Lincoln ever loved was Mary Todd and that the story of Lincoln's New Salem courtship of Ann Rutledge was a myth. To that end, she wrote an essay, "Sifting the Ann Rutledge Evidence," which cast unwarranted doubt not only on the Rutledge story but also on Herndon's Record. She argued that the testimony of former New Salem residents about Ann Rutledge was unreliable because the informants were old-timers with faulty memories, drooling on their bibs and making up stories out of whole cloth. She persuaded her husband to include that essay as an appendix to his four-volume magnum opus, *Lincoln the President*, even though the Ann Rutledge story has nothing to do with Lincoln's White House years. Because Professor Randall enjoyed enormous prestige (he served as president of the American Historical Association), and since he did not publicly reveal that "Sifting the Ann Rutledge Evidence" was, as he acknowledged privately, "very largely" the work of his wife, it was long regarded as an irrefutable demolition of the Ann Rutledge story. (Subsequent scholarship by Douglas L. Wilson, John Y. Simon, and John Evangelist Walsh has convincingly rehabilitated that story.) In her quest to vindicate Mary Lincoln, Mrs. Randall and her husband set Lincoln scholarship back half a century by discrediting not only Herndon's biography of Lincoln but also the invaluable archive of interviews, letters, and statements that he had compiled after Lincoln's death. The Randalls misled others into viewing the Herndon collection as a toxic nuclear waste dump rather than the gold mine that it truly is.

So, too did David Donald's 1948 biography of Herndon, based on a dissertation written at Professor Randall's suggestion and under his direction. Donald incorrectly maintained that "Mrs. Lincoln had always thoroughly disapproved of Herndon" and "there is no doubt that Herndon and Mary Lincoln cordially detested each other." Donald emphasized "Herndon's hatred" for Mary Lincoln and reported that "Herndon had never liked" her. (Decades later, Donald referred to Herndon's "dislike, verging on hatred" of Mary Lincoln.) But Donald was wrong. In 2001 Douglas L. Wilson, two-time winner of the Lincoln Prize (for *Honor's Voice: The Transformation of Abraham Lincoln* and for *Lincoln's Sword: The Presidency and the Power of Words*), correctly noted that there "is no factual basis for thinking that Herndon was openly or secretly hostile toward Mary Todd Lincoln prior to 1866, or vice versa, and no evidence to contradict his claim that she was always kind to him and that he, in turn, respected her. The evidence of his letters that refer to her, almost all written after Lincoln's death, suggests that while he often faulted her for her aristocratic ways and violent temper and that he believed Lincoln's home life was a 'domestic hell,' his mature view of her was complicated and heavily qualified, conceding to her many good qualities and valuable contributions. In spite of his reputation as her sworn enemy who in later years engaged her in 'open warfare,' a consistent theme in Herndon's correspondence from 1866 on is that Mary Todd Lincoln had been unfairly condemned as the sole source of difficulty in the Lincoln marriage, and that Lincoln, who was not an attentive and helpful husband, deserved a share of the blame. Herndon believed that they had married for the wrong reasons—she to land a successful politician and he to preserve his honor—and that this doomed their marriage. He further believed that she had changed over time—for the worse. They were not bad people, but they had a bad marriage. This caused Lincoln to be unhappy in his home life and Mary to sometimes behave as 'the female wild cat of the age.' In 1866, he had twice used a phrase that captures the essence of it: 'what *I know* and shall tell only ennobles both—that is to say it will show that Mrs L has had cause to suffer, and be almost crazed, while Lincoln *self sacrificed* himself rather than to be charged with dishonor.'"

David Donald's biography of Herndon is marred by numerous flaws and needs to be supplanted with a modern, scholarly, objective study by a historian who would avoid Donald's tendentious, hostile, outdated approach.

In *Mary Lincoln: Biography of a Marriage*, Ruth Randall utilized Donald's work. As Jason Emerson concluded, her biography's "overtly apologetic tone" and "its magnification of Mary's virtues and minimization of her vices" render it more a piece of "advocacy" rather "than an objective historical examination." Fawn Brodie called it "overprotective." The diligent Lincoln scholar Harry E. Pratt noted that "Mary Lincoln could not have found a kinder, more sympathetic or more indulgent biographer" than Ruth Painter Randall, even though she did concede that her subject "never quite grew up in some ways," had an "ill balanced personality," was "emotionally unstable" and "never too discreet." But those were minor concessions in a biography that verged on hagiography. Pratt, who had been a graduate student of Professor Randall's, delicately suggested that "readers may form conclusions which differ from Mrs. Randall's interpretation of the documented evidence—or even the author's evaluation of a particular source. The critical reader may feel that proper appraisal has not been placed on contemporary and reminiscent accounts."

Pratt may have been thinking of the way she interpreted the following reminiscence of a Springfield backyard neighbor, James Gourley, cited as proof of the Lincolns' "congeniality." Gourley reported that the Lincolns "got along tolerably well, unless Mrs. L got the devil in her." He added that she "was gifted with an unusually high temper" that "invariably got the better of her." If "she became excited or troublesome, as she sometimes did when Mr. Lincoln was at home, . . . he would apparently pay no attention to her. Frequently he would laugh at her, which is a risky thing to do in the face of an infuriated wife; but generally, if her impatience continued, he would pick up one of the children and deliberately leave home as if to take a walk. After he had gone, the storm usually subsided, but sometimes it would break out again when he returned."

The testimony of several other witnesses cited by Randall is similarly misrepresented. A good example is Benjamin Brown French, who served as commissioner of public buildings during Lincoln's administration and thus had frequent contact with the First Lady. (His duties made him "almost a member of the President's household," he wrote.) According to Randall, French "recognized that the bedrock" of Mary Lincoln's "character was a fundamental goodness and kindness of heart." He knew "like all who came in contact with Mrs. Lincoln," that "she was not the terrible woman pictured in malicious gossip. He was indignant at the '*vile slanders*' heaped upon her for political purposes." Some entries in French's journal and correspondence written in the early days of the Civil War do indeed support that view, but as time went by, French grew disenchanted with the First Lady. He wrote that in his dealings with her, "I always felt as if the eyes of a hyena were upon me, & that the animal was ready, if I made a single mismove, to pounce upon me!" He called her a "bundle of vanity and folly," deplored the way she "sought to put on the airs of an Empress," and composed verses satirizing her regal ways. In May 1865, after Mrs. Lincoln had left the White House, French confided to his journal: "She is a most singular woman, and it is well for the nation that she is no longer in the White house. It is not proper that I should write down, *even here*, all I know! May God have her in his keeping, and make her a better woman." Mrs. Lincoln, he complained, "has given me a world of trouble."

To buttress her argument that the Lincolns' marriage was happy, Randall cited what she called a "flock of witnesses close to the Lincolns" who "left testimony as to the happiness of their marriage." But like Gourley and French, many of the witnesses whom she summoned in fact gave evidence indicating that the marriage was unhappy (see Chapter 3).

APPENDIX

Numerous informants in addition to those cited by Herndon supported his view that the Lincolns' marriage was woe-filled. Among them were some of Lincoln's closest friends, including Orville Hickman Browning, who in 1875 told an interviewer that "many times" during the Civil War Lincoln talked to him "about his domestic troubles." As Browning reported, the president "several times told me that he was constantly under great apprehension lest his wife should do something which would bring him into disgrace." (This casts doubt on Richard Lawrence Miller's assertion that Lincoln's "statements about her . . . were always loyal, loving, and admiring.")

Also revealing are long-suppressed portions of Browning's extensive diary that became public in 1994. That diary had been published as a pair of large volumes in 1925 and 1933, but six passages were omitted because of references to Mrs. Lincoln. Browning's niece, who owned the diary, would not sell it to the Illinois State Historical Library in Springfield (now the Abraham Lincoln Presidential Library) unless the librarians would agree to forbid publication of, or public access to, those half-dozen passages. Reluctantly, the librarians complied, but in 1994 their successors reversed that decision. The preface to the published version of Browning's diary, edited by James G. Randall and Theodore Calvin Pease, describes the excisions as "passages of unimportant gossip." But they are essential for understanding how Mrs. Lincoln behaved as First Lady; all six passages dealt with her unethical conduct in that role. Arguably the most startling one was dated July 3, 1873. That day Browning met with David Davis, who had been appointed to the US Supreme Court by his good friend Lincoln. When Browning told Justice Davis "that all the charges against her [Mary Lincoln] of having pilfered from the White House were false," the judge demurred, stating "that the proofs were too many and too strong against her to admit of doubt of her guilt; that she was a natural born thief; that stealing was a sort of insanity with her, and that she carried away, from the White House, many things that were of no value to her after she had taken them, and that she had carried them away only in obedience to her irresistable propensity to steal."

(As coeditor of the diary, Professor Randall presumably saw those six passages, but he gives readers of his multivolume study, *Lincoln the President*, little idea of the problems that the First Lady's unethical conduct created for her husband and his administration. He even transcribed Horace Greeley's description of Mrs. Lincoln—"female president"—as "Senate president.")

Others who worked closely with Lincoln had unflattering things to say about his wife. Lincoln's two principal White House secretaries, John G. Nicolay and John Hay, referred to the First Lady as "the Hell Cat" and "her Satanic majesty," while the presidential physician, Dr. Robert K. Stone, called her "a perfect devil" (see Chapter 11). Lincoln's friend and political ally, Carl Schurz, stated flatly that the marriage "was the greatest tragedy of Mr. Lincoln's existence."

During Lincoln's administration, his wife did bring him into disgrace by padding payrolls and expense accounts, overspending the budget for White House improvements, accepting bribes and kickbacks, selling pardons and trading permits, leaking public documents, and consorting with shady characters (see Chapters 8–12).

Not only was she corrupt but she was also physically abusive. Testimony from neighbors, household servants, political associates, colleagues at the bar, and others indicates that Mrs. Lincoln had an uncontrollable temper which led her to strike not only her husband, but also her children and domestic servants (see Chapter 5).

Mrs. Randall tackled Herndon head-on, arguing that he "wanted to believe the worst about Mrs. Lincoln." In discussing Herndon's treatment of Lincoln's romance with Ann Rutledge, she wrote: "Herndon hated Mrs. Lincoln, but in his own self-justifying mind he considered that, in bringing out his deductions from the supposed romance to explain the 'unhappy' marriage, he was doing justice to her." But, like David Donald, she was wrong. Though substantial evidence unearthed since

Herndon's day has tended to corroborate his portrayal of the Lincoln marriage, historians have continued to support Ruth Randall's version of the story.

Jean H. Baker's defensive 1987 biography is usually regarded as the standard work in the field. A protégé of David Donald, Baker followed the line taken both by him and by Randall. To her credit, Baker attempted to explore Mrs. Lincoln's inner life, presenting evidence that she "suffered from the personality disorder of narcissism," a neurosis with roots in her troubled childhood (see Chapter 1).

Baker called the Lincolns' marriage a "success" partly because the "two uneven personalities" managed to form an effective political team. By struggling "to make herself her husband's chief adviser on patronage and appointments" she "meant to contribute to her husband's endeavors . . . the special intuition with which females—and none more than she—were endowed. . . . In her imaginative projection of their life together she had become his collaborator—a full-fledged, home-based counselor available for insightful judgments about the human motivations that were the core of politics."

A leading feminist historian, Anne Firor Scott, noted that Baker erred in portraying the "selfish, willful, grasping, and myopic" Mary Lincoln as an example of a nineteenth-century American woman unjustly "punished because she lived too soon." The "constraints society placed on nineteenth-century women were real," Scott observed, "but they did not prevent the extraordinary accomplishments of Elizabeth Cady Stanton, Julia Ward Howe, Lucy Stone, Hannah Tracey Cutler, or Paulina Wright Davis, to name only a few women of similar talents born within three years of Mary Todd who might also have been 'punished because [they] lived too soon.'" Scott thought that even Baker's highly defensive account of Mary Lincoln's behavior should cause readers to "feel that the fault lay not in her stars nor in the imposed limitations of what was certainly a male-dominated society but in herself. Gifted as she was, she might have used her talents for social benefit, but she was one of those who believe the world revolves around their own heads."

As Scott remarked, there is little evidence in Baker's book "that Mary Lincoln understood the depth of the nation's tragedy or the profound suffering it brought her husband. While he struggled with intractable generals and bickering politicians, she dressed herself like royalty and redecorated the White House at great, and unauthorized, expense. When thwarted, she indulged in temper tantrums. Such behavior is not pretty in tranquil times; in the midst of civil war it must have troubled even her closet friends." As First Lady, Mrs. Lincoln "used her position for personal gain in ways that today [1989] might evoke a special prosecutor." Scott sensibly maintained that "influence peddling is no more acceptable when practiced by a woman whose life has been full of sorrow than when it comes from a male presidential advisor."

As for Baker's contention that Mary Lincoln has suffered unfairly in "male-ordered" history, Scott argued that although "unsympathetic men trumpeted Mary Lincoln's failings, surely the behavior" narrated by Baker "must have offended any morally sensitive observer of either sex." Scott concluded that "[f]eminist historians can find many better cases" than Mary Lincoln "to illuminate the real (as opposed to the self-imposed) consequences of a male-dominated social order."

Lincoln biographer-cum-psychotherapist Charles Strozier noted that Baker "makes light of the abundant evidence of Mary's torments and rages, both in their childhood origin and in their overt expression in her relationship with Lincoln." That constituted "a failure on Baker's part to follow through on what she labels Mary's narcissistic character. Raging is one common hallmark of such a personality." Though "Baker was not required to make a diagnosis of Mary," nonetheless, "having made it, she is obliged to develop it in its full psychological complexity."

Baker conducted some research in unpublished sources but she failed to consult innumerable relevant manuscript collections, newspapers, and public records. In the introduction to a 2008 reissue of *Mary Todd Lincoln: A Biography*, she noted that new information had appeared in the twenty-one years since its original publication, but she did not mention important discoveries like the suppressed passages in Orville Browning's diary, the interview given by Browning in 1875, and the correspondence of White House employees in the records of the Senate Committee on Public Buildings, all of which had been published well before 2008. Moreover, she did not consult the papers of some earlier Lincoln biographers, among them Ida Tarbell, Albert J. Beveridge, Carl Sandburg, and William E. Barton.

Baker's book betrays signs of hasty composition, for it is riddled with factual errors, misspellings, and garbled citations. In 2017, Donna McCreary (author of *Fashionable First Lady: The Victorian Wardrobe of Mary Lincoln*; *The Kentucky Todds in Lexington Cemetery*; and *Lincoln's Table: A President's Culinary Journey from Cabin to Cosmopolitan*) stated in an online post: "At first glance, Jean Baker's book appears to be well researched and documented. It is neither. It is filled with mistakes, and sadly, since the book was first published in 1987, many other authors have used this book as source material. The former curator of the Mary Todd Lincoln House in Lexington, Kentucky [Lou Holden], told me that she found over 100 mistakes in the first two chapters of the book." She listed some of Baker's errors: "Just a few examples (of the hundreds) of incorrect information include:

> page 26: "Ann Maria Todd, the unmarried sister now in charge of his Lexington household." (Her name was Maria Logan Todd Bullock and she was married.)

> page 30: stepmother Betsey Todd pronounced Mary "a limb of Satan loping down the broad road leading to destruction." (This was said only by the slave woman, Mammy Sally.)

> page 89: "Her sister Elizabeth, who bore the name of their mother." (Mary's mother's name was Eliza, not Elizabeth.)

page 184: "During her wait she had made Tad a Zouave doll."
(The Zouave doll was a gift to the Lincoln boys.)

page 237: "and carried an ermine fan with silver spangles." (Fans
were not made of fur.)

page 309: (regarding the Chicago fire) "left behind a bundle of
her husband's personal letters. Like most Chicagoans, she probably spent the night -- and perhaps part of the next day—along
Lake Michigan." (She would have traveled through the fire to
get to the lake.)

"There are also many problems with the footnotes. There are documents
she claims to have used which do not exist. Quotes are misidentified as
being on a page of a book."

Illinois State Historian Thomas F. Schwartz also criticized Baker's
footnotes, calling them "an exercise in creative writing. Footnote style
is inconsistent, failing to follow any of the standard scholarly formats.
Manuscript collections are frequently omitted or incorrectly attributed.
Such multi-volume works as *Lincoln Day by Day* are cited without indica-
tion of the volume being cited. Other notes fail to offer any evidence other
than opinion." On p. 184, a letter from Schuyler Colfax to John G. Nicolay
is identified as a letter from Nicolay to Colfax; and some quoted passages
are inaccurate or invented. (An example appears on p. 203: "the New York
World's complaint that Lincoln 'in an unparalleled display of nepotism has
appointed his whole family to government posts.'" The citation is to the
World for 22 September 1864, but no such language appears in that issue
of the paper or any searchable newspaper.)

Schwartz also cited many other problems with Baker's biography: she
"uses the word 'epithet' (p. 8) when she really means 'epitaph.' Leonard
Swett is identified as Sweet (p. 266), and John Todd Stuart as John Todd

(p. 332)." The "dove on Eddie's tombstone becomes an angel (p. 126); Lincoln's silver-plated door nameplate becomes gold (p. 105); and John Wilkes Booth's dagger becomes a sword (p. 244)." Schwartz noted other flaws: throughout the book "[e]vidence is clearly misrepresented" and "speculations" are presented "in the form of declarative sentences." The result "is not a descriptive study of Mary Lincoln but a polemic in defense of her. Too many straw men are set up and knocked down."

Similarly, Betty Boles Ellison, a Kentucky journalist and historian, complained that Baker's biography "is filled with historical errors," many of which "occur in the first two chapters." Baker "seems to have a great many problems dealing with street names, Todd family names and family relationships," with the spelling of the name of a leading Kentucky historian (William H. Townsend, whom she repeatedly refers to as "Townshend"), and with the proper title of the lower house of the Kentucky state legislature. Mrs. Ellison was especially disturbed that Baker had been invited to speak at the Kentucky Historical Society's Boone Day Celebration: "It seems the Kentucky Historical Society could have found a Boone Day speaker who could at least get the facts correct regarding Kentucky history and, if the speaker writes about the state, make sure that person knows what he or she is writing about." (In 2014, Ellison herself published a biography of Mary Lincoln that, as Jason Emerson noted, is "filled with factual errors." He rightly called that book "an example of revisionism and presentism run amok, ascribing to Mary qualities, ideas, and characteristics she never had, could never have had at the time, and would rail against as ridiculous were she living today." It "is a feminist revisionist hagiography, based on shoddy research and mainly secondary sources—many of them unreliable." It begins with "a predetermined theory of Mary's greatness and infallibility" and "carries that idea through to the end." The author "offers no original thinking or research" but rather "unfounded suppositions, unproven accusations." In sum, her book provides "a complete misunderstanding of Mary as a person and historical character.")

Other errors in Baker's biography include the following: Lincoln, not Mary, broke their engagement (pp. 90–92); the Battle of Fredericksburg took place in 1862, not 1863 (p. 224); Volney Hickox is misidentified as "Vergie Hicks" (p. 123); Isaac Henderson, publisher of the New York *Evening Post*, sought a lucrative government office in New York, not Boston (p. 200); Herman Kreismann is misidentified as Henry Kreisman (p. 165); Carl Schurz is misidentified as a congressman, an office he never held (p. 240); Mary did not write the poem "Little Eddie" (p. 126); on p. 82 Edwin Bathurst Webb is described as twenty years older than Mary, but on p. 85 he is called fifteen years her senior (in fact the age gap was sixteen years).

Most egregiously, Baker garbled and badly misrepresented a letter by Elizabeth Blair Lee which is cited as proof positive of Lincoln's love for his wife. Here is Baker's version of that letter's text, written by Lee to her husband a few days after Lincoln's assassination: "Mary has her husband's deepest love. This is a matter upon which one woman cannot deceive another." Baker presented these two sentences as a direct quote from Mrs. Lee's letter, but they are not; rather, Baker lifted them almost verbatim from an inaccurate version of that letter in Elbert Smith's biography of Lee's father, Francis Preston Blair.

Elbert Smith's garbled paraphrase of Lee's letter, followed by an inaccurate quote from it, reads thus: "She [Elizabeth Blair Lee] knew that Mary had her husband's deepest love because this was 'a matter upon which one woman cannot deceive another.'" Mrs. Lee's letter actually reads: "Some have thought she [Mary] had not his [Lincoln's] affections but tis evident to me she had no doubt about it and that is a point about which women are not often deceived after a long married life like theirs."

Elbert Smith's paraphrase is obviously misleading; Elizabeth Lee "knew that Mary had her husband's deepest love" is not the equivalent of Elizabeth Lee stating her own belief that Mary "had no doubt about" having Lincoln's "affections." That Mary *thought* she had her husband's affections is hardly proof that she actually *did* have them and is far from a flat assertion by

Mrs. Lee that "Mary has her husband's deepest love." A more accurate paraphrase would have been something like this: "Elizabeth inferred that Mary had her husband's affection because Mary said so and because women married for as long as Mary had been wed are not often deceived about such matters."

Within quotation marks, Baker enclosed Elbert Smith's paraphrase ("Mary has her husband's deepest love") as if those words actually appear in Elizabeth Lee's letter, which they do not; moreover, Elbert Smith himself did not enclose them within quotation marks. Baker then enclosed within quotation marks the language that Elbert Smith inaccurately attributed to Mrs. Lee, who wrote "a point about which women are not often deceived after a long married life like theirs." Elbert Smith's version of those same words is: "a matter 'upon which one woman cannot deceive another.'"

Elbert Smith thus made two mistakes: a misleading paraphrase of the first part of Mrs. Lee's long sentence and a misrepresentation of the words (and meaning) of the second part. Baker erred by not checking the accuracy of Elbert Smith's summary of (and quotation from) Mrs. Lee's letter; erred by enclosing Elbert Smith's dramatic paraphrase within quotation marks ("Mary has her husband's deepest love"), mistakenly indicating that those words appear in Mrs. Lee's letter; and erred by quoting Elbert Smith's garbled, misleading version of Mrs. Lee's words (transforming "a point about which women are not often deceived after a long married life like theirs" into "a matter 'upon which one woman cannot deceive another.'") Such an inaccurate version of a key source is especially troubling because Baker relied heavily on the supposed testimony of Mrs. Lee to show that "Wartime observers of the Lincoln marriage detected the same mutual understanding that [Mrs.] Lincoln's sister Frances had noted about their relationship in Springfield." (As noted in Chapter 3, Frances Todd's testimony about the happiness of the Lincolns' marriage is highly suspect. During the same interview in which she claimed that Lincoln's marriage was happy, Frances insisted that her notoriously ambitious sister Mary was not ambitious.)

Baker's careless misrepresentation of Mrs. Lee's letter is tantamount to scholarly malpractice. The American Historical Association's "Statement on Standards of Professional Conduct" stipulates that "Historians should not misrepresent their sources. They should report their findings as accurately as possible."

In her error-filled, tendentious book, as Thomas Peet wrote, Baker "turns a blind eye to too much." Jason Emerson justly called it "a one-sided feminist—often accusatory and exculpatory—diatribe in which Mary is a saint." The author "portrays her as a female pioneer in a chauvinistic society—while simultaneously stating that Mary was no different than other women of her day." Moreover, Baker "misrepresents the role she played in her husband's political life," making it appear "far more important . . . than it was."

In *The President's Wife, Mary Todd Lincoln: A Biography* (1973), Ishbel Ross, author of many books about notable American women, anticipated Jean Baker's claim that Mary swayed her husband's "judgment in their early years together as she backed him determinedly in the significant decisions that led him finally to the Presidency." (Ross made a more valid point when she contended that Mrs. Lincoln "was a stimulant, for she prodded him into action when he seemed to lag.") Though a stout defender of Mrs. Lincoln, Ross acknowledged that her subject could be "pathetic," had an "unstable nature," whose "besetting sin" was "vanity, in the Biblical sense of the word."

The case for Mary Lincoln's importance as her husband's political advisor was effectively rebutted in Michael Burkhimer's essay, "The Reports of the Lincolns' Political Partnership Have Been Greatly Exaggerated," which pointed out that there is scant evidence to support it. Charles Strozier contended that "it is pure myth that she played a role in shaping Lincoln's views. She cheered him on, surely, and that was undoubtedly important for a man so chronically unsure of certain emotional things. But he stood aloof from her judgments and petty hatreds." Similarly, Dr. W. A. Evans, author of a 1932 study of Mrs. Lincoln which is still (in 2020) the best one yet published, concluded that Lincoln's "policies, plans, and methods of the presidential period were Lincolnesque. They give no evidence of his wife's influence. . . . Lincoln's outstanding mental characteristic was wisdom. His judgment was clear and cold. The decisions of Mrs. Lincoln were too much swayed by her likes and dislikes, prejudices, and other emotions to be designated as wise, or based on good judgment." Mark E. Neely concurred.

More recent studies than Jean Baker's are also disappointing. The flaws of her work appear in Catherine Clinton's thinly researched, superficial, tendentious *Mrs. Lincoln: A Life* (2009), which Jason Emerson aptly described as "an unoriginal rehash of previous writers' materials and conclusions" that "offers nothing new in fact or interpretation." As he noted, it "seeks to exculpate Mary Lincoln from previous historical criticism—to the point of ignoring Mary's proven faults, especially as first lady." Its "paucity of primary archival research," its "lack of scholarly depth," and its "failure to delve past the obvious surface stories of Mary's life" render it no more satisfactory than Baker's earlier work.

Kenneth J. Winkle's *Abraham and Mary Lincoln* (2013) is a slender volume in the Concise Lincoln Library published by the Southern Illinois University Press. Despite its title, the book contains surprisingly little on the Lincolns' marriage. There is much padding about such topics as Washington DC during the Civil War, antebellum social history, and Queen Victoria. Winkle whitewashes Mrs. Lincoln, ignoring the many scandals she was involved in and the physical and emotional abuse she administered to her spouse. It also fails to come to grips with other controversial aspects of the story, contains no psychological analysis, and is marred by some factual errors.

Another brief work, Stacy Pratt McDermott's *Mary Lincoln: Southern Girl, Northern Woman* (2015), "is a succinct overview of Mary's life" that "contains nothing new or groundbreaking," as Jason Emerson wrote.

The Lincolns: Portrait of a Marriage (2008) by Daniel Mark Epstein, a gifted poet, is exceptionally well written though poorly researched and argued. To his credit, the author does acknowledge that Mary Lincoln physically abused her husband, but he minimizes that aspect of the story. He garbles several other matters. In dealing with Lincoln's decision to break his engagement to Mary Todd, he accepts the highly dubious theory that Lincoln did so because he thought he had syphilis. Epstein also mishandles evidence about the real reason—namely, Lincoln's infatuation with the beautiful eighteen-year-old Matilda Edwards. The author claims that Mary Lincoln managed to keep her temper during the first dozen years of the marriage, ignoring abundant evidence that from early on in the marriage Lincoln stayed away from home as much as possible to avoid her temper tantrums.

Epstein's book reads like a novel, replete with colorfully imagined descriptions of flora, fauna, clothing, weather, furniture, wallpaper, landscapes, cityscapes, trees, and the like. The author often speculates about what people were thinking and pads his narrative with an account of Lincoln's activities unrelated to the marriage. That helps make *The Lincolns* a good read, but unconvincing as a serious work of history. Jason Emerson rightly called it "a hagiography of Mary Lincoln as a political partner and source of her husband's success" and an "unreliable book" based on "predetermined conclusions and poor research." Epstein's two main conclusions are demonstrably wrong: "First, these two people loved each other deeply, from the time they met in Springfield in 1839, until his assassination in 1865. The second is that Mary was extremely interested in Abraham's career and speeches; whenever they could, the two of them talked about these things. She was a strong political partner for him." (Epstein was similarly wrong in his book about Lincoln and Walt Whitman, in which he argued that Lincoln had read *Leaves of Grass*. The only source for that claim is a thoroughly discredited memoir.)

The Lincolns: Portrait of a Marriage, written by a poet, calls to mind an irreverent definition of romantic poetry: "the melodious expression of the patently untrue."

W. A. Evans's *Mrs. Lincoln: A Study of Her Personality and Her Influence on Lincoln* (1932), is, as Jason Emerson observed in 2019, "the best biography of Mary yet written." Dr. Evans concluded that she "was not responsible for many things she did and said," for she had a "pathologic personality" and her "mind was of the introvert type." (Somewhat quaintly, he explained that "Physicians now recognize diseased personalities. Among such is the introvert personality.") Her personality traits, he wrote, included "too great seriousness and an inability to laugh at herself; capacity to ridicule others, but not herself; lack of humor . . . inability to withstand restraint; a tendency to hysteria; and a disposition to disregard the point of view and feelings of others, to give offense, to resent criticism, to give way to anger, to remember hurts, to be revengeful." He concluded that "envy was a major" component of her personality.

Important insights and information are found in excellent recent studies which focus on various aspects of Mrs. Lincoln's life. A few such studies are contained in an uneven collection of essays, *The Mary Lincoln Enigma: Historians on America's Most Controversial First Lady* (2012). "There's Something about Mary: Mary Lincoln and Her Siblings" by Stephen Berry describes Mrs. Lincoln as "a diva of grief" and a "financial bulimic" and concludes that she "was a lot like her siblings" in "valuing display" and "demanding recognition at the point of a knife, or a tongue." A gifted wordsmith who has written an excellent study of the Todd family and has coedited some revealing correspondence of Mary's half-sister Elodie, Berry is especially insightful in describing the way that the city of Lexington shaped the Todds. (Mary's education is thoroughly explored in Randolph Paul Runyon, *The Mentelles: Mary Todd Lincoln, Henry Clay, and the Immigrant Family that Educated Antebellum Kentucky*.)

"'I Am So Fond of Sightseeing': Mary Lincoln's Travels Up to 1865" by Wayne C. Temple, retired chief deputy director of the Illinois State Archives, is a model of careful, richly detailed scholarship. In passing, Temple alludes to some of Mrs. Lincoln's corrupt actions as First Lady, including her pinching the salary of the White House stewardess and her padding of expense accounts. The corruption of Mrs. Lincoln as First Lady cries out for fuller treatment in the literature. Temple also alludes to another aspect of Mrs. Lincoln that is often glossed over: her temper. Temple rightly calls her outburst at a general's wife during her visit to City Point, Virginia, in March 1865 a "despicable tirade."

"A Psychiatrist Looks at Mary Lincoln" by James S. Brust carefully explores the troubled psyche of Mary Lincoln. Quite plausibly, he concludes that in all likelihood she suffered from bipolar disorder (manic depression). This diagnosis, he avers, should make her a more sympathetic character. In addition, she suffered from a "major depressive disorder with psychotic features."

An excellent specialized study is Jennifer Fleischner's beautifully written, thoroughly researched book, *Mrs. Lincoln and Mrs. Keckly: The Remarkable Story of the Friendship Between a First Lady and a Former Slave* (2003). Like Jean Baker, Fleischner emphasizes the devastating effect on Mary of the early loss of her mother, her father's remarriage to a woman unsympathetic to his children, and her subsequent losses. Mary understandably sought mother and father surrogates, and found one of the latter in Lincoln.

But unlike Baker, Jennifer Fleischner does not employ psychological analysis to palliate Mary Lincoln's bad behavior and more unfortunate qualities. (As Ann Firor Scott noted: "Self-absorption called a personality disorder is self-absorption still.") Fleischner freely acknowledges that Mary abused her husband, and she concludes that it would be "a mistake to consider her an early feminist. Mary did not consciously seek autonomous power in nondomestic roles, and her trespasses into male domains were the work of impulse, not principle. Women's rights did not interest her . . . Moreover, unlike political activists, Mary's concerns were never universal. She was interested in her personal rights, and she narcissistically saw her husband's advancement as her own."

Another gracefully written study is Douglas L. Wilson's *Honor's Voice: The Transformation of Abraham Lincoln* (1998). Based on wide-ranging research, it examines in depth Lincoln's life from the time he settled in New Salem at the age of twenty-two until his marriage at the age of thirty-three. The book covers his troubled courtship of Mary Todd and concludes that

APPENDIX

he broke off the engagement in 1841 because he realized that they were incompatible. But the following year he married her anyway, in obedience to the voice of honor, which insisted that once he had promised to marry her, he must follow through on that promise if she wanted him to do so. Wilson's account is far more plausible than the one offered in Ruth Painter Randall's 1957 monograph, *The Courtship of Mr. Lincoln*.

As noted in chapter 1, Wayne C. Temple's thorough study of Lincoln's religion, *Abraham Lincoln: From Skeptic to Prophet*, mentions in passing a possible explanation of why Lincoln wed Mary Todd, an explanation that supplements Wilson's treatment of that subject: that Mary may have seduced Lincoln just before the wedding and made him feel obliged to marry her immediately in order to preserve her honor.

There is a crying need for a modern, thorough, psychologically sophisticated biography of Mary Lincoln, based on extensive research in unpublished sources and written with W. A. Evans's goal of understanding rather than vindicating her.

The extensive reference notes can be accessed at the website of the University of Illinois Springfield, https://www.uis.edu.

ACKNOWLEDGMENTS

I n 1984, I began to conduct research on all aspects of Lincoln's life, and as a result I have come across a great deal of evidence about his marriage that specialists concentrating solely on that topic would likely miss. Over those thirty-six years, I have been the beneficiary of help from many generous friends, fellow scholars, family members, and librarians far too numerous to name here, though I cannot refrain from mentioning a few.

This book was largely written during a sabbatical leave granted by the University of Illinois Springfield, where I am indebted to my colleagues in the History Department and to Val Vaden, the philanthropist who underwrites the Chancellor Naomi B. Lynn Distinguished Chair in Lincoln Studies, which I have the honor to hold. The fund associated with that chair, along with the research fund of the College of Liberal Arts and Sciences of the University, enabled me to hire Kerry Ellard as a research assistant on this project. A long-time student of Mary Lincoln, she provided important information mined industriously and ingeniously from newspaper databases.

ACKNOWLEDGMENTS

Lewis E. Lehrman, an exceptionally generous philanthropist, has been unfailingly supportive over the years. In the Illinois capital many friends have been kind, most notably Sarah Thomas, John Paul, Mark Johnson, Bruce and Karen Finne, and Dick and Ann Hart.

My agent, Don Fehr of the Trident Media Group, skillfully helped me navigate the complicated world of modern publishing.

Finally, I cannot adequately express my profound gratitude to the beloved dedicatee of this work, Lois McDonald, who has enriched my life immeasurably for more than three decades.

Mystic, Connecticut

INDEX

INDEX

Gridley, Eleanor, 34–35
Griffin, Sarah Carroll (Sallie)
  (Mrs. Charles), 251–52, 254
Grimes, James, 125, 190
Grimsley, Elizabeth Todd, 22,
  59–60, 146, 148, 163
Gurley, Phineas D., 159, 197, 220

H
Hale, Albert, 197
Hall, A. Oakey, 200
Hall, Maria M. C., 211, 213
Halstead, Murat, 149, 198
Halsted, Oliver (Pet), 171–73
Hamlin, Hannibal, 229
Hammack, John, 186
Hanks, Dennis, 57
Hanks, Harriet, x, 54, 57, 67, 70,
  78–79, 91
Hanscom, Simon P., 175
Hardin, John J., 22, 24, 32, 84
Hardin, Lucy Jane, 22
Hardin, Martinette. *See* McKee,
  Martinette Hardin
Hardin, Sarah Smith (Mrs. John J.),
  26
Harlan, Mrs. James, 257
Harlan, Mary, 255
Harris, Ira, 228
Hatch, Ozias M., 142–43
Hay, John, 101, 158, 164–65, 183,
  246, 271
Hay, Milton, 83, 88, 96
Hayes, Lucy, 200
Heinzen, Karl, 201–2

Helm, Benjamin Hardin, 95, 146
Helm, Emilie Todd, 35–38, 54,
  70, 74, 95, 100, 146, 160, 216,
  222, 235
Henderson, Isaac, 113–14, 122,
  124–27, 134, 158, 277
Henry, Anson G., 25
Henry, Joseph, 221
Herndon, William H., ix–xi, 7,
  12, 19, 36, 39–40, 42–45, 50,
  57–58, 62–63, 68–69, 72–74,
  79–81, 83, 88, 90, 92–93,
  95–96, 101, 141, 145, 158–59,
  263–68, 270–72
Herndon's Lincoln (Weik),
  265–66
Hertford, Joseph, 183
Hickman, John, 166
Hitt, Robert R., 107
Hodder, Frank H., 42
Hogan, Mary, 63
Holden, Lou, 274
Honor's Voice (Wilson), 267,
  283–84
Hooker, Joseph, 171, 247–48
Hopkins, Samuel A., 139–40
House Book, The (Leslie), 61
house at Eighth and Jackson, 56,
  99–100
house on South Fourth, 52–53
Howard, Joseph, 180–81, 204
Howe, Julia Ward, 272

I
Illinois General Assembly, 104

150; reconciliation of, 32; wedding of, 33–34, 40–42, 46
Lincoln, Edward Baker (Eddy), 52, 61, 63, 87, 148
Lincoln, Mary Todd: abuse of Abraham by, viii–ix, 51, 53–54, 57–58, 60, 64, 71–74, 87–91, 141, 243–44, 252–57, 261, 264, 280–81, 283; abuse, physical, by, 51, 58, 62–64, 71–73, 76–79, 87–88, 90, 161, 257, 271; and adultery rumors, 137–38; advice to, 119; ambitions (financial), 98–99; ambitions (political), 81–84, 86, 88, 103–4, 108, 115, 121, 176, 263; ambitions (social), 98–100, 109–10, 112, 120, 178, 197–98, 210, 231; and animals, 80–81; avoided by other women, 50–51, 162; bibliography about, 265; and bipolar disorder, xi, 12–13, 283; and blackmail by, 184–86; and blacks, 61–63, 66, 232–41; and borderline personality disorder, 13; clothes and jewelry of, 101, 110, 113, 121, 165–66, 171, 175, 178–80, 182, 185–86, 198–200, 205–9, 212, 226, 239, 246, 273; Confederate sympathy of alleged, 176; as Congressman's wife, 85–86; as conservative politically, 237–38; conversation of, 203–5; and cooking, 101; and deaths

of relatives, xi, 17, 87; debts of, 178–84, 188; description of, 204–8, 226; and devilish nicknames for, 201, 246, 271; dishonesty of, 42, 140, 150–58, 160, 166–68, 170–73, 180–90, 192, 194–95, 197, 219, 230, 264, 270–71, 282; embarrassment caused by, 120, 123, 134, 141, 147, 149, 156, 158, 164, 166–68, 184, 186–89, 191–95, 198–99, 203, 207, 210–11, 230, 238, 242–57, 261–62, 264; and entitlement, sense of, 200, 202–3, 209, 214, 231, 244–45, 247, 250–51, 255, 257–58, 272; financial fears of, 179–80, 183–84, 187, 192; and flattery of, 121–22, 134–35, 163, 166, 170–71, 174–75, 180–81, 193, 199, 201, 204, 209, 212, 231, 237; gifts received by, 113, 121–22, 124, 131–36, 166, 171, 174, 179, 187, 202, 217–18; and grief of, 212–16, 222, 224; and half-siblings, 11; health of, 12, 54–55, 61; and hospital visits, 223–26; and housework, 56–58, 61–62, 95; indiscretions of 203, 207–11, 230, 237, 246–57, 261; and influence exercised by, 103–4, 111–12, 120–24, 127, 131–33, 136–37, 141, 145–49, 151–52, 156, 158, 160, 166, 170, 172–73, 177,

181–84, 186–87, 203, 218–20, 227–31, 236–37, 253, 272–73, 279–80; insanity of, 13–14, 160–61; and jealousy, 244–57; and journalists, 107, 110, 113, 209–10, 246; and letter writing, 93–94, 96; loneliness of, 55, 96–97, 162, 177; and love for Lincoln, 34–38, 97; and mental problems, vii, xi, 9–14, 59–60, 159, 161, 179, 187, 203, 255, 261, 282–83; mercurial nature of, 240; and migraines, xi, 54–55, 239; as money-loving, 192; as mother, 52, 55, 58–59, 75–80, 89; and narcissism, 13, 272–73, 283; and nervous breakdown risk, 159–60, 213; and paranoia, 59–60, 160; and parties, 171, 176, 207, 209–12; and patronage, 113–14, 121–24, 127, 131–34, 136–37, 139, 141, 143, 145–49, 152, 173, 183–84, 186–87, 218–20; pension for, 107, 237, 262; personality of, 50, 69, 74, 87–89, 95, 97–98, 105, 170–71, 190, 200, 202, 213–14, 222, 230–31, 282; positive impressions of, xi, 36–37, 61, 204–5, 223–24, 238, 267; and premenstrual stress syndrome, xii, 12; and presidential campaign, 108–110; and reactions to death of, 13–14; and resentment toward others, 105–7,

111–12, 203–4, 227–29, 237, 239, 245; rudeness of, 105–7, 112–13, 123, 149, 228–29, 233, 247, 250, 256–58; and sale of old clothes, 185–87; and servants, 54–55, 57, 59, 61–66, 71, 191–95, 198, 239–40, 247; sexuality of, 43, 46, 284; and shopping, 14, 101, 110, 131, 133, 136–37, 148, 156–57, 162, 178–79, 188–89, 198–99, 202, 224–25, 230; and showing off, 198, 206, 231; snobbish manner of, 201–2, 210, 212, 226, 230–31, 239, 247, 250; snubs Julia Trumbull, 105–7; and spiritualists, 217, 220–23, 226–27; and stepmother, xi, 9–11; stinginess of, 65–69, 101, 184–85, 191–95, 230; temper of, ix, 11, 14–15, 37, 50–51, 58, 62–64, 70–74, 77–79, 84–85, 87–91, 98, 113–14, 136, 161, 246–48, 250–57, 262, 264, 271, 273, 283; as thief, 14, 150–51; travel by, 177–78; unpopularity of, 196–204, 210–12, 214, 225–26, 230–31; and vacations, 163, 171–72, 175, 224–25; and White House refurbishing by, 187–91, 202, 271, 273. *See also* Todd, Mary
Lincoln, Nancy Hanks, 17
Lincoln, Robert Todd (Bob, Bobby), 13, 17, 41, 51–52,

55, 57, 59, 61, 63, 70, 75–76,
78–79, 86, 90, 97, 113–14, 129,
132, 148, 187, 216–17, 233,
236, 265
Lincoln, Sarah, 20
Lincoln, Thomas (Tad), 52, 58,
62, 75, 77–80, 94, 114, 172,
192, 209, 213, 216, 225, 248,
250–51
Lincoln, William Wallace (Willie),
79–80, 114, 172, 192, 209, 212,
225; death of, 13, 52, 70, 80,
159, 212–14, 216–17, 222–23
Lincoln the President (J.G. Randall), 266, 271
*Lincolns: Portrait of a Marriage,
The* (Epstein), 280–81
Lincoln's Sword (Wilson), 267
Lincoln's Table (McCreary), 274
Lippincott, Sara Jane (Grace
Greenwood), 208, 231
Littlefield, John H., 82
Logan, Mary S., 14, 231
Logan, Stephen T., 4

M
Madison, Dolley, 200
Mammy Sally, 238
manure, funds from, 153–54,
156–58
Marble, Manton, 157
Marietta (niece of Eliza Francis), x
Marshall, D.D.T., 124
Marston, Liza Irwin, 127–28, 134
Marston, Robert Irwin, 127–28

Marston, William Henry, 127–29,
133–34, 140, 158
Martin, Mr., 183
*Mary Lincoln: Biography of a
Marriage* (R.P. Randall), ix,
268–69
*Mary Lincoln: Southern Girl,
Northern Woman* (McDermott),
280
Mary Lincoln Enigma, The, 282
Mary Lincoln for the Ages
(Emerson), 265
Mary Todd Lincoln: A Biography
(Baker), 272–74
Matheny, Charles W., 143
Matheny, Elizabeth, 88–89
Matheny, James H., 33, 40–41,
74, 84, 88
Matteson, Joel, 104, 142
Matthews, Ellen, 62–63
McClellan, George B., 171, 229
McClernand, John A., 106
McClernand, Mrs. John A., 106
McClure, Alexander K., 114–15,
207, 261
McCoy, Joseph G., 96, 98
McCreary, Donna, 239, 274
McDermott, Stacy Pratt, 280
McIlvaine, Congressman, 85
McKee, Martinette Hardin, 22,
24, 32, 42
McManus, Edward, 138, 183,
228, 246
Meade, George Gordon, 166, 252
Mendosa, John F., 66–67

Taft, Julia, 80, 202
Taney, Roger B., 230
Tarbell, Ida M., 34–35, 266, 274
Taylor, Joseph, 144
Temple, Wayne C., 41–42, 266, 282–84
Tiger, Jacob, 63–64, 71
Todd, Alexander, 11
Todd, Ann (cousin), 28
Todd, Ann (sister), 16
Todd, Charles Stewart, 146
Todd, David, 15
Todd, Eliza, xi, 9–10, 20
Todd, Elizabeth Humphreys, xi, 9–11, 217
Todd, Elodie, 17, 35, 282
Todd, George R.C., 10, 15
Todd, John Blair Smith, 146
Todd, Levi (brother), 16
Todd, Levi (grandfather), 20
Todd, Lockwood, 145
Todd, Lyman Beecher, 70, 146
Todd, Mary: childhood of, xi, 9–12; childishness of, 7–9; courtship of Lincoln by, 6–9, 23, 32, 41–42; education of, 10, 20; family background of, 20; meets Lincoln, 3–4; paternal figure needed by, 9; personality of as young woman, 3–4, 7, 11–12, 17, 37, 50. *See also* Lincoln, Mary Todd
Todd, Mattie Dee, 15
Todd, Robert Smith, xi, 7, 9–11, 20
Todd, Samuel, 11

Todd family, psychological problems of, 15–17, 282
Tompkins, Mrs. Patrick, 85
Treat, Samuel H., x, 5, 75–76
Tripler, Eunice, 153, 206
Trumbull, Julia Jayne (Mrs. Lyman), 33, 105–7
Trumbull, Lyman, 81, 93–94, 104–7, 146, 190
Truth, Sojourner, 234, 240
Tuck, Amos, 147–48

U
United States, divisive groups in, viii
Upperman, James H., 154–55
Usher, John Palmer, 158

V
Van Bergen, Peter, 89
Vanderbilt, Cornelius, 128
Van Wyck, Charles H., 140
Villard, Henry, 107–8, 110, 113, 121, 163–64, 173, 182

W
Wade, Benjamin F., 150–51, 211, 227
Wadsworth, James S., 123
Wakeman, Abram, 130, 138, 186, 194
Wallace, Frances Todd, 5, 37–39, 41, 49, 70, 145, 215, 278
Wallace, William S., 49, 99, 145–46

Walsh, John Evangelist, 266
Ward, Sam, 134
Warren, Louis A., ix
Washburne, Elihu, 212
Washington, Martha, 209
Watt, Jane, 195
Watt, John, 138, 140, 151–58,
    166–68, 195
Webb, Edwin Bathurst, 42–43,
    277
Weber, George R., 144
Weber, John B., 60
Weed, Thurlow, 122, 124, 129,
    133, 135, 153, 155, 187
Weik, Jesse W., 57, 64–65, 83
Welles, Edgar, 114
Welles, Gideon, 13, 111, 114,
    124–26, 172–73, 182, 214, 238
Welles, Rosetta, 238–40
White, Horace, 107
White, Martha Todd, 147
White House: looting of alleged,
    150–51; receptions at, 194;
    refurbishing of, 187–91, 202,
    271, 273

Whitman, Walt, 281
Whitney, Henry C., 36–37,
    103–4, 231, 262–63
Whittlesey, Elisha, 155
Wickliffe, Margaret, 82
Wikoff, Henry (Chevalier), 163–
    72, 174–77, 181
Wilkinson, Morton, 190
Williams, George H., 243–44
Williamson, Alexander, 192, 225
Willis, Nathaniel P., 170–71
Wilmer, Richard H., 146–47
Wilson, Douglas L., ix, 32, 266,
    283–84
Winkle, Kenneth J., 280
Wood, Fernando, 149
Wood, William P., 160, 186
Wood, William S., 43, 134–40,
    151, 154, 158
Wool, John E., 165

Y
Yates, Richard, 93–94, 103, 138,
    143
Yates, William, 143